Documenting World Politics

As a central component of contemporary culture, films mirror and shape political debate. Reflecting on this development, scholars in the field of International Relations (IR) increasingly explore the intersection of TV series, fiction film and global politics. So far, however, virtually no systematic scholarly attention has been given to documentary film within IR.

This book fills this void by offering a critical companion to the subject aimed at assisting students, teachers and scholars of IR in understanding and assessing the various ways in which documentary films matter in global politics. The authors of this volume argue that much can be gained if we do not just think of documentaries as a window on or intervention in reality, but as theories that involve particular postures, strategies and methodologies towards the world they shed light on.

This work will be of great interest to students and scholars of International Relations, popular culture and world politics and media studies alike.

Rens van Munster is Senior Researcher, Danish Institute for International Studies (DIIS), Copenhagen.

Casper Sylvest is Associate Professor, Department of History, University of Southern Denmark.

Popular Culture and World Politics
Edited by Matt Davies
Newcastle University
Kyle Grayson
Newcastle University
Simon Philpott
Newcastle University
Christina Rowley
University of Bristol
and
Jutta Weldes
University of Bristol

The Popular Culture World Politics (PCWP) book series is the forum for leading interdisciplinary research that explores the profound and diverse interconnections between popular culture and world politics. It aims to bring further innovation, rigor, and recognition to this emerging sub-field of international relations.

To these ends, the PCWP series is interested in various themes, from the juxtaposition of cultural artefacts that are increasingly global in scope and regional, local and domestic forms of production, distribution and consumption; to the confrontations between cultural life and global political, social, and economic forces; to the new or emergent forms of politics that result from the rescaling or internationalization of popular culture.

Similarly, the series provides a venue for work that explores the effects of new technologies and new media on established practices of representation and the making of political meaning. It encourages engagement with popular culture as a means for contesting powerful narratives of particular events and political settlements as well as explorations of the ways that popular culture informs mainstream political discourse. The series promotes investigation into how popular culture contributes to changing perceptions of time, space, scale, identity, and participation while establishing the outer limits of what is popularly understood as 'political' or 'cultural'.

In addition to film, television, literature, and art, the series actively encourages research into diverse artefacts including sound, music, food cultures, gaming, design, architecture, programming, leisure, sport, fandom and celebrity. The series is fiercely pluralist in its approaches to the study of popular culture and world politics and is interested in the past, present, and future cultural dimensions of hegemony, resistance and power.

Gender, Violence and Popular Culture
Telling stories
Laura J. Shepherd

Aesthetic Modernism and Masculinity in Fascist Italy
John Champagne

Genre, Gender and the Effects of Neoliberalism
The new millennium Hollywood rom com
Betty Kaklamanidou

***Battlestar Galactica* and International Relations**
Edited by Iver B Neumann and Nicholas J Kiersey

Death of Feminism?
Is popular and commercial culture undermining Women's rights?
Penny Griffin

The Politics of HBO's The Wire
Everything is connected
Edited by Shirin Deylami and Jonathan Havercroft

Sexing war/Policing Gender
Motherhood, myth and women's political violence
Linda Ahall

Documenting World Politics
A critical companion to IR and non-fiction film
Edited by Rens van Munster and Casper Sylvest

Documenting World Politics

A critical companion to IR and non-fiction film

Edited by Rens van Munster and
Casper Sylvest

LONDON AND NEW YORK

First published 2015
by Routledge
2 Park Square, Milton Park, Abingdon, Oxon OX14 4RN

And by Routledge
711 Third Avenue, New York, NY 10017

Routledge is an imprint of the Taylor & Francis Group, an informa business

© 2015 Rens van Munster and Casper Sylvest for selection and editorial matter; individual contributors for their contributions.

The right of Rens van Munster and Casper Sylvest to be identified as the authors of the editorial matter, and of the authors for their individual chapters, has been asserted in accordance with sections 77 and 78 of the Copyright, Designs and Patent Act 1988.

All rights reserved. No part of this book may be reprinted or reproduced or utilised in any form or by any electronic, mechanical, or other means, now known or hereafter invented, including photocopying and recording, or in any information storage or retrieval system, without permission in writing from the publishers.

Trademark notice: Product or corporate names may be trademarks or registered trademarks, and are used only for identification and explanation without intent to infringe.

British Library Cataloguing in Publication Data
A catalogue record for this book is available from the British Library

Library of Congress Cataloging in Publication Data
A catalog record for this book has been requested

ISBN: 978-1-138-79778-9 (hbk)
ISBN: 978-1-315-75689-9 (ebk)

Typeset in Times New Roman
by Wearset Ltd, Boldon, Tyne and Wear

Contents

List of illustrations ix
Notes on contributors x
Acknowledgments xii

PART I
Setting the scene 1

1 **Introduction** 3
   RENS VAN MUNSTER AND CASPER SYLVEST

2 **Your film in seven minutes: neo-liberalism and the field of documentary film production** 23
   FRANCESCO RAGAZZI

PART II
Staging world politics 41

3 **Popular documentaries and the global financial crisis** 43
   CHRIS CLARKE AND JAMES BRASSETT

4 **Documenting financial assemblages and the visualization of responsibility** 58
   MARIEKE DE GOEDE

5 **Non-linearity in the ocean documentary** 78
   PHILIP E. STEINBERG

6 **Shots of ambivalence: nuclear weapons in documentary film** 95
   CASPER SYLVEST

viii Contents

7 Inside war: counterinsurgency and the visualization of violence 114
RENS VAN MUNSTER

8 The reflexivity of tears: documentaries of sexual military assault 133
ROBIN MAY SCHOTT

9 Meta-mediation, visual agency and documentarist reflexivity in conflict film: *Burma VJ* meets *Burke+Norfolk* 150
RUNE SAUGMANN ANDERSEN

10 *The Reckoning*: advocating international criminal justice and the flattening of humanity 166
WOUTER G. WERNER

11 Strange encounters: past, present, and future conceivable life 183
JUHA A. VUORI

PART III
Behind the scenes 199

12 Evil, art and politics in documentary film: interview with Joshua Oppenheimer 201
RENS VAN MUNSTER AND CASPER SYLVEST

13 Bridging research and documentary film: interview with Janus Metz and Sine Plambech 213
RENS VAN MUNSTER AND CASPER SYLVEST

14 After-image 223
JAMES DER DERIAN

List of QR codes 232
Index 233

Illustrations

Figures

4.1	A *flâneur* visits the Royal Bank of Scotland	66
4.2	The pipeline as incision in the landscape	69
4.3	The materiality of oil extraction	71
6.1	*The Atomic Café*, theatrical release poster, 1982	101
6.2	*Countdown to Zero*, theatrical release poster, 2010	105
7.1	A Danish soldier in shock after battle. Film still from *Armadillo*, dir. Janus Metz Pedersen	122
7.2	Captain Dan Kearney of Battle Company, 173rd US Airborne, meets with local Afghan elders in the Korengal Valley, Kunar Province, Afghanistan, 2008. Film still from *Restrepo*, dir. Tim Hetherington and Sebastian Junger	123
7.3	Specialist Misha Pemble-Belkin (l.) and fellow soldiers from Battle Company, 173rd US Airborne, during a firefight at Outpost Restrepo during combat in Afghanistan's Korengal Valley, Afghanistan, Kunar Province, 2008. Film still from *Restrepo*, dir. Tim Hetherington and Sebastian Junger	125
10.1	Theatre poster of *The Court* (without Jolie and Ferencz)	167
12.1	Behind the scenes of *The Act of Killing*	202
12.2	The waterfall scene in *The Act of Killing*	207
13.1	Niels Jørgen Molbæk and Sommai talk about their marriage. Film still from *Love on Delivery*, dir. Janus Metz	215
13.2	Saeng and her friend at a bar in Pattaya, Thailand. Film still from *Ticket to Paradise*, dir. Janus Metz	221

Table

1.1	A heuristic framework for analysis	10

Contributors

Rune Saugmann Andersen is a PhD candidate at the Centre for Advanced Security Theory, University of Copenhagen, and an external lecturer at the University of Helsinki. His research explores how media such as video, film and photography relate to security. He has published in *Security Dialogue*, *Journalism Practice* and JOMEC; his research video appeared in *Audiovisual Thinking*.

James Brassett is Reader in International Political Economy at the University of Warwick. His research interests include the ethics and politics of global governance and the theoretical and empirical dilemmas of cultural political economy. He is currently working on a book, loosely entitled *The Political Economy of the Global Event: Rationalities of Crisis for the Attention of Market Subjects*.

Chris Clarke is Assistant Professor in Political Economy in the Department of Politics and International Studies at the University of Warwick. His research interests are in the areas of the politics of financial markets, the ethics of Anglo-American economic citizenship, the history of economic ideas and the political economy of social lending.

James Der Derian is Michael Hintze Chair of International Security and Director of the Centre of International Security Studies at the University of Sydney. He has produced five documentaries, including *Human Terrain: War Becomes Academic* (2009) and *Project Z: The Final Global Event* (2014). He also writes books and articles on war, diplomacy and the media.

Marieke de Goede is Professor of Political Science at the University of Amsterdam, where she directs the European Union in a Global Order MSc program. She is the author of *Speculative Security: The Politics of Pursuing Terrorist Monies* and co-editor, with Louise Amoore, of *Risk and the War on Terror*. De Goede is associate editor of *Security Dialogue*.

Rens van Munster is Senior Researcher at the Danish Institute for International Studies and coordinator for the Peace, Risk and Violence research area. His research focuses on the politics of risk and catastrophe since the Cold War.

His most recent book is *Politics of Catastrophe. Genealogies of the Unknown* (with Claudia Aradau).

Francesco Ragazzi is Assistant Professor in International Relations at the Institute of Political Science, University of Leiden, and an associated researcher at the Center for International Study and Research (CERI) at Sciences Po Paris. His research interests cover sociological approaches to citizenship, migration and security in international relations.

Robin May Schott is Senior Researcher at the Danish Institute for International Studies in the section Peace, Risk and Violence. She is a philosopher working with feminist philosophy, ethics and political philosophy in an interdisciplinary key, and has written extensively on issues related to gender, conflict, war and sexual violence.

Philip E. Steinberg is Professor of Political Geography and Director of IBRU, the Centre for Borders Research, at Durham University. He researches spaces that elide state territorialization, including the ocean, the Internet and the Arctic. His most recent book is *Contesting the Arctic: Politics and Imaginaries in the Circumpolar North*.

Casper Sylvest is Associate Professor at the Department of History, University of Southern Denmark. His research interests are interdisciplinary, combining the study of politics, history, law and technology. He is currently writing a book with Rens van Munster on social and political thought during the thermonuclear revolution.

Juha A. Vuori is a Professor of World Politics (acting) at the Department of Political and Economic Studies, University of Helsinki, and an Adjunct Professor at the School of Management, Tampere University (Finland). His research interests combine International Relations, security studies, surveillance studies, history and China studies. He is the author of *Critical Security and Chinese Politics*.

Wouter G. Werner is Professor of Public International Law at the Centre for the Politics of Transnational Law, VU University Amsterdam. His research is focused on the politics of international law as well as international legal theory, with a thematic focus on issues of security and international criminal law.

Acknowledgments

This book was born out of the very simple observation that for all the attention currently given to popular culture in International Relations theory (IR), the genre of documentary film has been largely ignored. Although some scholars have turned to making documentaries, virtually no one had written about them! In 2012, we therefore decided to organize a panel on IR and documentary film at the joint ISA-BISA conference in Edinburgh. After the panel, we were approached by Simon Philpott, co-editor of Routledge's Popular Culture and World Politics series, who encouraged us to develop the panel into a book project. This was the beginning of an ongoing series of conversations between scholars who shared a fondness of documentary film, visuality and popular culture. A key moment in our discussions was a two-day workshop, which was held at the Danish Institute for International Studies (DIIS) in Copenhagen, May 2013. We are extremely thankful to all the workshop participants for presenting their work and for raising themes and questions, as well as for their strong commitment to this project. We have at times been demanding editors and we are grateful for the serious engagement with all of our requests and queries. We would also like to acknowledge the support from the Danish Research Council for Independent Research (DFF), who funded the workshop as part of our research program on Globality and Planetary Security (GAPS).

A few people deserve special thanks. Janus Metz, Joshua Oppenheimer and Sine Plambech generously granted us time for questions and interviews. They also helped us obtain permission to reproduce some of the copyrighted images printed in this book. James Der Derian kindly agreed to write the After-image. We would also like to thank the anonymous reviewers and series editors for useful comments and suggestions on the project. Rebecca Adler-Nissen, Nils Arne Sørensen, Martin Senn and Wouter Werner carefully read and commented on the introduction.

The project has benefited significantly from the research assistance provided by Ann Sophie Krogh Kjeldsen (Danish Institute for International Studies) and Simone Staal Jacobsen (University of Southern Denmark). Ann Sophie was invaluable in the early stages of the project and in organizing the Copenhagen workshop. In the final stages of completing this volume, Simone proofread the manuscript with great care, organized the referencing to films and provided the

QR codes at the beginning of each chapter. These codes can be scanned and will take readers directly to the trailers of some of the documentary films discussed in this volume. The idea for including QR codes was suggested by Wouter Werner.

Every effort has been made to contact copyright holders for their permission to reprint material in this book. The publisher would be grateful to hear from any copyright holder who is not acknowledged and will undertake to rectify any errors or omissions in future editions.

Rens van Munster and Casper Sylvest,
June 2014

Part I
Setting the scene

1 Introduction

Rens van Munster and Casper Sylvest[1]

As a central component of contemporary culture, films mirror and shape political debate. Reflecting on this development, scholars in the field of International Relations (IR) increasingly explore the intersection of TV series, fiction film and global politics.[2] So far, however, virtually no systematic scholarly attention has been given to documentary film within IR, despite the fact that this filmic form has close historical ties to politics and, in recent decades in particular, has explicitly contributed to the study and popular edification of international politics.[3]

Documenting World Politics seeks to fill this void. It offers a critical companion to the subject aimed at assisting students, teachers and scholars of IR in understanding and assessing the various ways in which documentary films matter in global politics. Two examples can serve to illustrate how documentary films construct certain issues as *global* and *transnational*, while simultaneously working as instruments of soft power and political campaigning. The first takes us back to 2007, when climate change reached the top of the global political agenda. One of the most striking leaps in this ascent of climate change to a matter of global concern – indeed, to an issue of the high politics of peace and security addressed at the 5663rd meeting of the UN Security Council – was the joint award of the 2007 Nobel Peace Prize to the Intergovernmental Panel on Climate Change (IPCC) and former US Vice-President Al Gore, whose slide-show on the dangers of climate change formed the spine of the Oscar-winning documentary *An Inconvenient Truth*. The recipients were lauded 'for their efforts to build up and disseminate greater knowledge about man-made climate change and to lay the foundations for the measures that are needed to counteract such change'.[4] Five years later, a 30 minute documentary about the Ugandan warlord Joseph Kony became the first film ever to receive more than 100 million hits on the web within a week. This controversial film, *Kony2012*, was part of an orchestrated media campaign produced by Invisible Children, a US-based non-governmental organization (NGO) determined to secure the arrest of Kony, who was indicted for war crimes and crimes against humanity by the International Criminal Court back in 2005.

As the chapters in this book illustrate, these two examples are not isolated events, but reflect a much wider trend of using film to frame themes of transnational or global reach. Even if such attempts are not always successful as filmic products or persuasive as political interventions, they make up an important, though largely neglected, aspect of global politics. In comparison to other artifacts of popular culture, documentaries are powerful instruments, because their claims to authenticity, truth or reality often translate into expectations of trustworthiness among audiences. The increasing popularity and commercialization of the genre, including recurrent debates about the truth and biases of individual productions, underline the elevated status that the documentary enjoys in the public domain. The chapters that follow examine the structural conditions under which contemporary documentaries are produced, provide critical readings of popular as well as less well-known documentaries on themes of central importance to IR and interview filmmakers about their aspirations and challenges in documenting world politics.

Documentary films are important for IR theory in two additional senses. First, documentaries not only seek to mobilize audiences, but also constitute analyses of international relations in their own right (Shapiro 2005; Sylvest 2013). As a cultural reference point, documentaries can have an impact upon the ways in which international politics is conceived in society more widely. In this context, it is also noteworthy that prominent IR scholars have recently turned to documentary filmmaking as a way of communicating their research.[5] This trend reflects a diversification in how research is communicated, as well as a belief that visual media, and particularly the documentary genre, can reach new and wider audiences. If at all, documentaries have been discussed mainly in terms of their content, as filmic counterparts to academic arguments in print. Much less attention is paid to the specific epistemological aspects of the documentary form. By contrast, this book considers the genre of documentary film an integral part of informed public and scholarly debates and urges readers to understand documentaries as visual theories that mediate particular understandings of world politics.

Finally, documentaries are particularly relevant for the teaching of IR (and other subjects) with film. A burgeoning IR literature on the benefits and challenges of using film, including documentary films, in the classroom suggests that engaging the sensory experiences of students leads to more effective and successful learning (Krain 2010; see also Gregg 1998; Simpson and Kaussler 2009; Swimelar 2013; Weber 2014). Such arguments are likely to correspond to the experiences of teachers who have developed active learning practices. Although some films in the documentary genre can be useful in transmitting information in an attractive and entertaining format, their classroom potential extends much further than that.[6] Keeping in mind the genre's complex relationship to truth and reality, we suggest that teaching with documentary films offers a rich opportunity for developing students' analytical and critical skills. As the chapters in this book demonstrate, discussions about the nature of the genre and *how* certain issues or events are represented in individual productions opens up a rich portfolio of theoretical and political questions in a form(at) that is motivating to students. Moreover, a critical pedagogy, which addresses 'the "how" questions involved not only in the transmission and reproduction of knowledge but also in its production', can help to bolster a reflexive ethics of skepticism in the classroom.[7] This view is expressed by Judith Butler (2010), who stresses how the framing of photography or film is a vital part of interpretation and reflection. Rather than instruction, the educational model promoted in this book is thus mainly one of facilitating perspectivism and critical thinking.

This introduction has four sections. First, we locate the core theme of the book within the study of popular culture and film in IR, as well as the rise of visual culture as a popular thematic within the humanities and social sciences more generally. The second section provides a brief history of the documentary film genre and defines its main characteristics. In the third section, we develop a heuristic framework to analyze the politics of documentary film at two levels: first, the sociological level of their production, circulation and impact; and, second, the film-theoretical level, which includes questions pertaining to filmmaking, representation and the ways in which films make reality visible. Finally, we outline the organization of the book and provide a snapshot of individual chapters.

Popular culture and world politics

Whether judged by scholarly research, publication outlets, educational opportunities or conference activity, the relationship between popular culture and world politics has emerged as a growth industry, particularly within the last decade. It is increasingly recognized that popular culture and world politics are deeply imbricated. Elements of such culture(s) are more than just pedagogical tools for teaching complex theories and concepts: they can trigger events; they reflect and shape ideas, norms and power relations in global politics; and they constitute sites of contestation, reproduction and innovation of political languages and imaginaries.[8] In particular, scholars influenced by the linguistic turn and what within IR, somewhat parochially, is termed the post-positivist philosophy of science recognize that cultural vocabularies, tropes and images can have constitutive effects – for example, by advocating, enabling or naturalizing the fundamental political beliefs, values, ideas or world views that inform policy and practice (Neumann and Nexon 2006: 17–20). Scholars departing from more mainstream theoretical positions have also pointed to the significance of popular culture. As Nye argues in his discussion of soft power: '[p]ictures often convey values more powerfully than words, and Hollywood is the world's greatest promoter and exporter of visual symbols' (Nye 2004: 47). In advancing and substantiating such claims across a range of cultural productions, the study of popular culture reflects an ambition to validate other kinds of research material and forms of knowledge than those that have traditionally dominated research activity within IR. In the words of Bleiker (2001: 511), the aspiration of the 'aesthetic turn' in IR scholarship is to take into account 'productive interactions across different faculties, including sensibility, imagination and reason, without any of them annihilating the unique position and insight of the other'.

The turn to popular culture in IR is taking place alongside a wider study of images and visual culture within the humanities and social sciences. The ubiquity of visual material in our political culture has created a demand for analytical tools to read (or rather, 'see' and 'watch') a good deal of the stuff that makes up world politics. A range of studies in IR engage with visual material as different as media footage, cartoons, photographs, children's drawings and visual symbols.[9] Taken together, they reflect a recognition that, as James Der Derian has put it (2010: 183), 'increasingly the world is comprehended and acted upon not through speech-acts but word-pictures'. Beyond IR, this trend is reflected in the field of visual culture, one of the most sprawling and dynamic interdisciplinary fields in the contemporary human sciences (see, for example, Heywood and Sandywell 2012). Although the contemporary adage that (post-)modernity is a uniquely visual age can easily be taken too far, the belief that images and practices of seeing and showing are strongly linked, if not intrinsic, to the contemporary production and communication of knowledge is certainly a strong one (e.g., Crary 2001; Foster 1988; Kleinberg-Levin 1999). That said, visual culture has so far proved resistant to any narrow(ing) definition of its subject, and diversity also reigns in terms of approaches and methodologies. Instead, it is often argued that the field is united by an attitude or sensibility (e.g., Smith 2008: x–xi). But at the very least it involves an examination of visual sensory experience and an interrogation of how vernacular practices, ocular cultures, scopic regimes and various forms of gaze function, what they produce and what forms of meaning-making they entail.

Recent work within visual culture indicates a growing interest in questions of global politics. A recent anthology on *Global Visual Culture* that focuses, *inter alia*, on questions of war, geopolitics and cultural dominance argues that

> [t]he production, circulation and deployment of historical narratives are key topics for visual culture ... these narratives are transmitted not only through language and writing, but are also embedded in architecture, art, mass media, and technologies of memory such as film, voice recording and photographs.
>
> (Kocur 2011: 3)

Visual culture, to paraphrase J. L. Austin (1962), is partly about the things we do with images, but it is also partly about what particular forms of visual media and practices are possible, culturally and politically. Contextualizing images and laying bare the powers of seeing and being seen are central to understanding such dynamics. To a leading scholar in the 'interdiscipline' of visual culture, 'visuality, not just the social construction of vision, but the visual construction of the social, is a problem in its own right that is approached, but never quite engaged by the traditional disciplines of aesthetics and art history, or even by the new disciplines of media studies' (Mitchell 2002: 179).

Film has been one of the most prominent visual genres taken up in IR, where the reading of films as reflecting or shaping world politics has emerged as the province of post-structuralists and/or scholars interested in teaching IR using film (e.g., Gregg 1998; Weber 2001; Shapiro 2009; Weber 2014; Swimelar

2013). Overwhelmingly, however, 'cinematic IR' (Holden 2006) has remained focused on fiction films, and to the extent that documentaries are included in the literature, they are either treated as being on a par with fiction film or regarded as uncontaminated transmitters of truth or reality. The first position is represented by Shapiro (2009: 77), who emphasizes the 'blurred boundaries' between fiction and documentary films, before proceeding to analyze the latter on a par with the former. There are, indeed, good reasons to be skeptical of too sharp a distinction between fiction and non-fiction, but ignoring the genre-specific characteristics of documentary is a strategy that ultimately raises more questions than it answers.[10] Why are documentaries a preferred medium of contemporary activism? Why do we recurrently debate questions of bias and distortion in relation to non-fiction films? And why do directors and producers consistently justify their work as distinct from fiction or journalism? The second position, that documentaries are somehow truthful or provide a transparent window on reality, is mostly prevalent in discussions of teaching IR using film (see, for example, Krain 2010; Swimelar 2013) and strongly appeals to our common intuition. However, even the most fleeting engagement with documentary filmmakers and the genre more broadly would quickly dispel this notion: the documentary is clearly *not* an innocent medium of transmission. Hence, a strong case can be made that documentary filmmaking needs to be taken seriously as a genre and a significant medium of representation in its own right. What, more specifically, do we expect from the documentary, where are its limits, where does its mysterious power and attraction reside and in what ways are such cultural productions political?

The history and characteristics of documentary film[11]

The starting point of *Documenting World Politics* is, then, that ignoring the significance, complexity and distinctiveness of documentary film – that is, by treating this genre merely as one among other visual forms – is to the detriment not only of students and scholars, but also of the wider public sphere which scholarship serves. However, it is not easy to condense the meaning of documentary film in a single definition. 'Documentary' is a deceptively straightforward word. The *Oxford English Dictionary* (OED) defines it as '[f]actual, realistic; applied esp. to a film or literary work, etc., based on real events or circumstances, and intended primarily for instruction or record purposes' and points out that since the nineteenth century documentary has included broader connotations about evidence, instruction and authenticity. These residues of meaning are also reflected in the etymological roots of the word, which stem from the document as the recording of events and the Latin verb *docere*, meaning 'to teach'.

Contemporary documentary filmmaking, however, is a diverse and sprawling industry that routinely transgresses these boundaries by taking on the characteristics of art, entertainment and journalism. Still, there is a common identity built around the expectations that are generated by classifying a film as a documentary: they are seen to embody a particular status in relation to truth and reality. In short, they embody a claim to authenticity.[12] A documentary's authority and political efficacy often derives from its implicit claim to record or depict reality, even if, in fact, it does not – hence the recurring outcries against documentaries such as *Kony2012* for willfully manipulating facts for political purposes. A prominent analyst of the documentary genre therefore suggests that, in contrast to fiction, 'documentary film has a kinship with those other non-fictional systems that together make up what we may call the discourses of sobriety, including science, economics, politics, and so on' (Nichols 1991: 3).

Nonetheless, documentary films enjoy a complex relationship with politics and reality, as well as with those late-modern *Sorgenkinder*, truth and authenticity. As cultural productions, they provide a particular way of seeing that is often taken to be true, real or authentic, and it is against that background that they inform or mobilize the public and, perhaps more subtly, structure beliefs among their audiences. To begin a consideration of documentary film by placing the claim to authenticity center stage does not, therefore, entail an acceptance of its truth-value. The documentary is born out of a tortured process, in which the aim of *presenting* the actual always (and necessarily) involves a *production* of that self-same actual (Nichols 2001; Chanan 2007; Aufderheide 2007). The view through the camera lens is the outcome of endless layers of decisions and techniques that, in conjunction with the subsequent editing, create, distort and twist the non-filmic. Some documentaries are quite adept in reflecting on their own particular qualities in this regard, so even when the relationship between truth/reality and representation is explicitly complicated, narrative and political force are often derived by playing precisely upon this ambiguity.[13] Hence, John Grierson's (1933: 8) classic definition of documentary as the 'creative treatment of actuality' is still a useful starting point.

The difficult relationship between documentary, truth and reality is integral to the genre and its history. The short film *Workers Leaving the Lumière Factory* (1895) by the Lumière brothers, which is generally recognized as the first documentary film, was staged, and at least three different versions exist today. Similarly, Robert J. Flaherty's influential and critically acclaimed *Nanook of the North* (1922) professed to chronicle Inuit life; yet Flaherty instructed his subjects to behave in ways that did not correspond to their everyday reality, but that supported the film's narrative of nature's innocence. When documentary filmmaking came to enjoy a close relationship with the prevailing political authorities, its partiality was more directly on display. In the Soviet Union, Dziga Vertov thought documentary film the most appropriate medium for the promotion of the communist revolution. By showing the 'unstaged' and 'unrehearsed' life that escaped other ways of seeing (theatre, painting, photography and the human eye), he considered the camera I/eye to present a vantage point that could create new perceptions of the world (see also Steinberg, this volume). Most (in)famously, perhaps, were Leni Riefenstahl's productions from the mid-1930s – including *Triumph of the Will* (1935) – that shaped public perceptions of the Nazi Party and contributed to the nationalistic beliefs that accompanied Germany's re-emergence as a Great Power.

The documentary played an equally political role in democracies. World War II, in particular, helped solidify the genre as a tool of propaganda (which was not always a pejorative term), education and advocacy. Frank Capra's series *Why We Fight* – designed to justify US participation in World War II – stands out as a landmark. In the same vein, John Grierson, the iconic figure in British and Canadian documentary film, claimed that documentaries could help mobilize citizens in social and democratic processes by providing insight into larger social structures that would otherwise escape the individual (Grierson 1966 [1946]; see also Brassett and Clarke, this volume). Against this background, it is hardly surprising that some observers in the post-war years regarded the documentary as a crucial tool in creating a better world by 'educating millions of people in knowing one another and thereby helping to shape a peaceful, cooperative world' (Pratzner 1947: 398).

Although the hopes and credibility invested in these types of documentary have been severely dented during the last half century, they are still used as tools in the PR (or public diplomacy) efforts of countries, large organizations and companies.[14] The genre has, however, witnessed a general move away from the grip of paternalistic and pastoral forms of government to become a preferred medium of independent, typically progressive filmmakers with distinct artistic and political ambitions. In large part, this is due to the technological possibilities that arose during the 1960s and 1970s, which made it financially possible to speak on behalf of the governed, rather than the governing. The ongoing reaction against officialdom at the time, particularly in the West, assisted this development and arguably came to fruition with the rise of *cinéma verité* and direct cinema.

Today, some continue to see an important democratic role for documentary (Kahana 2008). On this view, documentaries can enrich the public sphere by virtue of their ability to transgress the borders between officialdom and the citizenry and their respective languages. Clearly, one can question such a 'republican' vision of the documentary and its underlying progressive ethos, since film and television have been some of history's great forces in the production of both propaganda and political lethargy. Some contemporary documentaries embody more or less hidden contracts between creators and audiences, typically involving a 'feel good' element that can have apathetic effects.[15] Moreover, the increasing popularity and commercialization of documentary films described in Ragazzi's chapter (see Chapter 2) can involve a trade-off between subtlety and entertainment in contemporary productions (although this is not necessarily a zero-sum relationship).[16] Such trends are perhaps most vividly demonstrated in the emergence of a new form of documentary since the early 1990s, led by well-known figures like Michael Moore and Morgan Spurlock, in which filmmakers very actively stage and partake in what is documented (McCreadie 2008).

A heuristic framework for analysis

Given the rich tensions that emerge from this brief historical sketch of the genre and which are still on display in the wide variety of productions now on offer, we need tools that take us beyond naïve realism, yet provide analytical purchase. In this section, we present a heuristic framework of analysis that systematically organizes a set of questions that help us gauge the political role of documentary film, the importance of the field within which they are produced and the (sub-)genre characteristics of documentary filmmaking. Our framework takes inspiration both from Nichols' (2001) account of the various subgenres at work in documentary film and Platinga's (2005) anatomy of documentaries.[17] According to Platinga, in laying claim to reality documentary film combines two *forms*: saying and showing. The former refers to the filmmaker's explicit intention or ambition to influence the beliefs and attitudes of his/her audience (often through a voice-over or narrator), whereas the latter includes 'the images, sounds, and combinations thereof as reliable sources for the formation of beliefs about the film's subject', as well as more phenomenological filmic techniques seeking to (re)create a particular meaning or experience (Platinga 2005: 114–115). On this basis, it is possible to distinguish three distinctive operational modalities: (1) the documentary of *exposition* or *advocacy*, where saying is privileged over showing; (2) the *observational* documentary, where showing is privileged over saying; and (3) the *reflexive documentary*, where showing and saying are wilfully contradicted (see Table 1.1).

Table 1.1 A heuristic framework for analysis

	Exposition/ Advocacy	*Observational*	*Reflexive*
Operational modality	Saying over showing	Showing over saying	Showing contradicts saying (and *vice versa*)
Politics and ideology	Mobilization of audiences through exposition and narrative excavation	Spurring interpretation and reflection through disclosure of life-worlds	Facilitating new interpretations through the destabilization of (hegemonic) narratives
Theory and epistemology	Truth and knowledge is hidden behind false appearances	Truth and knowledge can be read off surface reality	Doubt/irony/ambiguity about what constitutes truth or about how knowledge of reality is produced and achieved
Examples of films discussed in this book	*Countdown to Zero* *The Reckoning* *Inside Job* *The Forgotten Space* *The Invisible War*	*Armadillo* *Restrepo* *Leviathan*	*Atomic Café* *Radio Bikini* *The Ambassador*

Introduction 11

This typology is a practical first step in approaching documentary film. This book develops the typology by adding two layers that are used in analyses of films throughout this book.[18] The first one deals with questions related to the politics and ideology of documentary film; the second concerns the relation between filmmaking, theory and epistemology.

Documentary film, politics and ideology

This analytical layer primarily asks questions about the politics and sociology of documentary films related to their conditions of production, funding and circulation patterns, and their effect in mobilizing audiences, typically but not exclusively in the public sphere, whether national or transnational. Central questions in this respect are the following:

- What are the political and economic conditions under which particular films are produced, disseminated and received?
- Does the film (explicitly or implicitly) have a political agenda? How is it revealed and pursued? What, if anything, cannot be said or shown?
- To what extent is the marketing, circulation and popularity of the film indicative of a political impact?
- What are the decisive political constrictions and possibilities of the medium of documentary film in this particular instance?

These kinds of questions are typically most pressing in relation to expositional documentaries that put forward a particular argument with a view to mobilizing their audiences behind a specific cause. They have a distinct narrative voice (in the form of the voice of God, a screen text or something similar) and follow a conventional narrative arc in which a social, political or economic problem or condition is identified and analyzed before a solution is provided (see, for example, the analysis of *Inside Job* or *The Reckoning*, this volume). In doing so, some productions of this type often seek to bolster their claims by referring to or making use of celebrities and widely acknowledged authorities.[19] Moreover, films made by activists or NGOs especially make a virtue of their political mission and are often accompanied by broader campaigns that can bolster their cause.[20]

These aspects of documentary filmmaking are also relevant for observational or reflexive documentaries, although they often require more intense efforts of interpretation that can rarely be restricted to this level of analysis. Moreover, such interpretations are often more open to dispute. Observational documentaries that seek to bring new (life)worlds into view are sometimes marketed as apolitical windows on reality, but the conditions of their production can have distinct political effects (see, for example, the analysis of *Restrepo* and *Armadillo* in van Munster's chapter, this volume). Reflexive documentaries, on the other hand, are often animated by a desire to destabilize or complicate conventional views. A classic example in this context is Errol Morris's Oscar-winning

The Fog of War (2003), a portrait of former US Defense Secretary Robert S. McNamara that also covers central questions concerning US foreign and security policy during the twentieth century. The politics of this film leaves a wide scope for interpretation, as the controversy it spawned testifies. Indeed, the reflexivity it seeks to generate may be seen as the quintessential political rationale of such interventions (Sylvest 2013; see also the interview with Joshua Oppenheimer, this volume).

At times, it is straightforward to trace the influence of films on political agendas. Some films explicitly generate media attention or shape political debates about international or global issues. For example, *Armadillo* triggered a public hearing with the Danish Minister of Defence on the possibility of Danish soldiers having committed war crimes in Afghanistan.[21] Other films are awarded explicit political recognition, allowing filmmakers or protagonists to become respected political actors in their own right (as was the case with *An Inconvenient Truth*). Yet other productions spur direct political action or legal change.[22] Much of the information needed to gauge this level of the politics of documentary film emerges from carefully contextualizing and analyzing the genesis of individual films or from accessing publicly available resources. Further, the ways in which the (documentary) film industry rewards particular productions at festivals and award ceremonies constitute useful public displays of support, appreciation and marketing. Box office numbers are available on public databases or websites (like the Internet Movie Database (IMDb), imdb.com), just as some details of institutional or financial support for documentary films can be gathered from press kits and credits.

A cautionary note is necessary, however. While some productions – for example, *An Inconvenient Truth* – receive considerable publicity and, according to some scholars, produce a real, traceable impact,[23] establishing the influences or reception of films in any direct or measurable fashion remains fraught with difficulty. To take just one example: in war films, it is surely right, as James Der Derian (2010: 181) has noted, that 'the cinematic aestheticisation of violence can glorify as well as vilify war, depending on how the spectator identifies with the protagonist and the investigator with the informant'. A similar indeterminacy can be detected in documentary films about a wide variety of topics, from climate change, migration and international criminal justice to films about more specific events, such as the Abu Ghraib prison scandal or the *real* cause of the collapse of the Twin Towers.

Filmmaking as theory and epistemology

The second, analytical level, which we term *filmmaking as theory and epistemology*, is strongly related to a view of documentaries as forming epistemologies or visual theories in their own right (van Munster and Sylvest 2013). The documentary impels us to think not only about the intentions of the maker and the political meaning of the filmic intervention in reality, but also about how reality is made perceptible in the first place, in effect asking 'how we see, how we are able, allowed, or made to see, and how we see this seeing and unseeing therein' (Foster 1988: 2). Core themes at this level concern *how* documentaries provide access to subjects and objects of global or international political interest. In this context, the emphasis shifts to the nexus between argumentative strategy and filmic technique. The analysis can involve a wide range of themes, stretching from camera technology to the relationship between documentary and art or aesthetics. From this perspective, films are primarily read as representations that are marked by, relatively free from or openly challenge the assumptions, narratives and blind spots at work in the public sphere.

This type of analysis typically engages the world of filmmaking and filmmakers. It deals in particular with the aspect of *how* the world and political arguments are framed and conveyed. Some of the central questions at this level are:

- By what narrative structure, filmic or non-filmic means is a political argument advanced or supported?
- What subjects are invoked in this particular film and how? Does the film speak on behalf of any particular group or entity?
- What is/remains outside the frame?
- How is the practice of filming, documenting or recording itself treated (if at all), and what kind of understanding of the camera does this treatment signify?
- What theories and/or epistemologies are involved in establishing authenticity, and how does filmic technique support or disrupt this quest?

To understand the epistemological workings of documentary film, it is helpful to think of well-known (IR) theories. Many *expository* documentary films operate in a theoretical modality that we are familiar with from Marxist theory and other theories that emerged out of Enlightenment thinking (including liberalism and some forms of realism). In its aim to expose false beliefs, it operates with a view of reality as double-layered: a surface reality, which consists of appearances that can be glanced; and a deeper reality of truth that requires narrative excavation (see also Boon 2008: 42). In this view, the documentary is not simply a method that describes what is apparent, but one that 'more explosively reveals the reality of it' (Grierson 1966 [1946]: 22–23). The images, sounds and other effects all support the objective of showing the hidden truth. The political efficacy of this type of documentary lies in its capacity to persuade or convince an audience about the real (but not immediately perceptible) state of affairs. Prominent examples of this type of film include *Fahrenheit 9/11*, *Inside Job*, *The Invisible War*, *Countdown to Zero* and *An Inconvenient Truth*. More subtle and less famous productions like *The Forgotten Space*, *The Red Chapel* or *Black Sea Files* also display traits of the expository documentary, because they posit an argument that is typically driven by the wish to enlighten or emancipate (see also Nichols 2001).

A second epistemological regime is more observational than argumentative. Recording reality as it unfolds, it does not seek to mobilize the spectator (too) directly; rather, the filmmaker typically tries to make her- or himself disappear, to become a fly on the wall, and 'calls on the viewer to take a more active role in determining the significance of what is said and done' (Nichols 2001: 111). Instead of looking for truth beneath reality, it operates according to an epistemological modality that reads truth off the surface. Films such as *Armadillo*, *Restrepo* and *Leviathan* share some traits with theoretical perspectives in IR, such as standpoint feminism, post-colonialism and critical theory, which also seek to enlarge our view of reality. For example, the feminist slogan that 'the personal is international' has sought to introduce the private and the social into a field of study where these issues were considered beyond the scope of reflection. By zooming in on diplomatic wives, prostitutes, sweatshops or rape, it is shown that the everyday shapes and is shaped by international politics (Enloe 2000). The documentary can be a powerful political vehicle in such quests, given its capacity to create emotional landscapes that only the best books can achieve. Here, documentaries are not just political because of the message they contain. Instead, politics is enacted through the camera's frame, where 'to be political ... is not a question of advancing an ideological position, militating for a cause or campaigning for anything' (Chanan 2007: 16), but of bringing something new to light.[24] The political efficacy of this arrangement depends on its ability to disclose something that previously was invisible.

Finally, documentary films can be assembled in more ambiguous ways, in order to stimulate reflection. As is the case with *The Atomic Café* or *Radio Bikini* (see the analysis in Sylvest's chapter, this volume), their epistemological modality is characterized by doubt, irony and a certain (self-)reflexivity. As such, their political efficacy is best understood in terms of their capacity to destabilize or undermine taken-for-granted notions by producing several (often contrasting) 'truths' or 'realities'. As such, this genre has much in common with the analytical ambitions of post-structuralism and critical theory in IR. They can be considered visual deconstructions of complexes of truth/power, where truth and reality are not given, but rather seen as the outcome of struggles between different rationalities, forms of knowledge and institutions.

In addressing how different documentary films contribute to visualizing, theorizing and (re)producing global politics in the public sphere, the chapters that follow help us make sense of the multiple ways in which documentary films are political.

Plan of the book

Documenting World Politics is divided into three main parts. Apart from this Introduction, the first part – Setting the scene – includes a chapter by Francesco Ragazzi that uses Bourdieusian sociology to analyze the conditions under which the revival of the documentary genre is currently taking place. This exercise is central to the ambition of the book, since as John Street has pointed out, '[t]o understand popular culture is to understand the conditions of its production' (Street 1997: 20). Ragazzi warns that the increasing popularization and commercialization of documentary film is likely to lead to a greater degree of filmic uniformity away from more experimental forms of filmmaking.

The chapters in Part II – Staging world politics – make up the bulk of the book. These chapters, written by experts in the field of IR who have a sensitivity towards and a strong interest in how cultural representations matter, provide critical readings of historical and contemporary documentaries on central aspects of international and global politics. In doing so, the chapters reflect on the politics of documentary film as political interventions and visual epistemologies. In Chapter 3, James Brassett and Chris Clarke critically examine recent documentaries of exposition about the financial crisis, including the Oscar-winning *Inside Job* and Michael Moore's *Capitalism: A Love Story*. They emphasize how these films both represent and (re)imagine global finance through visual political argument. In Chapter 4 we are presented with an altogether different perspective on international political economy, as Marieke de Goede shows how documentary films bring the materiality of financial assemblages into view and help us understand how responsibility is distributed and dispersed across the assemblage. Chapter 5, by Phil Steinberg, provides a critical reading of two recent documentaries – *The Forgotten Space* and *Leviathan* – demonstrating how they challenge and disrupt but also reproduce the traditional and deeply ingrained understanding of the sea in IR as a flat surface that both demarcates and underwrites the modern territorial order based on sovereign states.

The following four chapters deal with representations of weapons and violence. In Chapter 6, Casper Sylvest analyzes how nuclear weapons have been represented in documentary film since the dawn of the nuclear age. He argues that these representations both reflected and shaped the state of nuclear politics and that the very nature of these enigmatically destructive weapons embodies particular challenges for progressive documentary filmmaking. Chapter 7, by Rens van Munster, discusses observational documentaries produced in the context of embedded journalism and contemporary counterinsurgency warfare by paying particular attention to two remarkable productions about the war in Afghanistan, *Restrepo* and *Armadillo*. In Chapter 8, Robin May Schott takes up representations of rape and gender in contemporary documentaries on sexual military assault, including *The Invisible War* and *Operation Fine Girl*. Chapter 9, by Rune Saugmann Andersen, zooms in on the camera and particularly video footage as a weapon in contemporary global politics. In this context, Andersen juxtaposes the politics of *Burma VJ* (the acclaimed documentary about undercover video reporting of the 2007 protests against Burma's military junta) with that of *Burke + Norfolk*, a short documentary that problematizes war in Afghanistan.

The two final chapters in this part of the book deal, in different ways, with questions of norms and culture. In Chapter 10, Wouter Werner critically interrogates *The Reckoning*, a film about the International Criminal Court (ICC). Werner discusses both how the film expresses the wider mission of international criminal law in its representations of victimhood, justice and humanity and the political implications of such 'depoliticized' representations of legal institutions.

Chapter 11, by Juha Vuori, focuses on three recent Danish documentaries dealing respectively with totalitarian dictatorship, corrupt diplomacy and nuclear waste. The films share a deeper thematic, however: cultural exchange and communicating across time and space. Vuori provides a critical discussion of a problematique common to all three films – namely, the challenges of communicating across strangeness.

Since documentaries provide potentially powerful lenses on reality, Part III of the book – Behind the scenes – includes interviews with central practitioners in the field: the directors. Chapter 12 presents an interview with Joshua Oppenheimer, director of the much acclaimed *The Act of Killing* (2012) and *The Look of Silence* (2014), which revolve around issues of truth, representation and politics in documentary filmmaking. In Chapter 13 director Janus Metz and anthropologist Sine Plambech are interviewed about their experiences in bridging academic research and filmmaking during their collaboration on the migration films *Love on Delivery* (2008) and *Ticket to Paradise* (2008).

The book closes with an afterword by James Der Derian.

Notes

1 We would like to thank Rebecca Adler-Nissen, Martin Senn, Nils Arne Sørensen and Wouter Werner for useful comments on this introduction.
2 *Battlestar Galactica*, *Buffy the Vampire Slayer*, *Harry Potter*, *Lord of the Rings*, *Star Trek* and *The Truman Show* are just some of the movies that have drawn the attention of IR scholars. See Kiersey and Neumann (2013), Neumann and Nexon (2006), Ruane and James (2012), Weber (2014) and Weldes (2003).
3 There are exceptions – in particular, Aitken (2009, 2011). The general trend, however, is clear: documentaries are often ignored or treated on a par with fiction film.
4 Speech by Professor Ole Danbolt Mjøs, Chairman of the Norwegian Nobel Committee, 10 December 2007, available at www.nobelprize.org/nobel_prizes/peace/laureates/2007/presentation-speech.html (accessed 21 May 2013).
5 James Der Derian, the director of Brown University's global media project, has produced four documentaries with Udris Film (*Virtual Y2K*, *After 9/11*, *Human Terrain* and *Project Z*). Cynthia Weber is co-director of Pato Productions and the director of *I Am an American: Video Portraits of Unsafe US Citizens* (2007). See also the interview with Janus Metz and Sine Plambech in this volume.
6 Historically, of course, the genre of documentary film has been closely associated with an instructional model of education that still dominates the majority of television documentaries, and its influence is arguably noticeable in the widespread, though often unspoken, assumption among audiences (including university students) that documentaries neutrally transmit truthful knowledge. In contemporary documentary productions, this model can be discerned in cinematic techniques like the voice-over and in narrative arcs that posit questions and problems to which answers and solutions are subsequently provided (Nichols 2001: 91). Exposing students to these kinds of documentaries can be useful when assigning films for the purpose of teaching theories or central topics or events in world politics.
7 Denski (1991: 5). In recent years, the use of documentary films in higher education has been justified not only with reference to their informational value, but precisely by stressing their ability to provide new perspectives and facilitate critical thinking (e.g., Frank 2013). This model of learning in conjunction with documentary film challenges the idea that knowledge can be possessed and transmitted

unproblematically, and it points to the coexistence of different perspectives on experiences or issues. The following questions constitute a useful starting point for enabling student understanding of the role of documentary film in edifying debates about global politics: What expectations do you have of films classified as documentaries? This film is classified as a documentary. Why is this (not) an adequate classification? What do you learn about world politics from watching this film, and to what extent do existing (IR) theories help or hinder you in acquiring this knowledge? We suggest that questions of this nature be used in classroom teaching before proceeding to the actual analysis of films – for example, along the lines of the typology we develop in this introduction.

8 Cynthia Weber (1999, 2001, 2005) has produced some of the most important work in this field. See also Neumann and Nexon (2006), Drezner (2011) and Kiersey and Neumann (2013). Journals like *Millennium* and *International Studies Perspectives* also regularly feature articles about popular culture (spanning issues of theory, methodology, pedagogy, as well as many empirical studies). See, for example, Behnke (2006), Kangas (2009), Salter (2014), Blanton (2013) and Franke and Schiltz (2013). The Popular Culture and World Politics Network (PCWP) now runs an annual conference and educational programs, of which the MA in Popular Culture and World Politics at Newcastle University and the BA in Film and Visual Culture and International Relations at the University of Aberdeen are just two examples.

9 See, for example, Williams (2003), Vuori (2010), Hansen (2011), Lisle (2011) and Aradau and Hill (2013).

10 That something is amiss emerges, for example, from the insightful analysis of *An Inconvenient Truth* provided by a leading scholar in this branch of IR, Cynthia Weber. She argues that to present the argument about climate change – that is, that global warming, as well as the solutions to it, are anthropogenic – using the documentary film form is 'an incredibly smart move', since *An Inconvenient Truth* is harder to 'dismiss as over-the-top' (Weber 2010: 198). While the film has been subject to criticism (see, for example, Mellor 2009), the point is that the documentary form accords the film a distinctive status in the public sphere and gives it particular leverage in contributing to public policy debates.

11 Some of the material in this section draws on van Munster and Sylvest (2013).

12 Throughout this book we make no distinction between documentary and non-fiction film. Non-fiction predominantly refers to writing, as is evident from the definition of the OED: 'Prose writing other than fiction, such as history, biography, and reference works, esp. that which is concerned with the narrative depiction of factual events; the genre comprising this.'

13 Ironic or reflexive documentaries only function as such because they operate against the background assumption that documentaries are about truth and reality. Tellingly, the genre of fiction that insists on authenticity is referred to as 'mockumentary'. Genre mash-ups are prevalent in contemporary culture, such as in feature films, TV productions and advertising. For a good discussion of some of these issues, see Torchin (2008).

14 These types of production often employ a combination of news reports and mini-docs to communicate their *raison d'être* or to showcase the extent of their corporate social responsibility. Examples include ExxonMobil's Malaria Initiative (www.exxonmobil.com/Corporate/community_malaria_initiative.aspx, accessed 26 March 2014), the brand channel of NATO (www.natochannel.tv, accessed 26 March 2014) and the large-scale public diplomacy operation of America.gov, which is run by the US Department of State's Bureau of International Information Programs (www.america.gov/multimedia/video.html, accessed 26 March 2014).

15 We owe this point to Juha Vuori. For a discussion, see Godmilow and Shapiro (1997).

16 That said, many documentaries receive private or public support in ways that ensure that at some point they reach both cinema and television audiences, and there has

been a steady rise recently in documentaries achieving cinema distribution (Chanan 2007: 15).
17 In contemporary film studies it is common to divide documentaries into relatively coherent subgenres or modes. For example, Patricia Aufderheide (2007: 56–124) identifies six documentary subgenres – public affairs, government propaganda, advocacy, historical, ethnographic and nature – that mix form, theme and source. Bill Nichols (1991: Chapter 2) has focused more strictly on form and identifies four modes of documentary film: the expository, the observational, the interactive and the reflexive. Michael Renov (1993: 21–36) offers yet another inroad to the genre by identifying four 'fundamental and never entirely separated tendencies of documentary', which are: (1) to record, reveal or preserve; (2) to persuade or preserve; (3) to analyze or interrogate; and (4) to express.
18 Typologies like this one are useful for analytical as well as pedagogical reasons. They aid analysis by organizing data and are instructive in identifying and interpreting films that fit a curriculum or particular teaching objectives in either theme or form. The caveats that are often attached to typologies and classifications should, nevertheless, be repeated here: the classification is not exhaustive, nor are the distinctions completely watertight. Moreover, we fully expect (and welcome the fact) that use of the typology will identify limitations and generate critique.
19 For a critique of the use of celebrities in humanitarian campaigns, see, for example, Chouliaraki (2011) and Ponte and Richey (2011).
20 A good example here is Participant Media, a company run by Jeff Skoll, the former president of the internet trading company eBay. Its mission is to 'produce entertainment that creates and inspires social change' (www.ted.com/talks/jeff_skoll_makes_movies_that_make_change.html, accessed 26 March 2014). This ambition is also evident on Participant Media's website: www.takepart.com (accessed 26 March 2014). For a discussion of how NGO activism seeks to exploit the documentary form, see McLagan (2012).
21 The debate is publicly accessible on the website of the Danish Parliament. See www.ft.dk/Folketinget/udvalg_delegationer_kommissioner/Udvalg/Forsvarsudvalget/LydFraSamraad.aspx (accessed 21 May 2014).
22 A Danish documentary film on child adoption (*Adoptionens pris*, dir. Katrine Kjær, 2012) led Danish politicians to review and finally adapt the legal framework of adoption.
23 See, for example, Jacobsen (2011) for a discussion of the so-called 'Al Gore effect' in the context of *An Inconvenient Truth*.
24 The ideological possibilities of cinematic technology and technique were the focus of sustained analysis in film theory during the 1960s and 1970s. For a classic and influential statement, see Baudry (1974–1975).

Films

Adoptionens Pris (2012) Directed by Katrine W. Kjær. Denmark, Fridthjof Film.
After 9/11 (2003) [No director credited]. USA, Udris Productions.
An Inconvenient Truth (2006) Directed by Davis Guggenheim. USA, Lawrence Bender Productions and Participant Media.
Armadillo (2010) Directed by Janus Metz Pedersen. Denmark, Fridthjof Film.
Battlestar Galactica (2004–2009, TV series) Developed by Ronald D. Moore. USA, Series produced by David Eick.
Black Sea Files (2005) Directed by Ursula Biemann. Switzerland, partly available at: www.youtube.com/watch?v=bNlPZfpObMk (accessed 28 May 2014).
Buffy the Vampire Slayer (1997–2003, TV series) Created by Joss Whedon. USA, Mutant Enemy Productions.

Burke + Norfolk: Photographs From the War in Afghanistan (2011) Directed by Simon Norfolk. UK, available at: www.tate.org.uk/context-comment/video/burke-norfolk-photographs-war-afghanistan (accessed 28 May 2014).

Burma VJ (2008) Directed by Anders Østergaard. Denmark, Kamoli Films and Magic Hour Films.

Capitalism: A Love Story (2009) Directed by Michael Moore. USA, Overture Films and Paramount Vantage.

Countdown to Zero (2010) Directed by Lucy Walker. USA, Lawrence Bender Productions, Nuclear Disarmament Documentary and Participant Media.

Fahrenheit 9/11 (2004) Directed by Michael Moore. USA, Fellowship Adventure Group and Dog Eat Dog Films.

Harry Potter (2001–2011) Directed by Chris Columbus, Alfonso Cuaròn, Mike Newell and David Yates. UK and USA, Warner Bros., 1492 Pictures, Heyday Films, P of A Productions Limited and Moving Picture Company.

Human Terrain (2010) Directed by James Der Derian, David Udris and Michael Udris. USA, Udris Film, Global Media Project and Oxyopia Films.

I Am an American: Video Portraits of Unsafe US Citizens (2007) Directed by Cynthia Weber. USA, available at: www.youtube.com/watch?v=SPHSRniWdys&list=PLE90B11721CB936A7 (accessed 28 May 2014).

Inside Job (2010) Directed by Charles Ferguson. USA, Sony Pictures Classics.

Kony2012 (2012) Directed by Jason Russell. USA, Invisible Children.

Leviathan (2012) Directed by Lucien Castaing-Taylor and Véréna Paravel. France, UK and USA, Arrete Ton Cinema and Le Bureau.

Lord of the Rings (2001–2003) Directed by Peter Jackson. USA and New Zealand, New Line Cinema, WingNut Films and The Saul Zaentz Company.

Love on Delivery (2008) Directed by Janus Metz. Denmark, Cosmo Doc.

Nanook of the North (1922) Directed by Robert J. Flaherty. USA and France, Les Fréres Revillon and Pathé Exchange.

Operation Fine Girl: Rape Used as a Weapon of War in Sierra Leone (2001) Directed by Lilibet Foster. USA, WITNESS.

Project Z (2012) Directed by Philip Gara. USA, Global Media Project, Littoral Media and Oxyopia Production.

Radio Bikini (1988) Directed by Robert Stone. USA, Crossroads, Robert Stone Productions, Spark Media and WGBH.

Restrepo (2010) Directed by Tim Hetherington and Sebastian Junger. USA, Outpost Films and Virgil Films and Entertainment.

Star Trek (1966–1969, TV series) Created by Gene Roddenberry. USA, Desilu Productions, Norway Corporation and Paramount Television.

The Act of Killing (2012) Directed by Joshua Oppenheimer. Denmark, Final Cut for Real.

The Atomic Café (1982) Directed by Jayne Loader, Kevin Rafferty and Pierce Rafferty. USA, The Archives Project.

The Fog of War (2003) Directed by Errol Morris. USA, Sony Pictures Classics, Radical Media and SenArt Films.

The Forgotten Space (2010) Directed by Allan Sekula and Noel Burch. The Netherlands and Austria, Wildart Film.

The Invisible War (2012) Directed by Kirby Dick. USA, Chain Camera Pictures.

The Reckoning: The Battle for the International Criminal Court (2009) Directed by Pamela Yates. USA, Skylight Pictures.

The Red Chapel (2009) Directed by Mads Brügger. Denmark, Danmarks Radio and Zentropa Productions.
The Truman Show (1998) Directed by Peter Weir. USA, Paramount Pictures and Scott Rusin Productions.
Ticket to Paradise (2008) Directed by Janus Metz. Denmark, Cosmo Doc.
Triumph of the Will (1935) Directed by Leni Riefenstahl. Germany, Leni Riefenstahl-Produktion and Reischspropagandaleitunf der NSDAP.
Virtual Y2K (2000) [No director credited]. USA, Udris Productions.
Why We Fight (2005) Directed by Eugene Jarecki. USA, France, UK and Canada, Arte, BBC Storyville, Canadian Broadcasting Corporation and Charlotte Street Films.
Workers Leaving the Lumière Factory (1895) Directed by Louis Lumière. France, Lumière.

References

Aitken, R. O. B. (2009) '"To the Ends of the Earth": Culture, Visuality and the Embedded Economy', in Jacqueline Best and Matthew Paterson (eds) *Cultural Political Economy*. New York: Routledge, 67–90.

Aitken, R. O. B. (2011) 'Provincialising Embedded Liberalism: Film, Orientalism and the Reconstruction of World Order', *Review of International Studies*, 37, 1695–1720.

Aradau, Claudia and Andrew Hill (2013) 'The Politics of Drawing: Children, Evidence, and the Darfur Conflict', *International Political Sociology*, 7, 368–387.

Aufderheide, Patricia (2007) *Documentary Film: A Very Short Introduction*. Oxford: Oxford University Press.

Austin, J. L. (1962) *How to do Things with Words*. Oxford: Clarendon Press.

Baudry, Jean-Louis (1974–1975) 'Ideological Effects of the Basic Cinematographic Apparatus', *Film Quarterly*, 28, 39–47.

Behnke, Andreas (2006) 'The Re-enchantment of War in Popular Culture', *Millennium*, 34, 937–949.

Blanton, Robert G. (2013) 'Zombies and International Relations: A Simple Guide for Bringing the Undead Into Your Classroom', *International Studies Perspectives*, 14, 1–13.

Bleiker, Roland (2001) 'The Aesthetic Turn in International Political Theory', *Millennium: Journal of International Studies*, 30, 509–533.

Boon, Timothy (2008) *Films of Fact: A History of Science in Documentary Films and Television*. London: Wallflower Press.

Butler, Judith (2010) *Frames of War: When Is Life Grievable?* London: Verso.

Chanan, Michael (2007) *The Politics of Documentary*. London: British Film Institute.

Chouliaraki, Lilie (2011) *The Ironic Spectator: Solidarity in the Age of Post-Humanitarianism*. Cambridge: Polity Press.

Crary, Jonathan (2001) *Suspensions of Perception: Attention, Spectacle, and Modern Culture*. Cambridge, MA: The MIT Press.

Denski, Stan W. (1991) 'Critical Pedagogy and Media Production: Theory and Practice of the Video Documentary', *Journal of Film and Video*, 43, 3–17.

Der Derian, James (2010) '"Now We Are All Avatars"', *Millennium*, 39, 181–186.

Drezner, Daniel W. (2011) *Theories of International Relations and Zombies*. Princeton: Princeton University Press.

Enloe, Cynthia (2000) *Bananas, Beaches and Bases (updated edn)*. Berkeley: University of California Press.

Foster, Hal (ed.) (1988) *Vision and Visuality*. Seattle: Bay Press.
Frank, Jeff (2013) 'The Claims of Documentary: Expanding the Educational Significance of Documentary Film', *Educational Philosophy and Theory*, 45, 1018–1027.
Franke, Ulrich and Kaspar Schiltz (2013) '"They Don't Really Care About Us!" On Political Worldviews in Popular Music', *International Studies Perspectives*, 14, 39–55.
Godmilow, Jill and Ann-Louise Shapiro (1997) 'How Real is the Reality in Documentary Film?', *History and Theory*, 36, 80–101.
Gregg, Robert W. (1998) *International Relations on Film*. Boulder: Lynne Rienner.
Grierson, John (1933) 'The Documentary Producer', *Cinema Quarterly*, 2, 7–9.
Grierson, John (1966 [1946]) *Grierson on Documentary*, ed. F. Hardy. London: Faber and Faber.
Hansen, Lene (2011) 'Theorizing the Image for Security Studies: Visual Securitization and the Muhammad Cartoon Crisis', *European Journal of International Relations*, 17, 51–74.
Heywood, Ian and Barry Sandywell (eds) (2012) *Handbook of Visual Culture*. London: Berg.
Holden, Gerard (2006) 'Cinematic IR, the Sublime, and the Indistinctness of Art', *Millennium*, 34, 793–818.
Jacobsen, Grant D. (2011) 'The Al Gore Effect: An Inconvenient Truth and Voluntary Carbon Offsets', *Journal of Environmental Economics and Management*, 61(1), 67–78.
Kahana, Jonathan (2008) *The Politics of American Documentary*. New York: Columbia University Press.
Kangas, Anni (2009) 'From Interfaces to Interpretants: A Pragmatist Exploration Into Popular Culture as International Relations', *Millennium*, 38, 317–343.
Kiersey, Nicholas J. and Iver B. Neumann (eds) (2013) *Battlestar Galactica and International Relations*. Abingdon: Routledge.
Kleinberg-Levin, David Michael (ed.) (1999) *Sites of Vision: The Discursive Construction of Sight in the History of Philosophy*. Cambridge, MA: The MIT Press.
Kocur, Zaya (ed.) (2011) *Global Visual Cultures: An Anthology*. Oxford: Wiley-Blackwell.
Krain, M. (2010) 'The Effects of Different Types of Case Learning on Student Engagement', *International Studies Perspectives*, 11, 291–308.
Lisle, Debbie (2011) 'The Surprising Detritus of Leisure: Encountering the Late Photography of War', *Environment and Planning D*, 29, 873–890.
McCreadie, Marsha (2008) *Documentary Superstars: How Today's Filmmakers Are Reinventing the Form*. New York: Allworth Press.
McLagan, Meg (2012) 'Imagining Impact: Documentary Film and the Production of Political Effects', in M. McLagan and Y. McKee (eds) *Sensible Politics: The Visual Culture of Nongovernmental Activism*. New York: Zone Books, 305–319.
Mellor, Felicity (2009) 'The Politics of Accuracy in Judging Global Warming Films', *Environmental Communication*, 3, 134–150.
Mitchell, W. J. T. (2002) 'Showing Seeing: A Critique of Visual Culture', *Journal of Visual Culture*, 1, 161–181.
van Munster, Rens and Casper Sylvest (2013) 'Documenting International Relations: Documentary Film and the Creative Arrangement of Perceptibility', *International Studies Perspectives*, DOI: 10.1111/insp. 12062.
Neumann, Iver and Daniel H. Nexon (eds) (2006) *Harry Potter and International Relations*. London: Rowman & Littlefield.
Nichols, Bill (1991) *Representing Reality*. Bloomington: University of Indiana Press.

Nichols, Bill (2001 [2010]) *Introduction to Documentary (second edn)*. Bloomington: University of Indiana Press.

Nye, Joseph S. (2004) *Soft Power: The Means to Success in World Politics*. New York: Public Affairs.

Platinga, Carl (2005) 'What a Documentary Is, After All', *The Journal of Aesthetics and Art Criticism*, 63, 105–117.

Ponte, Stefano and Lisa Richey (2011) *Brand Aid: Shopping Well to Save the World*. Minneapolis: University of Minnesota Press.

Pratzner, Wesley F. (1947) 'What Has Happened to the Documentary Film?', *Public Opinion Quarterly*, 11(3), 394–401.

Renov, Michael (1993) 'Toward a Poetics of Documentary', in M. Renov (ed.) *Theorizing Documentary*. London: Routledge, 12–36.

Ruane, Abigail E. and Patrick James (2012) *The International Relations of Middle-earth. Learning from Lord of the Rings*. Michigan: University of Michigan Press.

Salter, Mark B. (2014) 'Teaching Prisoners' Dilemma Strategies in *Survivor*: Reality Television in the IR Classroom', *International Studies Perspectives*, 15, 359–373.

Shapiro, Michael J. (2005) 'The Fog of War', *Security Dialogue*, 36, 233–246.

Shapiro, Michael J. (2009) *Cinematic Geopolitics*. London: Routledge.

Simpson, A. W. and B. Kaussler (2009) 'IR Teaching Reloaded: Using Films and Simulations in the Teaching of International Relations', *International Studies Perspectives*, 10, 413–427.

Smith, Marquard (ed.) (2008) *Visual Culture Studies*. London: SAGE.

Street, John (1997) *Politics and Popular Culture*. Philadelphia: Temple University Press.

Swimelar, Safia (2013) 'Visualizing International Relations: Assessing Student Learning Through Film', *International Studies Perspectives*, 14, 14–38.

Sylvest, Casper (2013) 'Interrogating the Subject: Errol Morris' *The Fog of War*', in H. Bliddal, P. Wilson and C. Sylvest (eds) *Classics of International Relations*. Abingdon: Routledge, 240–249.

Torchin, Leshu (2008) 'Cultural Learnings of Borat Make for Benefit Glorious Study of Documentary', *Film & History*, 38, 53–63.

Vuori, Juha (2010) 'A Timely Prophet? The Doomsday Clock as a Visualization of Securitization Moves with a Global Referent Object', *Security Dialogue*, 41, 255–277.

Weber, Cynthia (1999) 'Going Cultural: Star Trek, State Action, and Popular Culture', *Millennium: Journal of International Studies*, 28, 117–134.

Weber, Cynthia (2001) 'The Highs and Lows of Teaching IR: Using Popular Films for Theoretical Critique', *International Studies Perspectives*, 2, 281–287.

Weber, Cynthia (2005) *Imagining America at War: Morality, Politics and Film*. London: Routledge.

Weber, Cynthia (2014) *International Relations Theory: A Critical Introduction (fourth edn)*. London: Routledge.

Weldes, Jutta (ed.) (2003) *To Seek Out New Worlds. Exploring Links between Science Fiction and World Politics*. Basingstoke: Palgrave.

Williams, Michael C. (2003) 'Words, Images, Enemies: Securitization and International Politics', *International Studies Quarterly*, 47, 511–531.

2 Your film in seven minutes

Neo-liberalism and the field of documentary film production

Francesco Ragazzi

I yearn for something more radical from major 'doc' fest programmers (and filmmakers), especially in North America. Call it my mid-life crisis. RIP Chris Marker, but what of the young Markers? Could they find a slot in a mainstream documentary film festival? Would we recognize it if we saw it? Would we worry about audience walk-outs?

(Sean Farnel, former director of Hot Docs)[1]

Introduction

Documentary films about world politics have never been so successful commercially. Michael Moore's *Fahrenheit 9/11*, a first-person film dealing with US foreign policy in the aftermath of the 9/11 attacks, won the Palme d'Or in Cannes in 2004 and grossed US$222.2 million worldwide.[2] Al Gore's *An Inconvenient Truth*, documenting the impact of contemporary consumerism on the climate and released on 24 May 2006, generated US$49.7 million worldwide. Of course, these figures do not compare to the successes of blockbusters such as *Avatar* (dir. James Cameron 2009, US$2,021 million worldwide) or *The Dark Knight Rises* (dir. Christopher Nolan 2012, US$1,084 million worldwide). But *Fahrenheit 9/11* made four times as much as, for example, *The Motorcycle Diaries* (dir. Walter Salles 2004, US$57.6 million worldwide), a film that competed in Cannes the same year.

Of course, these are exceptions. Even successful documentary films that reach an audience beyond the usual film buffs hardly make similar figures. *Restrepo* (dir. Sebastian Junger and Tim Hetherington 2010) and *Armadillo* (dir. Janus Metz 2010), two successful documentary films about the war in Afghanistan, earned respectively US$1.4 million and US$2 million worldwide. Alex Gibney's *Taxi to the Dark Side* (2007), the Oscar-winning film about the killing of an Afghan driver by American soldiers in a secret detention facility, grossed US$294,000, a figure similar to Errol Morris's film on the Abu Ghraib scandal in Iraq, *Standard Operating Procedure* (2008), which grossed US$324,000 worldwide. *5 Broken Cameras* (dir. Emad Burnat and Guy Davidi 2011), an Oscar-nominated film about Israeli policies in the occupied territories based on the personal archives of a non-violent Palestinian activist, released in May 2012, grossed US$104,000. After decades of being considered a marginal genre, documentaries have been back in fashion for the past ten years or so.

On the other hand, documentary films have never been so conventional in their form. The films just cited are good examples: they follow a style of either participatory documentary, in which the director is placed in front of the camera and interacts or even generates situations (Michael Moore, Morgan Spurlock) – the classic format of alternating interviews and archival footage (Gibney, Morris) – or a fly-on-the-wall, observational style footage (Junger and Hetherington, Metz), or both. Successful, marketable, contemporary documentaries do not present themselves as *possible* representations of reality; similarly, they seldom question the capacity of the media to problematize reality. On the contrary, they claim to document reality so that a certain type of truth – suspect connections of the Bush family with Saudi Arabia, the effects of mass consumption on the environment, the absurdities of everyday war, US army black sites, the torture that takes places inside them – can be *revealed*. To this end, they mostly rely on a narrative dramaturgy reminiscent of a fiction film: the stories are focused on a character (or the director), a challenge to overcome, a journey to carry out.

Today, there are few documentary filmmakers who reject unreflexive, character-driven narratives and fiction film-like narrative arcs (Steyerl 2008); Alan Berliner (*Intimate Stranger* 1991; *Nobody's Business* 1996), Avi Mograbi (*Avenge But One of My Two Eyes* 2005; *Z32* 2008), Renzo Martens (*Enjoy Poverty* 2009), Lucien Castaing-Taylor and Véréna Paravel (*Leviathan* 2012) are among this group. Less known to the general public than the directors mentioned earlier, they are the heirs to the directors who made documentary film a recognized form, distinct from both cinema and journalism, such as Jean-Luc Godard, Frederick Wiseman, Albert and David Maysles, Alain Resnais, Georges Franju, Jean Rouch, Michel Brault, Pierre Perrault, Richard Leacock and Barbara Koople. In their time, documentary film directors – in particular, those directing documentary film productions in the 1960s and 1970s – worked to emancipate the documentary form from the genres of governmental propaganda and broadcast educational programs. The genre was unstable, undefined in terms of its funding, its production model and its diffusion channels and was certainly as unprofitable as it is today. Yet it was the point of convergence of a larger literary, artistic and intellectual movement interested in questioning the validity of grand narratives (Lyotard 1984), the power of images and the relationship between representations of truth and practices of power (Deleuze 1983).

As Mike Wayne (2008) has argued in his analysis of documentary film as 'method' – and drawing on the parallels that the present book establishes between the academic subfield of International Relations (IR) and the field of documentary film production – the successful documentary films we celebrate today fall, in large part, into what scholars working from within the critical tradition of social science would categorise as 'positivist'. The question here is not so much whether the current, highly visible documentaries present an objective, disincarnated truth deprived of a point of view – they generally do offer a subjective, emotional approach to their subjects – but that the point of view they adopt, the people they interview and the story they tell is presented to the viewer as *the truth* regarding this particular person or story, rather than a mediated representation of reality constituted within determined parameters of capturing, altering and editing. Or, as Corner puts it, the approach according to which

> the epistemological and affective identity of a sequence of organized images and sounds is that of a *discourse* (an authored account, a descriptive version) rather than a *representation* as such, even though it is grounded in a sequence of representations.
>
> (Corner 2008: 23 [emphasis in original])

In other words, while those of us who work from within critical approaches in International Relations write from a reflexive, anti-foundationalist perspective, the documentary films we show in class might often be based on the very assumptions we criticize.

Why has the genre undergone this evolution? Have documentary film directors, allured by the temptation of profit and mass success, given up on the hard task of interrogating contemporary forms of representation? While some individual directors might have made these decisions consciously while others consciously resist them, my argument in this chapter is that the recent commercial success and narrativization of documentary film language are two phenomena that largely escape the choices of individual directors, being better explained by the evolution of the field of documentary film production over the past fifty years. In a nutshell, the revival of documentary film has gone hand in hand with the loss of its autonomy as a specific field of cultural production.

In order to illustrate this argument, I shall divide this chapter into two sections. First, I shall explain my approach to the field of documentary film production as a specific subfield, outlining two successive evolutions within it: autonomization and heteronomization. Second, I present ethnographic notes on the International Documentary Film Festival (IDFA) in Amsterdam – the largest industry event in the field of documentary film production – as a site in which the logics of the field can be analyzed.

The documentary field: from autonomization to heteronomization

It is only quite recently – around the beginning of the 1990s – that the field of European documentary film production established itself as an autonomous professional field, with dedicated funding streams, production companies, festivals, pitching fora, markets, commissioning editors, agents, consultants and training programs. The revived popularity of the documentary film genre during the same period is no coincidence and can largely be explained by changes that have affected the social conditions of the production of such films – namely, the privatization of national broadcasters that happened a decade earlier, the development of the European funding scheme MEDIA and a broad range of other national and European initiatives dedicated to developing the documentary film market. This market-oriented approach to documentary film has allowed for the revival of the genre, but has relegated the non-narrative forms of documentary film to a prestigious yet commercially marginalized subgenre: 'auteur' or 'experimental'. In this section, I first outline some key concepts borrowed from Bourdieu's sociology of the field of cultural production. I then sketch two key processes in the evolution of the documentary field: first, its *autonomization* as a site of production, including the development of an independent documentary language around the 1960s and 1970s; and second, its *heteronomization* – namely, its submission to the higher economic imperatives of broadcasters and public national and European film funds since the 1990s.

Field, autonomy, heteronomy

Following Bourdieu (1983, 1998), I approach the field of documentary film production as a subfield within the broader field of cultural production (alongside the intellectual, literary, artistic, scientific, religious and educational fields). Contrary to a purely economistic vision of the relations of domination in society, Bourdieu posits that relatively autonomous sections of society or fields produce their own principles of hierarchization between dominant and dominated agents within their own field. In the fields of cultural production, this means, for example, establishing the criteria of who will be considered 'good', 'mediocre', 'pure' or 'sold out'. The structure and the boundaries of a field are constantly renegotiated by the interactions of the agents within a field – for example, a new 'avant-garde' will make the old 'avant-garde' seem dated and out of fashion, changing the governing principles of hierarchization. It is, therefore, a dynamic rather than static concept of social configurations (Bourdieu and Wacquant 1992: 94–114).

Fields are composed of dominant and dominated social agents, but fields also partake in relations of domination between each other. Bourdieu conceptualizes a field as *autonomous* when the principle of hierarchization is structured around the capitals that are specific to it. For example, the field of mathematics is relatively autonomous, in the sense that only mathematicians determine the criteria for what differentiates good from bad math. Other fields, such as the field of journalism, are very much dominated by other fields, such as the field of politics and the field of economy. Good journalism, according to the specific logic of the field, involves good reporting and investigation. But the logics of politics and economics also prevail: journalists are under political pressure to publish politically salient information, but also under economic pressure to sell. This produces alternative criteria against which journalism can be judged: whether it is politically relevant and whether it sells. This is what Bourdieu defines as a *heteronomous* field: a field that is permeable to the principles of the hierarchization of other fields (Bourdieu 1983: 320).

Grounded in the study of the literary field in nineteenth-century France, Bourdieu finds that the field of cultural production is characterized by a certain degree of heteronomy, in that it is at all times dependent on the economic logic of the bourgeoisie, and later that of the general public, whose capital it needs to sustain itself economically. The field of cultural production, writes Bourdieu, is therefore traversed by at least three competing principles in the hierarchization and legitimation of artistic works: first, the recognition specific to the field – that is, recognition granted by peers, corresponding to logics of the self-sufficient world of 'l'art pour l'art' or art for art's sake; second, the principle of bourgeois legitimation – namely, the established and institutionalized taste of the upper class, consecrated in places such as academies and salons; and finally, the principle of hierarchization and legitimation agreed by ordinary consumers (the 'masses', the 'people'). It is around this triple scale of legitimation that the distinctions are made between those who remain 'pure' to the art (specific logic), those who 'sell out' (i.e., please the bourgeois logic) and those who produce 'kitsch' or 'vulgar' art (i.e., please ordinary consumers) (Bourdieu 1983: 331).

The autonomization of documentary film as a subfield of cinema

After World War II, the documentary genre established itself as a legitimate artistic form by demarcating itself from two fields: the field of power, in which the documentary served the function of propaganda, and the field of journalism, in which documentaries were conceived as educational programs.

Many of the important documentary films of the 1930s and 1940s were either government commissions funded with the objective of legitimizing governmental policies or revolutionary films produced to undermine them. Leni Riefenshtahl glorified Nazism in *Triumph of the Will* (1935). Joris Ivens and Henry Storck glorified the struggle of the Belgian working class in *Misère au Borinage* (1933). Pare Lorentz's *The Plow That Broke the Plains* (1936), produced by the US Farm Security Administration, exalted the merits of the New Deal. Capra's *Why We Fight* series (1942–1945), commissioned by the US Department of Defense, was produced to convince the American public of the justice of the war effort. In their form and editing, these films are characterized by both the presentation of images as objective, universal evidence and the substitution of the dogmatic principle with the real or more precisely the assimilation of the dogma to the real (Niney 2002: 71).

After World War II, documentary films were integrated into the programming of television broadcasts. The role of the documentary in post-World War II broadcast television was not far removed from the wartime aim of educating the masses, and it evolved into the genre of paternalistic programs designed by the intellectual elites to 'educate the masses'. In the UK Grierson employed a team of directors dedicated solely to the development of documentary films, with the objective of creating 'uplifting' films. A left-wing Calvinist, he durably established the genre via television programs, in which, as Fraser (2012: 18) argues,

> people strove for humanity, and into which the rest of us could enter, thus seeing our sense of ourselves, as democrats and human beings, significantly

enlarged by the experience. Viewing such singular, ordinary lives, audiences would experience a degree of solidarity.[3]

The emancipation of documentary film as a form of its own took place at the beginning of the 1960s through a heterogeneous movement of filmmakers located in different countries dedicated to questioning and disrupting the grand ideological narratives produced by the propagandist or educational uses of the form. The movement was made possible by technical innovations: the diffusion of portable, quiet 16 mm cameras that were more sensitive to light, as well as small-scale Nagra sync-sound recording devices. It involved the emergence of 'Free Cinema' in the UK, 'Direct Cinema' in the US, 'Candid Eye' in Canada, 'Cinéma-Direct' in Quebec and 'Cinéma-Vérité' in France. While all these movements aimed at problematizing the relationship between image and reality, they did so in radically different ways. While US Direct Cinema, as exemplified in Drew's *Primary* (1960), a film about the competition between John Kennedy and Hubert Humphrey over the candidacy of the Democratic Party, was original in the access and intimacy provided by the new technical means, the French Cinéma-Vérité movement, in dialogue with the New Wave and the likes of Jean-Luc Godard, aimed to question the notion of truth altogether.

In *Night and Fog*, a film about concentration camps (dir. Alain Resnais 1955), or later in *Sans Soleil* (dir. Chris Marker 1983), commentary is not detached and 'objective', but questions, analyses and contrasts the images in order to question and assess their validity. Jean Rouch, in *Moi, un Noir* (1958), juxtaposes images of Nigerian immigrants in Ivory Coast with the improvised commentary of one of the characters, Amadou Demba (Niney 2002: 110). In *Sympathy for the Devil* (1968), Jean-Luc Godard contrasts, among others, scenes of the Rolling Stones' recording of 'Sympathy for the Devil' in a music studio with a staged scene of Black Panther activists reading revolutionary literature and customers in a bookshop selling Nazi books. In other parts of the world, the de-centering and de-structuring of the traditional narrative forms of documentary film have been carried out by directors such as Santiago Alvarez in Cuba, for example, with *Now* (1965), a film about racial discrimination in the US, and *LBJ* (1968), a film-collage about Lyndon Johnson in a form reminiscent of Dziga Vertov's early harsh editing, which questions images of pro-war propaganda through non-linear forms of editing. In Brazil, Glauber Rocha's *História do Brasil* (1973) revisits Brazil's history of economic domination by the US in a pure Marxist tradition, until the voice-over is interrupted and replaced by a dialogue between the director and another interlocutor, who discuss the validity of certain interpretations of history, while archival images continue to be shown.

Contrary to documentary films' social conditions of development during the 1930s and the 1940s, which was driven by funding from institutions such as the Empire Marketing Board (UK), the National Film Board (Canada), the Farm Security Administration (US) or public broadcasters such as the BBC in the UK or the ORTF in France, documentary film directors could experiment with the form and engage in the production of essayistic, 'avant-garde', non-narrative, non-linear films. This is because the field had established itself autonomously within the broader field of cinema. The principles according to which films were judged were the criteria of artistic value, political commitment and form. Several important documentary film directors of the time (Resnais, Marker, Godard, Rocha) were already or became fiction film directors. The definition of documentary as cinema, while it allowed a demarcation from both 'propaganda' and 'reportage', also provoked its temporary demise (McLane 2012: loc 4889). When the *Nouvelle Vague* receded at the end of the 1970s, and with the focus of the cinematographic industry on more commercially viable films, the genre progressively marginalized the documentary until the late 1980s and early 1990s.

Heteronomization of the field

The revival of the documentary coincided with a series of structural factors, which on the one hand allowed the unprecedented production and diffusion of documentary films, yet on the other hand severely influenced the field towards commercial standards of production. Three transformations in particular influenced the evolution of the field: the emergence of private television channels, the externalization of documentary film production to independent producers and the active development of a publicly funded documentary film market.

Educational documentaries within the system of publicly owned television channels had almost disappeared by the end of the 1970s and the beginning of the 1980s. Documentary film slots were rare and generally located far from prime time slots. A first transformation was the outsourcing of television programming to private, so-called 'independent' production companies. Applying new techniques of public management, the outsourcing of programs to external companies officially allowed the large television corporations more flexibility in their programming so as to provide opportunities for emerging talent and to diversify their sources of production. This was a time when important documentary film production companies such as Les Films d'Ici (France), Wall to Wall (UK), Passion Pictures (UK) and Eye Still Films (Canada) established themselves. While broadcasters retained control over content by appointing commissioning editors to link producers and broadcasters, it was now up to the production companies to produce content that would generate interest from broadcasters.

The second important transformation was television's new economic model. With the appearance of new television channels such as Channel 4 in the UK or TF1 and Canal+ in France and the diminishing levels of funding dedicated to public broadcasting by states, television increasingly relied on advertising. Advertisers wanted to know how much impact their commercials had, and TV ratings were introduced (e.g., the Nielsen ratings in the United States) as a measure of a program's popularity. The economic rationale behind this change was also one of risk aversion: it allowed the responsibility for successful programs to be switched from the broadcaster to the producer. If a program failed, the producer could easily be changed without significant repercussions to the broadcaster. While some television channels maintain a public service remit of information and education (the BBC and Channel 4 in the UK, France Televisions in France), this new model inevitably tilted the criteria for the selection of programs from the paternalistic educational style to programs that appealed to broader audiences.

The third important evolution, which accompanied the two previous ones, involved a change of approach within the field of documentary film: from arts to industry. Public support for the arts was generally conceived as a disinterested policy of support for cultural production. Yet public support for documentaries, as exemplified in the 1990s with the development of the main European funding body for documentary films – namely, MEDIA – was concerned with the development of a market to facilitate the establishment and functioning of an economic network of producers and buyers, which could generate employment, profits and commercial returns. The MEDIA fund has carried out this policy since the 1990s through a series of targeted funding streams: funding for documentary-specific training programs, for documentary-specific festivals and markets, for technological innovation and for the development, as well as the distribution, of selected documentary films primarily *as television programs*. In the context of these developments, certain institutions, from the previous cinematographic approach to the documentary, have been retained, and certain institutions still provide funding for documentaries as films: the CNC (Centre National pour la Cinematographie, France), the National Film Board (Canada), the Independent Television Service (ITVS, US) and the Sundance Institute (US). In order to illustrate the effects of the heteronomous nature of the documentary field on the types and genres of documentary film productions, I now present ethnographic notes on the functioning of the International Documentary Film Festival (IDFA) in Amsterdam.

IDFA as a point of entry to an analysis of the documentary field

I use the festival as an entry point into the contemporary field of documentary film production. The festival, launched in 1988 with the support of the European Union and the Dutch Film Fund, is not only an occasion for directors and producers to showcase films and win awards, it is also one of the key annual sites of the documentary film industry for financing current projects and selling finished productions. I first analyze the pitching forum as a privileged site of the production of hierarchies regarding what constitutes a 'good' documentary, before turning to the festival programming as a mode of disciplining, consecrating and marginalizing documentary styles.

The 'pitching forum' as a site of the reproduction of heteronomous hierarchies

At the time of writing, the 'pitching forum', or simply 'the Forum', is physically located in a refurbished theater close to the main screening theaters of the festival in Kloveniersburgwal Street, Amsterdam. The forum lasts three days and is one of the main reasons why most documentary film professionals gather in Amsterdam in November each year. In a large room surrounded by observers, teams of producers and directors have seven minutes to 'pitch' (present) their film; they receive about the same amount of time to gather feedback and possibly establish a meeting for the one-on-one afternoon sessions. The program is dense: in the three days of the forum, twenty projects are presented. The organizers of the forum carry out the first screening of projects. At IDFA, projects need to have 25 percent of their financing in place, which restricts the field of candidates. Projects are chosen on the basis of their ability to attract funding.

On the other side of the table, the main target audience is composed of about forty commissioning editors. While they are dominated within their professional field of television networks – they are perceived as being in charge of a marginal type of programming in terms of audience, revenue and prestige – the commissioning editors are the dominant agents of the documentary field, since they have the power to make or break film projects by investing in them or not. They personify the heteronomy of the field: they often do not possess sufficient symbolic capital to be authoritative in the eyes of documentary filmmakers, yet they have the power to make the most important decisions.

The contemporary financing model of documentaries is, indeed, in great part based on the ability to attract funds from broadcasters. A typical documentary project costs between €150,000 and €300,000. While producers can raise finance from regional, national or European funds, these funds generally cover the initial stages of the development of the project and rarely cover more than a fraction of the overall cost of the film. Producers are therefore dependent upon the type of commitment they can obtain, in advance, from broadcasters. The amount that commissioning editors can invest in projects depend on the size of their broadcasters' countries (and therefore the budget allocated by the broadcaster to documentaries), the strand they represent and the level of involvement they want to have in the film: a co-production[4] with ARTE's Thema strand can mean a commitment of €80,000–150,000, while a pre-buy[5] from the Swedish broadcaster SVT will be closer to €5,000–6,000. This means that the producers and broadcasters generally have to co-produce – that is, attract financing from different broadcasters to ensure the completion of the budget. In this configuration, the influence of commissioning editors in deciding which projects will or will not receive funding is uneven, but often critical.

By aiming at opening up the market of documentary commissions to independent producers, the forum relies on the idea that 'anyone has a chance' and that much of the task consists in pitching 'convincingly'. For this purpose, a certain number of 'pitching tutors' provide training in how to pitch (how to best present an idea to the broadcasters, how to emphasize the strong points of a project, etc.). Tutors, typically former commissioning editors, producers and festival executives, who are socialized into the tastes of the commissioning editors, constitute a second step in the screening process and in tailoring documentary film projects to the tastes of the commissioning editors. While at IDFA the capacity of these tutors to change a project is limited, in European training initiatives such as Documentary Campus or Eurodoc, in which producers and filmmakers meet with tutors over longer periods of time, their influence is much stronger. During tutoring sessions, presenters are asked to emphasize the emotional nature of their projects and to present the compelling nature of their characters and the strength of the narrative arc. These, among others, are the features that commissioning editors seek out during the main presentation.

From the perspective of classical economic liberalism, the forum can be thought of as nothing more than the financial market for documentaries: producers in need of capital looking for investors. But the forum is both less and more than a market. The pitching forum is not entirely a free market, because a very large part of the transactions take place outside its bounds. Most established documentary film producers, who have longstanding relations with commissioning editors, will pitch directly in editors' offices, on the margins of the festival or in more informal locations of professional socialization such as the hotel bar. Second, the forum is more than a place of encounter for economic actors, because by publicly providing repeated judgments about what might get financed and what might not (all pitching forums are made in public, and the public is mostly made up of other filmmakers and producers), the forum is the mediated location for the expression of the commercial system of the hierarchy of documentary films.

Finally, for the audience – that is, the other producers who are only spectators of the pitches – the forum more closely resembles a stock exchange, providing a useful sense of what 'sells' and what does not in terms of topics ('We don't take climate change docs anymore'; 'We've filled out slots for human interest stories') or genres and subgenres ('We had too many personal stories docs last year'; 'We're not really looking for docu-fiction anymore') . Implicitly, however, it establishes the range of possibilities that are or are not acceptable for television. A certain number of formats will be excluded. Black and white films or films shot in any other format than HD or below contemporary standards of production are automatically excluded (unless they are classics or show unprecedented footage, they cannot be aired in an era of HD television). Films below fifty-two minutes or over seventy minutes are excluded or have to be re-edited in order to fit a programming slot.

More importantly, by repeatedly asking questions about certain features of the documentary, commissioning editors outline the criteria of what for them constitutes a 'good' film. First, a documentary must have one or two main characters. The question 'Who is your main character?' pre-emptively announces the possible failure of the pitch, since it is considered a basic element for every film. The character must be compelling: funny, tragic and/or emotionally attractive. 'Can your character hold fifty-two minutes?' is another regular question. The character must face a challenge that will lead him or her through a quest: 'What is the story arc of the film?'; 'What will happen next?' By formulating this series of questions, which are repeated pitch after pitch, commissioning editors are not only asking the producer whether their product fits their financial plans, they are producing and enacting the heteronomous set of values and norms imposed by the field of television on the field of documentary production. The linear, character-driven, emotionally compelling, narratively structured form of documentary is not a choice, but the parameter within which the documentary field as a whole is called upon to operate, since it relies almost entirely on television funding. All other films are relegated to the category of 'experimental' or 'festival films' – that is, films that are unlikely to be funded by a broadcaster.

Commissioning editors are well aware of the limitations they impose on the field, and they acknowledge in particular that these features are in opposition to the hierarchical principles of the classification of films that would otherwise be specific to the field. Yet they, too, respond to external constraints and must defend their choices to their superiors within television channels, who are in most cases concerned with ratings and audience performance. Their choice of documentaries is therefore not a choice of style, but corresponds to features that have been established on the basis of audience research: what it takes to 'hook' the audience and ensure that it stays engaged and does not change channel. Furthermore, in contexts where broadcasters cannot fully commission a film and are forced to engage in international co-productions, the choice of universal stories ensures that the audience can relate to the film. That this vision for the documentary is a dominant one within the field does not mean that all commissioning editors have the same taste. Nordic broadcasters (DR, SVT, NSK, YLE) are considered to be more open to unconventional documentaries. British broadcasters (BBC, Channel 4) are known to privilege a strong story over a beautifully shot film. Southern European broadcasters (RAI, TRT, ERT) are known to choose more commercially formatted films. But the choice of a compelling character, the presence of a strong narrative, the choice of a debated issue, even the choice of the film's title – these are all elements aimed at reassuring the commissioning editor that his choice will be a good one.

Documentary projects that fit the 'experimental' or 'festival' category can find funding beyond the world of broadcasters. At the commissioning editors' table, film funds such as the US-based ITVS or the Irish Film Board have been known to fund original projects. Other national film funds, such as France's National Center for Cinematography, the Danish Film Institute or the Polish Film Institute, are among those who support alternative types of documentary. But increasingly, this support is conditioned or determined by the ability of independent producers to secure additional funding from the MEDIA program or from international broadcasters. In addition to this, and rather paradoxically, the commissioning editors' category of 'festival films' is generally not a category of films that are actually screened at festivals. In the following section, I elaborate on this paradox.

The festival as a site of consecration and marginalization

One would expect the 'festival' section of IDFA – namely, the selection and screening of films in a broad range of competitions – to be more attuned to the autonomous rules of the field. After all, this is the privileged moment in which juries composed of fellow documentary filmmakers judge and reward the best documentary films produced that year. In reality, the selection process, the hierarchy of competition sections and the awarding of prizes are not entirely independent of the production circuit, but are equally dominated by considerations of profitability and audience. Here again, the heteronomous character of the field marginalizes non-narrative, non-character-driven films.

For a selection of about 250 films per year, a festival like IDFA receives 2,500–3,000 submissions every year. According to De Valck and Soeteman, who interviewed IDFA's director, Ally Derks, the selection process consists of an initial pre-selection carried out by seven trusted pre-selectors (Dutch film professionals, who hold positions as chief editor, film critic, film fund advisor or film scholar), who suggest to the festival director a preliminary list of 500 films. Derks then selects 250 films from this list, which participate in the festival, and establishes the distribution of the films that will go into the competitive and non-competitive sections of the festival (de Valck and Soeteman 2010: 296). In 2012 the competitive sections were Feature-Length Documentary, Mid-Length Documentary, First Appearance, Student Documentary, Dutch Documentary, DocLab Competition for Digital Documentary Storytelling and DOC U Competition. Non-competitive sections were Best of Fests, Masters, Panorama, DocLab, Paradocs, Expanding Documentary, Kids & Docs, IDFA's Top 10 and Retrospective.[6]

While in principle all films have the same chance of being selected, in practice some films have already been flagged by festival selectors (and/or pre-selectors): they are either films from established or popular documentary filmmakers whose premieres the festival is eager to attract or they can be films that have generated attention in pitching forums across the documentary financing circuit. Indeed, most festivals send dedicated scouts to other festivals and industry events so as to secure the premieres of upcoming directors or promising projects. As former director of Hot Docs (the North American equivalent of IDFA) Sean Farnell explains:

> If you're an independent documentary filmmaker who has sent an unsolicited submission to a film festival, and you've actually been selected to present your work at said festival, well, first: mazel tov! You've defied the odds. You're in the ten percent. Or, more like five. Or less.[7]

One of the reasons driving the active scouting is that documentary film festivals increasingly compete with one another. IDFA, in Europe alone, must compete with at least three major festivals taking place at the same time of year: Dok Leipzig (Germany, in October–November), CPH Dox (Denmark, in November) and Docslisboa (Portugal, in November), as well as other major festivals, such as the Thessaloniki Film Festival (Greece, March), Visions du Réel (Switzerland, April), the Sheffield Documentary Film Festival (UK, in June) and Sunny Side of the Doc (France, June). Documentary film festivals are therefore compelled to raise their profiles by showcasing the trendiest directors.

A second important preoccupation of the festivals is to attract audiences. In a period of budget cuts, directors must increasingly justify the funding they receive from the European Union or national funding bodies in terms of attendance and profitability. The first lines of Ally Derks' commentary on the 2012 edition of IDFA are revealing in this respect:

> The Festival is on target to reach over 200,000 admissions and to generate over €1 million in box-office returns by the weekend. That, Derks contends, is a very solid performance at a time when other Dutch festivals have been losing audiences in a tough economic climate.
>
> 'We really thought we could sell 10% less because of the experiences of other film festivals, but now we will have more ... we are already even with last year. It helps that IDFA isn't just a 'highbrow, academic film festival.'
>
> Alongside the doc enthusiasts, Ajax FC fans were lured to screenings of *The King – Jari Litmanen* (with the Finnish player himself in attendance to greet his admirers). With everybody from Rwandan drummers (accompanying *Fight Like Soldiers Die Like Children*) to pop idol Rick Springfield (*An Affair of the Heart*) providing the soundtrack, there was also plenty of music at the 2012 IDFA. Yes, Derks acknowledges, the budget cuts and threatened closure of the Dutch Cultural Media Fund have been on festival-goers' minds. 'But we are a documentary community, so we don't give up easily.'[8]

The reliance on the financing circuit for scouting and the increasing pressure on festivals to be profitable and attract large audiences naturally tilts festival directors towards more narrative films, which are considered to be more easily digestible for the audience. Again, it is less a matter of personal taste and more to do with the structural constraints of the field – in this case, the constraints of management and the hierarchical principles imposed by the need to please a 'broader public'.

One result of this double set of considerations is to privilege narrative films in selections for the most competitive and prestigious sections of the festival (Feature-Length, Mid-Length and First Appearance). Films which fall into the 'auteur' or 'experimental' categories are relegated to the more marginal Paradox section. While for many directors the mere fact of being selected at IDFA signifies the acquisition of prestige within the field, the logic of sections determines one's ability to convert reputational capital into economic capital. Indeed, De Valck and Soeteman suggest conceptualizing 'specialized festivals', such as IDFA, as sites of distribution or prestige (awards) – that is, field-specific capital, which can then more or less conveniently be reconverted into economic capital (film sales). In this context, jury deliberations and the criteria according to which prizes are distributed (to those documentaries that have not been relegated to the Paradox section) should reflect the principles of hierarchization that are specific to the field.

In their study of the deliberations that led to the attribution of the Best Feature Length documentary between 1988 and 2006, de Valck and Soeteman found that the discussions between jurors were organized along three main themes (de Valck and Soeteman 2010: 298). The first issue of contention was structured around 'aesthetic versus political criteria' – that is, whether a film should be privileged because of originality or appealing formal choices or because of its political message and topicality. A second range of discussions was organized around 'TV aesthetics versus cinematic aesthetics'. While this distinction is rather vague – which 'cinema' aesthetics were jurors referring to? – it is a distinction that is often made by documentary professionals, generally to designate camera work rather than dramaturgy: it does not say much about the structure of narration or the focus on character-driven stories. Finally, the last point of discussion concerned 'truth value'. Here, the discussions were not focused on the capacity of documentaries to question their relationship to the truth, but on the much more trivial question of whether what was shown actually took place or not (de Valck and Soeteman 2010: 298).

What this analysis reveals – in particular, the third set of remarks – is that the question of reflexivity and the status of 'truth' – in one word, the critical aspect of documentaries that was so central to filmmakers in the 60s and the 70s– are entirely absent from the deliberations. The analysis also points to the undecided status of cinematographic criteria of hierarchization and legitimation versus the criteria of television. The mere fact that the term 'cinematographic' is used without any qualifiers – as opposed to designating one specific school or genre of cinema – reveals the distance that is established by professionals between the field of documentary and the field of cinema as a whole.

In sum, as exemplified by its logics of selection, classification in sections with lower or higher prestige and the logics of the distribution of reputational capital through prizes, film festivals reproduce in large part the structure of the documentary as a heteronomous field, dominated by the logics of mass audience participation that dominate the fields of broadcast television and public cultural funding.

Conclusion

As Hito Steyerl put it:

> The documentary form, conventionally and content-wise an instrument to criticize power, transformed itself in terms of form into a power instrument saturated with power/knowledge. Having become widespread in the field of art, the 'discourses of sobriety' (Nichols 1991) – science, economy, education, etc., whose affinity to documentary forms was meant to ensure their proximity to social reality – began exercising the same governmental, administrative, regimenting and regulating functions of power/knowledge as they did in the other social spheres.
>
> (2008: 58)

In this chapter, I have argued that the current dominance of the narrative, truth-telling form of documentary can largely be explained by the heteronomization of the field of documentary production, which has been both revived by and submitted to the logic of broadcast and cinematographic commodification. In sum, the current evolution should not be explained by the fact that contemporary filmmakers are 'selling out' – although this might be the view of filmmakers or producers who draw on the specific logic of the field, positioning themselves in the field as the proponents of a 'purer' approach to documentary – but rather through the social conditions of the production of contemporary documentary film, which since the 1990s have increasingly been dominated largely by the subfield of TV broadcasting and, to a lesser degree, by the subfield of cinema production. This heteronomization of the field over the past twenty years – a process that was partly responsible for the revival of the genre – has professionalized the 'trade' and marginalized critical documentary film productions by relegating them to the marginal categories of 'auteur', 'experimental' or 'avant-garde'. While such films and their directors still exist, they are generally produced and consumed outside the dominant institutions of the field (outside TV broadcasting, major cinema distribution, major festivals), by individuals who do not (entirely) depend on the field for their livelihood and artistic recognition (university professors, filmmakers with a day job, etc.).

To be sure, the fact that formal experimentation and research have been marginalized in the field of documentary production does not mean that critique is entirely absent from current films, nor that reflexive, atypical films cannot achieve commercial success. The force of the field is not deterministic. The recent success of Joshua Oppenheimer's *The Act of Killing* (2012) – a film documenting the atrocities in mid-1960s Indonesia through a complex mise en abyme of regime torturers through a film about themselves – is a testimony to the possibility for contemporary documentary filmmakers to develop a language of critique that is compatible with the requirements of the market. A whole string of films, at the forefront of which are Errol Morris' *The Thin Blue Line* (1988) and *The Fog of War* (2003), have been able to smuggle in critique through visual irony and double entendre. On the one hand, this reinforces the argument developed here – namely, that the domain of conceivable formal choices has been reduced. On the other hand, one could argue that, under this form, critique is only possible if it is 'smuggled' in in a more consumable form that can reach a broader audience.[9]

What remains to be seen is how the emergence of new forms of financing (Kickstarter, Indiegogo) and online distribution (Netflix, Amazon, Apple, but also smaller, DIY platforms like Distrify, VHX.tv) will affect the field of documentary film, as they are likely to end the domination of broadcasting over documentary. There are, however, many reasons to be pessimistic. For one thing, the passage of entire cultural sectors like music or print under the domination of online distribution – transformations which were announced as the democratization of content creation and distribution – has reinforced inequalities in the market by promoting mainstream cultural productions and bringing diminishing revenues to smaller independent producers and publishers (see the small revenue offered by platforms like iTunes, Spotify, Deezer or Pandora to musicians or by Amazon Kindle, Apple iBooks or Barnes & Noble's Nook to authors). Second, the reduced financial capacities of broadcasters have favoured the emergence of agenda-driven actors and foundations (BRITDOC, Puma, etc.), who, under the cover of a well-meaning progressive agenda of depoliticized 'change', are likely to bring the entire field one step further away from the critical investigations it currently lacks.

Notes

1 'Notable Unfiction 2012', *Ripping Reality*, available at: http://goo.gl/6CZUP (accessed 4 May 2013). Chris Marker (1921–2012) was a French documentary filmmaker. He is best known for *La Jetée* (1962), *A Grin Without a Cat* (1977), *Sans Soleil* (1983) and *A.K.* (1985).
2 'Fahrenheit 9/11', *Box Office Mojo*, available at: http://goo.gl/xcHo6 (accessed 4 May 2013). All the following box office figures are taken from the Box Office Mojo website, available at: www.boxofficemojo.com/ (accessed 4 May 2013).
3 While both in the age of propaganda and the golden era of television, documentaries were subjected to both the constraints of the state and the ethos of a paternalistic uplifting mission, it was nonetheless a moment of technical and aesthetical innovation, with the production of films such as *Drifters* (dir. John Grierson 1929) and *Fires Were Started* (dir. Humphrey Jennings 1943) – both considered masterpieces.
4 A type of investment in which the broadcaster has a say early in the film, generally during production.
5 A type of investment in which the broadcaster is involved at a later stage in the film, generally post-production.
6 'Program Sections', available at: www.idfa.nl/industry/festival/program-sections.aspx (accessed 5 May 2013).
7 Sean Farnell, 'Towards a Filmmaker Bill of Rights for Festivals', *POV Magazine*, 16 November 2012, available at: http://povmagazine.com/articles/view/towards-a-filmmaker-bill-of-rights-for-festivals (accessed 10 March 2014).
8 'Big is Beautiful', available at: http://goo.gl/SyvNu (accessed 5 May 2013).
9 See also Andersen's contribution on *Burke + Norfolk* and van Munster's analysis of *Armadillo* in this volume.

Films

5 Broken Cameras (2011) Directed by Emad Burnat and Guy Davidi. Palestine, Israel, France and The Netherlands, Alegria Productions, Burnat Films and Guy DVD Films.
A Grin without a Cat (1977) Directed by Chris Marker. France, Dovidis and Iskra.
A.K. (1985) Directed by Chris Marker. France, Greenwich Film Productions, Herald Ace and Nippon Herald Films.
An Affair of the Heart (2012) Directed by Sylvia Caminer. USA, Yellow Rick Road Productions, Dolger Films and Doverwood Communications.
An Inconvenient Truth (2006) Directed by Davis Guggenheim. USA, Lawrence Bender Productions and Participant Media.
Armadillo (2010) Directed by Janus Metz Pedersen. Denmark, Fridthjof Film.
Avatar (2009) Directed by James Cameron. USA and UK, Twentieth Century Fox Film Corporation and Lightstorm Entertainment.
Avenge But One of My Two Eyes (2005) Directed by Avi Mograbi. France and Israel, Les Films d'Ici, Israel Film Council and New Israeli Foundation for Cinema and Television.

Drifters (1929) Directed by John Grierson. UK, Empire Marketing Board and New Era Films.
Enjoy Poverty (2009) Directed by Renzo Martens. The Netherlands, Inti Films Renzo Martens.
Fahrenheit 9/11 (2004) Directed by Michael Moore. USA, Fellowship Adventure Group and Dog Eat Dog Films.
Fight Like Soldiers Die Like Children (2012) Directed by Patrick Reed. Canada, White Pine Pictures.
Fires Were Started (1943) Directed by Humphrey Jennings. UK, Crown Films Unit.
História do Brasil (1973) Directed by Glauber Rocha. Cuba and Italy.
Intimate Stranger (1991) Directed by Alan Berliner. USA, Cine-Matrix Film.
La Jetée (1962) Directed by Chris Marker. France, Argos Films.
LBJ (1968) Directed by Santiago Àlvarez. Cuba.
Leviathan (2012) Directed by Lucien Castaing-Taylor and Véréna Paravel. France, UK and USA, Arrete Ton Cinema and Le Bureau.
Misère au Borinage (1933) Directed by Joris Ivens and Henri Storck. Belgium.
Moi, un Noir (1958) Directed by Jean Rouch. France, Les Films de la Pléiade.
Night and Fog (1955) Directed by Alain Resnais. France, Argos Films.
Nobody's Business (1996) Directed by Alan Berliner. USA, Cine-Matrix Film.
Now (1965) Directed by Santiago Àlvarez. Cuba.
Primary (1960) Directed by Robert Drew. USA, Drew Associates and Time.
Restrepo (2010) Directed by Tim Hetherington and Sebastian Junger. USA, Outpost Films and Virgil Films and Entertainment.
Sans Soleil (1983) Directed by Chris Marker. France, Argos Films.
Standard Operating Procedure (2008) Directed by Errol Morris. USA, Participant Media.
Sympathy for the Devil (1968) Directed by Jean-Luc Godard. UK, Cupid Productions.
Taxi to the Dark Side (2007) Directed by Alex Gibney. USA, Jigsaw Productions and Tall Woods.
The Act of Killing (2012) Directed by Joshua Oppenheimer. Denmark, Final Cut for Real.
The Dark Knight Rises (2012) Directed by Christopher Nolan. USA and UK, Warner Bros., Legendary Pictures, DC Entertainment and Syncopy.
The Fog of War (2003) Directed by Errol Morris. USA, Sony Pictures Classics, Radical Media and SenArt Films.
The King – Jari Litmanen (2012) Directed by Arto Koskinen. Finland, Marianna Films.
The Motorcycle Diaries (2004) Directed by Walter Salles. Argentina, USA, Chile, Peru, Brazil, UK, Germany and France, FilmFour, Wildwood Enterprises, Tu Vas Voir Productions, BD Cine, Inca Films S.A., Sahara Films, Senator Films Production and Sound for Film.
The Plow That Broke the Plains (1936) Directed by Pare Lorentz. USA, Resettlement Administration.
The Thin Blue Line (1988) Directed by Errol Morris. USA, Channel 4 Television Corporation and Third Floor Productions.
Triumph of the Will (1935) Directed by Leni Riefenstahl. Germany, Leni Riefenstahl-Produktion and Reischspropagandaleitunf der NSDAP.
Why We Fight (series) (1942–1945) Directed by Frank Capra, Anatole Litvak and Anthony Veiller. USA, Signal Services (US Army) and Signal Corps Army Pictorial Service.
Z32 (2008) Directed by Aci Mograbi. France and Israel, Les Films d'Ici.

References

Bourdieu, Pierre (1983) 'The Field of Cultural Production, or: the Economic World Reversed', *Poetics*, 12(4–5), 311–356.

Bourdieu, Pierre (1998) *On Television*. New York: New Press.

Bourdieu, Pierre and Loic J. D. Wacquant (1992) *An Invitation to Reflexive Sociology*. Chicago: The University of Chicago Press.

Corner, J. (2008) 'Documentary Studies: Dimensions of Transition and Continuity', in Thomas Austin and Wilma de Jong (eds) *Rethinking Documentary*. Maidenhead: Open University Press, 82–94.

Deleuze, Gilles (1983) *Cinema 1*. Paris: Les Editions de Minuit.

Fraser, Nick (2012) *Why Documentaries Matter*. Oxford: Reuters Institute for the Study of Journalism, University of Oxford. Available at: https://reutersinstitute.politics.ox.ac.uk/publications/risj-challenges/why-documentaries-matter.html (accessed 1 June 2013).

Lyotard, Jean Francois (1984) *The Post-Modern Condition*. Minneapolis: University of Minnesota Press.

McLane, Betsy A. (2012) *A New History of Documentary Film*. New York: Continuum (Kindle edn).

Nichols, Bill (1991) *Representing Reality*. Bloomington and Indianapolis: Indiana University Press.

Niney, Francois (2002) *L'épreuve du réel à l'écran*. Bruxelles: De Boeck.

Steyerl, Hito (2008) 'Politics of Truth. The Wal-Martization of Documentary Practice', in Benda Hofmeyr (ed.) *The Wal-Mart Phenomenon: Resisting Neo-Liberal Power through Art, Design and Theory*. Eindhoven: Lecturis Eindhoven, 55–64.

de Valck, Marijke and Mimi Soeteman (2010) '"And the Winner Is …": What Happens Behind the Scenes of Film Festival Competitions', *International Journal of Cultural Studies*, 13(3), 290–307.

Part II
Staging world politics

3 Popular documentaries and the global financial crisis

Chris Clarke and James Brassett

Introduction

Recent years have seen a rise in the popularity of documentary films on finance and the recent financial crisis. Titles such as *Inside Job* (dir. Charles Ferguson 2010) and *Capitalism: A Love Story* (dir. Michael Moore 2009) have enjoyed mainstream circulation. Others such as *Four Horsemen* (dir. Ross Ashcroft 2012) have taken the centrality of the financial crisis in the popular imagination as an opportunity to reflect on the wider structural context of capitalism.

Such films present a dilemma for critical international political economy (IPE). On the one hand, they have an important pedagogical function that arguably complements the idea of organic intellectuals in neo-Gramscian IPE. Concepts such as 'financialization' and 'depoliticization' are used and developed in everyday narratives. On the other hand, however, these films also partake in the *political economy of critique* – that is, the marketability, profitability and branding of certain lines of critical argument. Corporations such as Amazon, Paramount and Sony have been content to fund, distribute and otherwise support these documentaries. In this sense, documentaries about global finance have become an important if ambiguous element in the performance of capitalism, fostering reflexivity and a capacity for normative (re)production.

Rather than accept a simple divide, whereby critical documentaries are seen as either 'good' educational stories that change the way we think about global finance or 'bad' legitimation devices that serve only to tranquilize dissent by turning critical thought into a commodity, we think it is important for students of IPE to enter into a negotiation over the politics of such forms of representation. Documentary films are interesting in this regard precisely because they straddle the gap between representation and the represented through their claim to authenticity (Nichols 1991). Documentaries seek to *relate* the individual and the story, providing an (apparently) authentic view of reality and asking the viewer to reflect on his or her own perceptions. On this view, apparently natural facets of market interaction – including concepts such as 'the consumer', 'the global' and, indeed, one might argue, 'the market' per se – become a cultural achievement, represented and performed through 'reel histories' of the market.

In the wake of the global financial crisis, it is necessary to interrogate documentaries about global finance as cultural performances. We wish to probe the tension between films as *representing* global finance on the one hand, and films as *producing* global finance on the other. The former is seemingly the intention of critical documentaries, while the latter is perhaps an unintended result that works through the naturalization and socialization of individuals as critical market subjects.

On our reading, all the films present a warm image of the period before global capitalism became financialized, stressing a nostalgic longing for an embedded liberal compromise. By privileging a particular Anglo-American experience of global capitalism, there is a tendency to represent capitalism through a series of limiting dichotomies. Principally, finance becomes either a *disembedded*, abstract world of global finance or an *embedded* regime of nationally controlled finance. This constitutive binary is, we argue, an important but seldom exposed limitation on the critical imagination of global finance.

The argument develops the broad idea of documentaries as an element in the performance of finance, before introducing three films under consideration: *Inside Job, Capitalism: A Love Story* and *Four Horsemen*. This involves engaging with the *possibilities* and *limits* of the films, examining the potential for resistance to and the subversion of global capitalism. We suggest that, for all their undoubted worth, the films are trapped within a certain image of financialized global capitalism, which understands the world economy through the conventional binaries of IPE: state/market, national/global, embedded/disembedded and financial/productive, etc. We suggest that such binaries blunt the radical pedagogical intent of the films.

Our central argument therefore highlights the performance of critique at the heart of documentary films: how the viewer is asked to think 'differently' about finance. For us, the image of the economy to which the critical viewer is supposed to respond is a central dilemma in thinking about global finance. In this way, the documentaries are themselves rendered as elements in the naturalization of finance, limiting the imagination of global finance to minor adjustments along a set of continuums that neither problematize the underlying ontology of finance, nor unpick its ongoing expansion into everyday common sense. In various ways, the three films showcase a nostalgic longing for the post-war embedded liberal order. The everyday experience which the viewer is asked to relate to is largely a US-centric one, presented as universal even though it is deeply parochial. Critique thus becomes a crucial element in the performance and reproduction of finance.

Documentaries and finance, documentaries as finance

An important precursor to the study of contemporary documentaries about global finance can be found in the work of Rob Aitken (2009, 2011), who presents a genealogy of the cinematic production of the embedded liberal compromise. IPE textbooks traditionally map the embedded liberal compromise as a specific post-war period that is then superseded by the rise of high finance (Broome 2014;

Helleiner 2014; O'Brien and Williams 2013). Embedded liberalism is presented as an attempt to harness the twin goals of global free trade and domestic insulated finance, a compromise between labor and capital, as well as between liberal multilateralism and economic nationalism. Ideally, finance would be reined in through capital controls, while fiscal policy would ensure the proper functioning of the real economy of production and trade.

Aitken looks to uncover a different basis to the national economy in the emergence of documentary film as a form of cultural governance. He pays particular attention to the documentary maker John Grierson, who had a deep interest in documentary film and in how it could insert 'individuals directly into a global space ... by cultivating a mode of self and citizen – and a kind of worldly being – in which individuals could confront their own roles as agents in a new world' (Aitken 2009: 69). In this way, film was thought to be 'a technology capable of cementing a link between the abstract world of international life and the intimate site of everyday experience' (Aitken 2011: 1703). This was a period in which the idea of the economy as a national entity began to emerge, and Aitken shows how a (similarly) nationalizing media was intrinsic to such processes. Aitken (2009: 74) points out that Grierson's active support of Keynesian ideas of central planning, national scale and international context also required *intimacy*: 'Speaking intimately and quietly about real things ... will be more spectacular in the end than the spectacle itself.'

The intimacy between the individual at home and the world abroad was a way to cultivate reflexivity: people were encouraged to think about and reflect upon their role in the market. Critical IPE often portrays reflexivity as an inherently good thing (Cox 2006; Farrands 2002): it is important to step back from the assumed market-centrism of 'reality' in order to think and act differently. However, through his study of documentary film, Aitken shows that reflexivity is integral to the narratives of modern consumers. In the propaganda of the Empire Marketing Board, for instance, which sought to inculcate responsible citizen consumers to 'buy Empire' and thus support their own country and engage in consumption to maintain the standards of British civilization, there is a similar sentiment that moralizes consumption. During the embedded liberal compromise, Grierson presided over documentary films that encouraged people to 'remember the unemployed' and promote 'national growth' (Aitken 2009: 79). The economy is thus imagined in moral terms, as an arena in which individuals can lead a good and just life.

Developing this idea of the reflexive viewer, we might propose that the social governance dimension of the documentaries examined by Aitken has come to be augmented by the growth of the idea of the *critical* individual. The individual viewer is rephrased as a responsible *critic* of global finance per se. Extending Aitken's argument, the intimate nurturing of reflexivity is now enlisted in the service of anti-globalization stories that seek to re-found the normative dimension of global capital through a responsible and critical individual viewer.

Following Aitken, we might begin to think about the common elements of IPE (markets, institutions, consumers, scale, etc.) as *already represented images*.

In terms of documentary film, the need to involve viewers in the narrative frame of the documentary means that certain artistic tropes are deployed, not least of which is the desire for 'relatability' or the ability for the individual to relate to the narrative.

It all used to be so different!

Turning to our contemporary documentaries, *Inside Job* presents the tragic story of what happened to Iceland during the global financial crisis. It depicts the Icelandic experience as one of ruin brought about by the spread of global finance. Viewers are told that pre-crisis Iceland almost had an 'end of history status'. Immediately, the film asks the viewer to feel sorrow for the plight of the Icelandic people, who seemingly fell victim to the excesses of finance. Crucially, though, the Icelandic case is presented at the beginning of the film not only as a microcosm of the crisis, but also a set of experiences to which 'we' can relate. Just as Iceland lost its end of history status, so, too, the US has lost its way over the last forty years. *Inside Job* instructs the viewer:

> After the Great Depression, the United States had 40 years of economic growth, without a single financial crisis. The financial industry was tightly regulated. Most regular banks were local businesses, and they were prohibited from speculating with depositors' savings. Investment banks, which handled stock and bond trading, were small, private partnerships.

Much of the early narrative of *Inside Job* revolves around a distinction between an old system, understood as a more socially equitable, safe, tamed and productive form of capitalism, and a new system, in which finance in general and global investment banks in particular come to dominate. In the new system, scale is immediately presented as a problem: 'In the old system, when a homeowner paid their mortgage every month, the money went to their local lender'; whereas in the new system, 'when homeowners paid their mortgages, the money went to investors *all over the world*'. A nationalized frame for understanding finance is presented: the old/new (i.e., good/bad) is reflected in the national/global binary of scale.

This line of argument is confirmed by the director's accompanying book, in which, for example, director Charles Ferguson (2012: 3) argues that the Occupy Wall Street protesters 'were deeply right about one thing: over the last thirty years, their nations have been taken over by an amoral financial oligarchy'. This question of the old/new system becomes very important for the film's narrative arc: 'For decades, the American financial system was stable and safe. But then something changed. The financial industry turned its back on society, corrupted our political system and plunged the world economy into crisis' (narrator, *Inside Job*). Financiers are posited as people the viewer should not relate to, and American audiences are instead asked to relate to the people of Iceland, who have suffered a similar fate under the hands of finance since *their* deregulatory period.

Love Story also engages with the question of scale. Early scenes show in intimate detail the fear of an American family as they await the arrival of police to evict them from their home, having fallen victim to the foreclosure crisis. As the police surround their house and ram the backdoor to gain entry, the young woman who is filming sighs, '[t]his is America folks, what you're watching right here'. Scenes of eviction feature stories of house repossession to show how the 'ordinary' people of America are left with nothing, including a comic misunderstanding when a foreclosure victim is 'surprised' at being evicted thirty days earlier than he thought, because now 'somebody else' already owns the house.

By focusing on the foreclosure crisis, *Love Story* presents capitalism as the ruthless logic of finance. For instance, vulture firms feed off foreclosure victims, legally and ethically, because capitalism allows them to take advantage of others' misfortunes.

Arguably, *Love Story* is the most straightforwardly anti-capitalist of the films analyzed, especially in its discussion of the absurdity of the discourse of free enterprise. In fact, we are told by Michael Moore that his hometown priest told him that capitalism itself is a sin. Yet, echoing *Inside Job*'s nostalgia for the old system, Moore tells the viewer that when he was growing up he loved capitalism, which was acceptable in a past era, because of the high tax rates that funded nationally provided social goods.

In *Love Story*, Moore tells the viewer that his 'love affair with capitalism' became skewed with the election of Ronald Reagan as a 'corporate spokesman', the embodiment of the takeover of the country by Corporate America and Wall Street. This historic moment marked the fact that the US would never be the same again, as borrowed money and debt became the order of the day: ordinary Americans have to come to terms with debt, eviction and exploitation. To make his case, Moore refers to his first film, *Roger and Me* (1989), to show industrial decline and invites his father to speak about his memories of working at a sparkplug plant. Intimacy is cultivated through such stories, with the film seeking affective care towards ordinary/everyday people struggling in the face of corporate and financial power.[1]

A major trope used at the beginning of both *Love Story* and *Four Horsemen* is the comparison between the decline of the US and the decline of the Roman Empire. At the beginning of *Four Horsemen*, a 'we' is introduced into the narrative referring explicitly to the US as an imperial state: '*We* had fifty percent of the world's GDP, *we* were making 54,000 airplanes a year, 7,000 ships ... and *we were the new Rome.*' The film is enunciated in universalist tones – that is, the crisis affects *everyone, everywhere*, while in fact the substance might be more accurately understood in provincial form. *Four Horsemen* presents the story of the financial crisis through the lens of the West, with a similar longing for an older, safer system of capitalism. Interviews with David Morgan, a precious metal analyst and consultant, tell viewers that '[t]he baby boom generation ... has gone and done the biggest misallocation of capital in the history of mankind'. The economist and author John Perkins argues that:

> Over the last 30 or 40 years, capitalism has taken this extreme form and a lot of it goes back to the economist Milton Friedman from the Chicago School and Ronald Reagan and Margaret Thatcher and others buying into these policies that really encourage people to take on huge amounts of debt.

The director, Ross Ashcroft, also has an accompanying book entitled *Four Horsemen: The Survival Manual*. It confirms the narrative of the film about the corruption of the old system, while suggesting a parallel between the Anglo-American experience and the rest of the world in crisis:

> [O]ver the last three decades, no country has been untouched by the process of economic globalization that Reagan and Thatcher set in motion. And, while there have been some benefits in countries where there was previously little hope of development, the main 'achievement' has been the adoption of a fatally flawed economic system *by virtually every nation*.
> (Braund and Ashcroft 2012: 25 [emphasis added])

This economic 'experiment' was quite simply an 'attempt to extend power and control in much the same way as the empires of old' (Braund and Ashcroft 2012: 25). Although *Four Horsemen* portends to not find 'conspiracies everywhere', its questioning of the 'systems we've created' presents a stark understanding of capitalism that pitches an equally simplistic politics of capitalism as either embedded or disembedded (in the interests of the elite). On the one hand, Ashcroft guards against believing in 'some far-off golden age' that never existed (Braund and Ashcroft 2012: 34). On the other hand, both the film and *The Survival Manual* look back to the post-war settlement:

> Each time Enlightenment ideals have encouraged new policies to tip the balance in favour of the struggling majority, the vested interests of elite power have pushed back hard. Their biggest act of retaliation has come with the economic reforms of the last three decades, a reaction to *the inclusive economic and social policies of western governments in the period after 1945*. Ordinary people have had little option but to keep accepting these changes.
> (Braund and Ashcroft 2012: 10 [emphasis added])

However, there is still, at the same time, the cultivation of a sense of responsibility to the economy: someone outside of our own immediate experience represents what is happening to the economy, which in turn deserves our care. In the case of *Inside Job*, this is introduced as the Icelandic victim, while in *Love Story* and *Four Horsemen* it tends to be the ordinary hard-working American.

The market is political

A key problem for developing a *political* approach to the market is precisely the assumption that the market exists as a natural phenomenon independent of cultural presentation. By seeking to grapple with the 'already represented' nature of these ideas and images, this section seeks to uncover the critical potential and limits of documentary filmmaking.

Perhaps the most obvious value of these films is how they each challenge the idea of the market as a self-organizing, natural and/or benign presence in the world. Moore's *Love Story* actively nurtures the idea that capitalism is a manmade, unstable system, which is prone to crises and involves a rapid redistribution of capability. Political intervention is required to make and sustain market operations, a point which all three films stress in relation to the 2008 US bank bailouts. Finance and, indeed, capitalism are described as a set of power relations: knowledge, society and culture are secondary to the rapacious interests of finance. In one vignette, *Love Story* suggests that 'right now the legal system is on the side of the Banks', and the US Treasury is said to be basically an arm of investment bank Goldman Sachs. Likewise, *Inside Job* refers to a 'Wall Street Government' and seeks to uncover the decisions and non-decisions over regulation that allowed for the excessive rise of finance, resonating with the way in which *Four Horsemen* laments the repeal of the Glass–Steagall Act that separated the high street and investment functions of banks. Thus, it can be argued that all three films place the concept of power at the heart of the market. Corporations lobby government, lawyers work for high fees and government knows how to retain its tax dollar.

Having embedded markets in a political world, each of the documentaries provides an account of the alternatives, which are presented in two principal ways: through the performativity of the film and its producers and through the *agency of viewers*. Interestingly, all three films have an interactive dimension, which includes wider forms of critical pedagogy and agenda setting. For instance, on the website of *Love Story* there are links to the Occupy Wall Street protests and an agenda for change.[2] *Inside Job* and *Four Horsemen* have companion books written by their respective directors. In his book, Ferguson (2012: 329–330) implores people to 'take to the streets; support Occupy and likeminded organizations; run for office … and support candidates who do seem to care'. Similarly, in *The Survival Manual*, reference is made to 'The 27 Principles' put forward as part of a 'collaborative project' available on the *Four Horsemen* and 'Renegade Economist' websites (Braund and Ashcroft 2012: 246).

The effect of this strategy is hard to predict: people who watch the film, log on and catch clips on the Internet will all take away something different. Nevertheless, the films all identify civil society groups as potential progenitors of change, especially those seeking to effect change through either local or national government. Protestors are depicted at anti-globalization rallies, *Love Story* presents an argument for 'being a squatter in your own home' and Moore finishes with the now popular Occupy slogans: ' "we" have 99 per cent of the votes, while "they", the wealthy, only have 1 per cent'. When he went to see the original US Constitution, rather than a blueprint for a capitalist economic system, Moore comes away asking 'Welfare? Union? *We*? … what if the workplace were a democracy?' and looks to businesses with democratically controlled and worker-owned management structures.

Perhaps *Inside Job* and *Four Horsemen* go furthest in making concrete proposals. *Inside Job* suggests that an aggressive form of regulation in the banking industry should take both incentives and illegal practices seriously. *Four Horsemen* makes a number of suggestions for monetary reform. In fact, in the question and answer section of *The Survival Manual* featuring selections from sessions with director Ross Ashcroft after screenings of *Four Horsemen*, he claims that:

> The gold standard is a wonderful metaphor for a filmmaker.... In the film we use gold as a metaphor for sound money, free of interference from governments or markets. Under the right circumstances, sound money could be achieved through a commodity-backed currency, or via a transparent fiat currency.
>
> (Braund and Ashcroft 2012: 255–256)

These points aside, none of the films are directly prescriptive in the sense of proposing a *particular* model or endgame, but rather each seeks to enlist the reflexivity of the individual viewer to find points of intervention for themselves.

Thus, critical documentaries suggest – indeed, perform – a degree of agency and reflexive thought on the part of viewers. Put simply, if we can think of capitalism as something made and not given, then it is possible to stimulate and encourage political agency for change. However, for all that these films stimulate important debates, denaturalize the market and propose alternatives, there are several limits performed throughout all three films.

The limits of documentary politics

A key sense in which these critical documentaries – indeed, knowledge about the global financial crisis in general – have developed a flawed understanding of the market is in their understanding of the crisis as central to finance. It is simply problematic that each film orientates around the crisis: foreclosure, sub-prime, banking. The effect is to produce a sense of calamity, an event that marks the descent of capitalism, as if the previous period can be seen as positive, as an 'ascent'.

For instance, the depiction of the sub-prime crisis as a massive tsunami, tidal wave, disaster and so on turns it into 'a global event', which requires a rapid (humanitarian) response, with all the emergency logics entailed (Brassett and Clarke 2012). In other words, the complex assemblages of cultural and political rationalities that make up finance – developed through the films – are overlooked in favor of a politics of exception. We are left with the tranquilizing figure of tragedy: something must be done, but nothing can be done.[3]

> Christine Lagarde (*Inside Job*): And I clearly remember telling Hank [Paulson]: we are watching this tsunami coming. And you are just proposing that we ask which swimming costume we are going to put on.

Love Story has a distinct position on the crisis, showing how the US Government ramped up the 'terror factor' in advance of the bailout debate and how the subprime crisis is still seen as a *singular* event which requires a response – whether it be regulation, bailout, or otherwise. *Four Horsemen*'s accompanying *Survival Manual* plays to a similar image of crisis.

This event-alization of politics has profound implications for how we conceive of time, space, ethics and political possibility. For the event to operate in finance requires that finance (including specific relationships between individuals, property and the state) is naturalized and detracts from broader questions of definancialization, de-linking and other alternatives. Maintaining the metaphysical fiction of the financial crisis allows for a curious (re-)naturalization of finance: as a community of (apparently non-political) individuals that require rescue (*that require finance to be rescued from itself*). Tragic critique tranquilizes critique.

All three documentaries suggest that, *after all this education*, what we actually need is to return to the golden era of the embedded liberal compromise: a US-centric vision, where the particular romance of the embedded liberal period is read through the perceived failings of the current period. Thus, while capitalism is about power, there would seem to be a particular type of capitalism that works in a 'nice', almost harmless way. It is a particular type of global capitalism, financialized global capitalism gone speculative, that is at issue. As Ferguson (2012: 115) writes, there has been 'a major cultural change in global banking, and in its treatment by regulators and law enforcement authorities. Since the 1980s finance has become more arrogant, more unethical, and increasingly fraudulent'. Likewise, *Four Horsemen* laments the loss of the Bretton Woods system of exchange rates.[4]

Returning to the issue of authenticity, a common technique for achieving relatability between complex stories and individual viewers is to *individualize* the narrative – that is, to place the perceived failings of capitalism in the hands of one or two heroes or villains whose decisions matter. In this way, the viewer can engage in a moral play: *Would I do that? Would I behave that way?* The aim is to show a relatable sense of individual decision. If the viewer can contemplate being in the position of a CEO or Wall Street banker, it is not through a discussion of financial engineering, *but through money and sex*. Most explicitly, *Inside Job* presents an aesthetic of banking reminiscent of Oliver Stone's *Wall Street* (1987): gleaming skyscrapers adorn high-powered individuals. Bankers, policy-makers and academics are portrayed as living a high life of exciting experiences with vast amounts of money.

At one level this makes sense, as the political critique of *Inside Job* is centered on the incentive structures of contemporary banking. High incentives imply low levels of whistleblowing. However, at another level, investment bankers receive special treatment as exotic Others: six-figure bonuses, sports cars and so on. Indeed, one Icelandic banker even buys a pin-striped private jet (!). In this way, the personal mores of bankers are brought into question. They are all (apparently) men, who regularly take cocaine and visit strip clubs and prostitutes.

Indeed, the film interviews a high-class prostitute about her business relations with Wall Street bankers said to run into the thousands. The objective appears to be to portray a particular form of immoral financier, a footloose, non-embedded metaphor for capitalism: 'In an industry in which drug use, prostitution and fraudulent billing of prostitutes as a business expense occur on an industrial scale, it wouldn't be hard to make people talk if you really wanted to' (narrator, *Inside Job*).

Furthermore, this individualization ironically works towards further care for the abstracted: the economy 'out there'. The films present a juxtaposition between distant/abstract objects and the everyday/immediate form, similar to what Aitken (2011: 1704) refers to as the 'delicate balance between the particular and the universal' in filmic internationalism. Thus, Moore's deeply individualized depiction of the foreclosure crisis highlights the intricacies of the web of global finance and those who are tied to it. At the same time, the juxtaposition is always already embodied or located within a particular experience or economic frame. Capitalism is Anglo-American, embedded finance is safe and successful and so on.

Documenting and resisting 'the economy'

On the one hand, then, a successful element of the films is their engagement with global finance through a questioning of how we come to know finance. Resistance and subversion are fostered through an individual capacity to rethink the accepted wisdom of the place of markets in our everyday lives. 'Everyone is an economist', according to the *Survival Manual* (Braund and Ashcroft 2012: vii), while *Inside Job* (narrator) asks the viewer to challenge the idea that what the 'men' who caused the crisis do 'is too complicated for us to understand'. On the other hand, however, the reflexive individual is depicted in relation to the economy in a potentially problematic way. The very idea of the economy emerges through the films as an intimate relationship between individuals and the world, which asks them to develop a critical sense of responsibility for the economy.

Approaches to rethinking, or 'un-thinking', the totalizing abstract image of the economy might focus on modalities of resistance that can challenge the (authorial) authority of the market in multiple ways, not by posing a better system (and thus accepting its systemic fiction), but by envisaging the possibility of alternatives. As Marieke de Goede (2005: 176) argues:

> Dissent and resistances to financial practices should not be understood as a subversive collective, working in unison toward the eventual overthrow of financial orthodoxies. Resistances themselves work in different, contradictory, and insecure ways [anti-debt campaigns such as] Jubilee question[s] the contemporary logic of credit and debt; multiple moneys can represent a conscious rejection of contemporary finance, but can also be complementary currencies, coping strategies, or inadvertent appropriations of supposedly

neutral money; money art disturbs the image of finance as dwelling in the sphere of science and rationality.

On this view, resistance might present unanticipated openings in the narrative of finance. Take, for instance, Michael Moore's attempt to address a new politics of housing. Imploring viewers to think about the links between the financial crisis and foreclosure evictions engages with the relationship between debt and the housing market in a way that might provoke new avenues for intervention. For example, in all the public discussion of embedding big finance, the idea of rethinking the links between finance and housing has been largely ignored. On this view, it might be suggested that, despite the moral demonization of finance and financiers that accompanied the crisis, the actual product of sub-prime credit is not necessarily the problem. What should be questioned is not sub-prime per se, but the specific practices of securitization, the bundling and re-bundling of risk, that led to the expansion of sub-prime lending.

Unfortunately, the practice of securitization has been left largely unscathed by even the most reformist of the numerous commissions on financial reform (FCIC 2011). The moral certitude of seeing the crisis as tragic and emplacing a previous order of finance as legitimate arguably distracts from the discussion of other possibilities, such as desecuritization or, on an individual level, definancialization. Such questions might disrupt the ever-more commonsensical conflation of private homes with financial investment and open up the kinds of housing debates suggested by Moore. Such debates might revisit the social possibilities of squatting, #OCCUPY and traveler communities or even address the idea of alternative currency communities, barter and local exchange trading as a basis for understanding the economic dimension of housing.

In this regard, one significant element in the films revolves around their discussion of sites of knowledge about the economy. The way we imagine and seek to understand the economy has significant implications for what the economy can *do* and *be*, especially if viewers are encouraged to imagine it and perform it differently. Perhaps most simplistically, the aim of *Four Horsemen* is put forward in *The Survival Manual*: 'Once *you understand* how the economy works, *you will be liberated* from its constraints' (Braund and Ashcroft 2012: 37 [emphasis added]). Moreover, Braund and Ashcroft (2012: 43, 59) claim that the academic discipline of economics helps reinforce the injustices of the current economic system and that it has 'nothing to offer' in the way of radical change. The viewer is told: 'Milton Friedman, his protégées the Chicago Boys and the neoclassical ideology beat the classical approach to economics and became the framework for what we today call capitalism.' The film can then act as a corrective form of education: 'We need context from people who speak the truth in the face of collective delusion.'

In *Love Story*, as we are told that capitalism is immoral and obscene, the structure of propaganda that surrounds the system is explained using the imagery of hypnosis. Moreover, in a vignette on 'bright minds', Moore claims that the best way for heavily indebted students to pay back their college loans is to work for the banks, working on products such as derivatives and credit default swaps, in 'destructive' jobs that do not contribute to the 'common good'. Then, providing both a critique of the complexity of finance and the position of top academics in facilitating Wall Street practices, Kenneth Rogoff of Harvard University is shown falling over his words when explaining what financial derivatives are.

Similarly, *Inside Job* attempts to politicize the failure of academic economics, framed in terms of conflicts of interest and 'pay to play' activities in academia: big name economists receiving consultancy fees from top financial firms and being paid to write academic papers (Ferguson 2012: 241). This does not necessarily politicize global finance itself, but makes a milder claim about the intersections between high finance, government and top US colleges. However, director Charles Ferguson (2012: 21) points out that '[m]any viewers of *Inside Job* commented that the most surprising and shocking element of the film was its revelations about academic conflicts of interest'.[5]

In this way, we might see *Inside Job* as bringing into doubt the authority of respected knowledge of the economy such that the viewer is left with more reflexive questioning. Indeed, *The Survival Manual* actually makes reference to this: 'The cowardly attributes of many neo-classical economists are showcased in Charles Ferguson's excellent film, *Inside Job*' (Braund and Ashcroft 2012: 120). On this view, the task may not be so much to think in terms of resistance *to* 'The Economy', but how we might *rethink* the assumed (moral) relationship between 'it' and the subject, the consumer and the viewer.

Conclusion

This chapter has engaged with readings of the global financial crisis in contemporary documentary film. Certain lines of response, usually containing a pedagogical aspiration to induce a sense of responsibility for 'the economy', are recommended in such films. We accounted for the possibilities and limits of resistance, while suggesting that the radical potential of the films can be found, in part, in their more contingent engagements with practices of knowing the economy. While certain elements of these films succeed in fostering critical reflexivity, they also cultivate an attitude of responsibility 'to the economy', which blunts the critical edge of this reflexivity.

At issue is the legitimacy of such a system, the production of subjects capable of understanding how to live within its terms and the various rationalities that sustain it. Such an assemblage performs a complex global economy as morally and functionally straightforward: the individual-global becomes a key subject. In turn, the films also cultivate a particular and potentially regressive vision of 'the economy' that the viewer is compelled to act responsibly towards. We present them here in terms of the national/global scale, the state/market divide and embedded/disembedded finance.

All three films mobilize everyday stories in ways that foster affective care towards others. In a sense, this provides for critical reflexivity and thinking 'outside of the self'. Along these lines, *The Survival Manual* claims that '[e]mpathy is the revolutionary emotion' and suggests that '[e]nlarging the scope of our moral concern is the key to progress' (Braund and Ashcroft 2012: 194, 248). However, the films present a deeply nationalistic frame for understanding 'global' finance. While *Love Story* is focused on the collapse of corporate America, *Inside Job* and *Four Horsemen* read the crisis almost entirely through a US focus. So while the everyday stories induce affective care, the limits of this seem to be implicitly at the border, with all that this entails for truly reforming a supposed 'global' finance.

The state/market divide, while much discussed in IPE, is also implicitly woven through the films. While the films do politicize the economy by showing the decisions and non-decisions that produce a purported Wall Street Government, they also limit the imagination of alternative economies through an exceptional logic: the crisis is so big that only rapid reaction to embed finance is conceivable. The films thus showcase a nostalgic longing for an embedded financial settlement. This dichotomy is not necessarily a major problem, as national re-embedding and definancialization might be an appropriate response to the crisis. Yet, the limitations of this world view are revealed when we think about the type of economy that the viewer is being asked to act responsibly towards.

The films tend to present a stark contrast between national embeddedness and the anarchy of free-floating global finance, while neglecting the contingent and contradictory elements of the latter. From tax havens to Bitcoin, shadow banking to local currencies, finance *does not* fit an either/or embedded/disembedded frame. Indeed, as Christopher Holmes (2012: 475–476) has noted, the distinction between embeddedness and disembeddedness is not so much an empirical proposition about the extent to which markets exist as it is 'a distinction between two different ideational structures within which economic action can take place'. On this view, the language of critique is being performed in a manner that confirms many of the limitations that arguably brought us to this point.

Notes

1. Further examples include young people incarcerated in private prisons for very minor misdemeanors, work and pay conditions in the airline industry and 'dead peasant' life insurance policies taken out on unwitting employees.
2. Available at: http://michaelmoore.com/books-films/capitalism-love-story (accessed 22 May 2014).
3. See also the chapters by de Goede (on political economy and distributed responsibility) and Sylvest (on nuclear politics) in this volume.
4. What these accounts overlook is that embedded liberalism was fraught with its own problems and tensions. Idealizing the period of 'embedded liberalism' of the 1950s and 1960s as one of progressive social relations ignores the gendered (and racialized) politics of finance of the time. During that period, access to credit was highly unequal, with practices such as red lining, where whole neighborhoods were refused access to credit, being widespread. Further, it was also a period during which the global economy was structured and institutionalized in accordance with the vision of the successful powers – a process that led to highly unequal patterns of indebtedness and fiscal autonomy for much of the twentieth century.

> In 2011 two Harvard professors decided to show my film in their class. When Summers learned of this, he contacted the professors and demanded the right to come to the class and comment on the film. They agreed, on condition that they invite me to comment as well. When I agreed to come, Professor Summers decided that he didn't need to appear after all.
>
> (Ferguson 2012: 251)

Films

Capitalism: A Love Story (2009) Directed by Michael Moore. USA, Overture Films and Paramount Vantage.
Four Horsemen (2012) Directed by Ross Ashcroft. UK, Motherlode.
Inside Job (2010) Directed by Charles Ferguson. USA, Sony Pictures Classics.
Roger and Me (1989) Directed by Michael Moore. USA, Dog Eat Dog Films and Warner Bros.
Wall Street (1987) Directed by Oliver Stone. USA, Twentieth Century Fox Film Corporation.

References

Aitken, Rob (2009) '"To the Ends of the Earth": Culture, Visuality and the Embedded Economy', in Jacqueline Best and Matthew Paterson (eds) *Cultural Political Economy*. New York, NY: Routledge, 67–90.
Aitken, Rob (2011) 'Provincialising Embedded Liberalism: Film, Orientalism and the Reconstruction of World Order', *Review of International Studies*, 37(4), 1695–1720.
Brassett, James and Chris Clarke (2012) 'Performing the Sub-Prime Crisis: Trauma and the Financial Event', *International Political Sociology*, 6(1), 4–20.
Braund, Mark and Ross Ashcroft (2012) *Four Horsemen: The Survival Manual*. London: Motherlode.
Broome, André (2014) *Issues and Actors in the Global Political Economy*. Basingstoke: Palgrave Macmillan.
Cox, Robert (2006) 'Problems of Power and Knowledge in a Changing World Order', in Richard Stubbs and Geoffrey Underhill (eds) *Political Economy and the Changing Global Order (third edn)*. Oxford: Oxford University Press, 39–50.
Farrands, Christopher (2002) 'Being Critical about Being "Critical" in IPE: Negotiating Emancipatory Strategies', in Jason P. Abbott and Owen Worth (eds) *Critical Perspectives on International Political Economy*. Basingstoke: Palgrave, 14–33.
Ferguson, Charles (2012) *Inside Job: The Financiers Who Pulled Off the Heist of the Century*. Oxford: Oneworld.
Financial Crisis Inquiry Commission (FCIC) (2011) *The Financial Crisis Inquiry Report: Final Report of the National Commission on the Causes of the Financial and Economic Crisis in the United States*. Washington, DC: Financial Crisis Inquiry Commission.
de Goede, Marieke (2005) *Virtue, Fortune, and Faith: A Genealogy of Finance*. Minneapolis, MN: University of Minnesota Press.
Helleiner, Eric (2014) 'The Evolution of the International Monetary and Financial System', in John Ravenhill (ed.) *Global Political Economy (fourth edn)*. Oxford: Oxford University Press, 174–197.

Holmes, Christopher (2012) 'Problems and Opportunities in Polanyian Analysis Today', *Economy and Society*, 41(3), 468–484.
Nichols, Bill (1991) *Representing Reality: Issues and Concepts in Documentary*. Bloomington, IN: Indiana University Press.
O'Brien, Robert and Marc Williams (2013) *Global Political Economy: Evolution and Dynamics (fourth edn)*. Basingstoke: Palgrave Macmillan.

4 Documenting financial assemblages and the visualization of responsibility

Marieke de Goede[1]

> The signing of big deals entails a million small contracts and negotiations.
> (*Black Sea Files*, dir. Ursula Biemann 2005)

Arranging perceptibility in political economy

A powerful scene in the 2010 documentary *Inside Job* (dir. Charles Ferguson), which analyzes the 2007/2008 financial crisis and its fallout, provides a crisp explanation of what it calls the 'securitization food chain'. A mere three minute scene, offering some simple graphics and a few well-chosen quotes from experts, explains the historical background and technical arrangement of the complex derivatives – called Mortgage Backed Securities (MBSs) – that played an important role in the crisis. MBSs bundled, repackaged and (re)sold mortgages and other small household debt to global investors and are now widely regarded as one important element underlying the crisis, for the repackaged loans dispersed risk in ways that were poorly understood by, or indeed hardly understandable to, those who invested in them. Even though *Inside Job*'s explanation of MBSs is doubtlessly oversimplified, the scene is important and compelling for the ways in which it makes arcane financial product innovation accessible and comprehensible to the average cinema-goer. Its 'arrangement of perceptibility' opens up the 'black box' of financial technical knowledge and reconnects it with wider questions of politics and moral legitimacy (van Munster and Sylvest 2013: 5; MacKenzie 2005).

This chapter focuses on documentary films that are broadly in the realm of political economy and the financial crisis. In particular, the chapter explores the question of how these films render visible complex political economies and arrange the perception of responsibility. Global economies involving speculative investments, financial derivatives, transnational pipeline deals, export networks and technical consumer standards are both seemingly distant from mundane lives and largely incomprehensible to the uninitiated viewer. The films discussed in this chapter aim to render these complexities accessible and comprehensible in order to draw the (Western) viewer into understanding and critique. The selected films can be understood as contributing to the work of 'perspectivism' and 'decentering' that for Shapiro (2009: 5–6) are key elements in cinema. For

Shapiro there is a capacity for political work in cinema and the visualization of 'movement' that exceeds the capacities of language and linguistic meaning to render interconnected and 'vulnerable lives' intelligible (2009: 40–41). Thus, the films may be understood as contributing to the work of politics and the creation of what Ute Tellmann calls a 'critical visibility' (2009: 7).

At the same time, the films discussed in this chapter engage their viewers in radically different ways. Though they all reflect on the ways in which lives are interconnected and rendered vulnerable through the distant spans of political-economic assemblages, the ways in which they apportion responsibility and engage their viewers through framing, narrative and editing are very different. With the help of Jane Bennett's notion of 'distributed responsibility', the chapter analyzes and critiques selected films to tease out these differential engagements.

Ranging from an Oscar-winning box-office hit to a multi-channel video essay that was shown mainly within a museum space, the selection of films discussed in this chapter is admittedly eclectic. What unites them is their attention to the dispersed, transnational subject matter of contemporary political economy and the complex questions of politics and blame that they bring to bear. The chapter will take as its starting point a reading of the much-lauded film *Inside Job*, in which complexity is visualized, but where blame is ultimately positioned with bad politics and big banking. It subsequently discusses the Dutch documentary *The Food Speculator*, which sets in scene a childish innocence vis-à-vis the financial markets, as a way of approaching its distant geographical and political relations. Finally, the chapter moves to explore a set of slightly different films – Ursula Biemann's *Black Sea Files* and Hubert Sauper's *Darwin's Nightmare* – where politics and responsibility are much more diffusely located, and where the non-human comes to play an important role in the assemblages being visualized and critiqued.

Documenting and Assembling

In contrast to understanding finance and the economy as hierarchically ordered and clearly demarcated systems, recent literature in the broad discipline of international political economy (IPE) has drawn attention to the multiple ways in which 'global finance' is interconnected with, and enacted within, everyday lives (Aitken 2006; Best and Paterson 2009; Langley 2008). These approaches can broadly be seen to disentangle the overarching conceptual containers of political economy – like 'global finance' or 'financial derivatives' – to study their technical arrangements, mundane performativities and modern subjectivities. As Donald Mackenzie (2005: 558) has emphasized, these approaches draw attention to the 'details' of financial-economic complexities, though they are never 'mere details'. They involve attentiveness to the questions 'how does the "small" structure the "big", and how is the "big" inscribed in the "small"?'

One conceptual notion that compellingly captures the multiple interconnections and daily enactments of global political economies is that of an *assemblage* (e.g., Anderson and MacFarlane 2011; Ong and Collier 2005). In her analysis of the North American blackout, for example, Jane Bennett conceptualizes political agency in terms of an assemblage, which she distinguishes explicitly from a 'system' or a 'network'. If the notion of a 'system' would assume a hierarchical order and purposeful management, the assemblage, in contrast, entails a partly unpredictable coming together of forces – both human and non-human – to produce particular outcomes. 'While individual entities and singular forces each exercise agentic capacities', Bennett (2005: 447) writes, 'isn't there also an agency proper to the groupings they form? This is the agency of assemblages: the distinctive efficacy of a working whole made up, variously, of somatic, technological, cultural, and atmospheric elements.' In the case of the blackout, which cut power supplies across north-east America for up to two days in August 2003, Bennett examines the complex relations between regulators and energy producers, political decision and deregulation, the development of energy needs and the technology of the grid. Instead of pinpointing the causes of the blackout, Bennett (2010: 28) suggests that there was 'not so much a doer (an agent) behind the deed (the blackout) as a doing and an effecting by a human-nonhuman assemblage'.

The assemblage as conceptualized by Bennett brings into focus the situated details and non-human arrangement of global political-economic formations, and includes an attentiveness to the distributed nature of power. Such a perspective on a socio-financial event like the credit crisis, for example, would acknowledge its complex causality, involving not simply capitalism's 'bads', but more precisely its contested historical ideological developments, underlying cultural notions of homeownership, contingent financial product development and the important role of ever-faster technological financial trading (e.g., Langley 2008, 2013; Lenglet 2011). Connecting distant relations and long-term historical strings of events is a key feature of the documentaries analyzed in this chapter.

In this sense, the work of *assembling* and *documenting* may be thought of as closely related. As David Campbell shows, the boundary between documentary photography and fiction has always been fragile and contested. Even if documentary photography has historically conceived of its work as 'showing' the truth (rather than constructing it), iconic documentary photographs were often selected and staged, including, for example, pictures of the 1930s 'dust bowl' famines (Campbell 2002). Importantly, this is not the same as saying that they are 'faked or forged' (Campbell 2002: 6), but it does mean drawing attention to the political work of documenting, and to the importance of analyzing the economy of circulation of visual material.[2] Furthermore, as Judith Butler (2009: 67) reminds us, documentary framing should not be thought of as a purely 'subjective act'. For Butler (2009: 67), the intentions of the photographer or documentary maker are only partially relevant in the production of meaning, and are exceeded by the ways in which 'the photograph itself becomes a structuring scene of interpretation'. Though there are differences between the medium of the photograph and documentary film, the point to be drawn out in relation to both concerns the mediated nature of visual representation and the understanding of documenting as an active assembling, the effect of which is nevertheless partly unpredictable.

Distributed responsibility and unruly viewing

An intriguing but under-analyzed aspect of the way in which Bennett writes about the assemblage is the accompanying notion of *distributed responsibility*. If Bennett deliberately seeks to articulate conceptual language that problematizes agency and renders power dispersed rather than possessed, a critique of the assemblage would be that it renders power invisible (e.g., Atia 2013, 2007). If no 'doer' behind 'the deed' is ever identified, how can powerful institutions be held to account, be it the histories of the privatization of the electrical grid in Bennett's example of the blackout or the histories of predatory lending and mortgage securitization in the example of the contemporary credit crisis (e.g., Aitken 2006; Langley 2008)? 'Must a distributive, composite notion of agency thereby abandon the attempt to hold individuals responsible for their actions or hold officials accountable to the public?' as Bennett herself asks (2010: 37). To address this question, she offers the notion of distributed responsibility as a way to avoid and counter a 'moralized politics of good and evil, of singular agents who must be made to pay' (2010: 38). In contrast to the desire for blaming and punishment, the notion of distributed responsibility '*broadens* the range of places to look for ... the sources of harmful effects' and looks to 'long-term strings of events' (2010: 37 [emphasis added]). In other words, the notion of distributed responsibility seeks to avoid 'easy' scapegoating and draws attention to multiple potential sites of responsibility.

A notion of distributed responsibility is particularly important in critiquing financial practice, where historically scapegoating of the wayward trader, the irrational speculator or the excessive investment has worked to reaffirm and rescue the normality of speculative practice (de Goede 2005; Sinclair 2010). Having publicly punished and jailed the rogue trader, banned the speculative excess and reaffirmed rationality, the financial system could be restored without an examination of its fundamental assumptions and gendered logics. For example, as Jacqueline Best has shown in relation to the Asian crisis, post-crisis analyses overwhelmingly suggested that it was caused by emerging economies' underdeveloped regulatory systems (2010: 30). Proposals in the wake of the crisis emphasized knowledge, risk assessment and rationality in order to address perceived shortcomings, but did not, in Best's words (2010: 44), recognize the 'limited capacity for financial markets to process sophisticated information' or address the inadequate accountability of financial institutions for their risk decisions. In brief, financial politics has a durable history whereby scapegoating and blaming serve to rescue and reinstate the legitimacy of the wider system. Bennett's notion of distributive responsibility offers an attractive starting point to think of ways of dealing differently with guilt, blame and political responsibility in this context.

Visualizing financial-economic practices as an assemblage does not just bring different elements into focus, but arguably entails a particular relationship with audiences. As Vuori discusses in this collection, documentary film may produce varied effects in audiences, including a 'feel-good' effect, which allows viewers to feel engaged with the world's problems and inequities, but which simultaneously puts them in a 'heroic' position of distance and moral superiority. An alternative 'ethos of engagement with the world' (Anderson and MacFarlane 2011: 126) may be found in particular kinds of photographic practices that *resist* positioning viewers in 'an authoritative, distanced and privileged position', as Debbie Lisle (2011: 875) suggests. Such alternative practices of visualization recognize that 'the act of paying attention can be dangerous and unruly, and can therefore never be fully disciplined or driven towards an instrumental political end' (Lisle 2011: 875). Lisle herself discusses the photographs of Simon Norfolk as examples of affective visualizations that refuse 'any kind of final account' in similar ways to Campbell's analysis of the work of Sebastião Salgado (Lisle 2011: 883; Campbell 2003; also Simon 2012; Andersen, this volume). In Lisle's reading, some of Norfolk's photographs have the capacity to disrupt 'familiar ways of looking' and to produce an 'elongated space of contemplation' (2011: 881). Most important, perhaps, about such ethical viewing is a collapse of the distance between viewer and viewed, and the exposition, 'if only momentarily', of the viewers' own 'culpability in, and vulnerability to, the experiences of others' (Amoore 2006: 263).

Though the purpose here is not to prescribe or tease out fully the conditions of possibility for an unruly viewing as discussed by Lisle – as if that were ever possible – let me briefly discuss two elements through which the films discussed in this chapter will be analyzed and assessed. First, both Ragazzi (in this volume) and Butler (2009: 74–100) emphasize the importance of a film's reflection on its *own* constitution of the frame as a key element in enabling ethical viewing responses through its invitation to the viewer to participate in the process of meaning-making. In contrast to 'conventional' documentary productions with a linear plot and clear characterizations of good-and-bad, Ragazzi (this volume) discusses the tradition of documentary filmmaking that acknowledges its own process of production, thus producing a space for critical reflection on its claims. In a comparable way, Biemann conceives of her documentary *Black Sea Files* as producing 'visual intelligence', thus acknowledging, as I will suggest, the participatory and contestable nature of its interpretation.

Second, ethical viewing as discussed by Lisle requires, or at least seems to benefit from, an avoidance of notions of spectacle or trauma as the 'standard calculus' of the representation of disaster (Campbell 2003: 72). Representing human crisis as traumatic is to some extent unavoidable as a way of producing political recognition, but it is also limiting ethically and politically: 'the reproducibility of the event can prevent us from experiencing and understanding the event', writes Campbell (2003: 72). In relation to the financial crisis, Brassett and Clarke (2012) have argued compellingly that the trauma narrative has largely facilitated a *therapeutic* response, which has evoked 'passive and needy' financial subjects that are ultimately 'emptied of ... political agency'. In this reading, the therapeutic response replaces political and more profound systemic critiques of financial speculation.

Summing up, then, my analysis of the films in this chapter focuses on two elements. First, drawing on notions of the assemblage, my analysis focuses on the ways in which these films render visible the distant connections and cascading effects forged through contemporary financial-economic practice and thus the ways in which they visualize complex causalities of crisis and profound inequity. A key question here concerns how (if at all) the filmmaker puts herself inside the frame of these global assemblages. Second, my analysis questions the films' engagement and their potential to 'jolt the viewer' out of existing modes of interpretation (Lisle 2011: 874). Exceeding existing modes of interpretation is, by nature, unpredictable, but as defined here they may entail a rejection of the template of crisis or spectacle, which distances the viewer from the viewed. It entails, most importantly, a reflection on distributed responsibilities, which escapes linear stories of 'good' and 'bad' – or 'perpetrator' and 'victim' – in order to draw a multiplicity of actors and spaces into narratives of responsibility, including the viewer him-/herself.

Inside Job

Without doubt, one of the best-known and most-watched films about the credit crisis is the 2010 documentary *Inside Job* by Charles Ferguson. This film became a box-office hit, festival favorite and winner of an Oscar for Best Documentary Feature Film. It investigates the complex causes behind the financial crisis, understood as a spectacular disaster and 'meltdown' with global ramifications. 'The global economic crisis of 2008 cost tens of millions of people their savings, their jobs and their homes', states the film's opening motto, '*This is how it happened*' (emphasis added). The film's pre-credit opening offers an incisive and crisp exploration of the role of Icelandic banks in setting the stage for the crisis to unfold. This is a detailed and delicate analysis of the crisis' preamble, immediately followed by – and, indeed, creating quite a contrast with – the fast-paced, visually dazzling and musically vibrant opening credits of the film. Peter Gabriel's *Big Time* ('I'll be a big noise / With all the big boys') creates an affective atmosphere of greed and luxury, reminiscent of Tom Wolfe's 1980s Wall Street critique, *Bonfire of the Vanities* (1987).

The film's format turns on 'talking heads' – that is, interviews with some of the main US players during the time of the 1990s–2000s deregulation and market innovation phases. A few key critical voices marginal to the mainstream carry the film's narrative of critique. If documenting entails an active assembling, it is interesting to reflect on who carries the narrative: with few exceptions, the interviewees in the film seem to be selected on the basis of their pre-crisis foretelling of something amiss in the financial system. They are cast as the ones who saw the crisis coming. These talking heads are interspersed with graphs and figures, video material from public hearings and images of text being highlighted, apparently excerpts from the reports discussed in the film. Matt Damon's voice-over is a flat, disinterested, factual, but slightly outraged narrator. The result is a curious mix of a seemingly disinterested presentation of economic facts, figures and (prescient) reports together with the spectacular, affective exposure of greedy bankers and lax regulators.

The assemblage followed and pursued in the film consists of two axes. First, the film focuses on the long-term string of events underpinning the deregulatory moves that enabled the speculative products underlying the credit crisis to emerge. The historical parts of the film trace the beginnings of these moves with the Reagan administration, Volcker's tenure as Fed president in the 1980s and the departure from Glass–Steagal in 1999. Unfortunately, the film loses interest with this important historical trail quite quickly, and this part of the film becomes interspersed with vague but spectacular suggestions of financial corruption, money laundering and general criminal tendencies on Wall Street.

Second, the film explores the interconnectedness of global financial investment and the ramifications of Wall Street speculation-gone-wrong on distant localities and the livelihoods of Mississippi pensioners, Chinese migrant workers and European mortgages. The main body of the film, and where it does its most effective work in terms of critiquing the credit crisis, is where it explains crisply and accessibly the 'securitization food chain', as discussed in the introduction to this chapter. The film investigates the main conditions of possibility for the acceleration of the trade in credit derivatives and lays bare a system where banks earn through generating fees from selling as many deals as they can. This generates massive private gains through short-term profit, while long-term societal risk is dispersed and disowned.

The film draws upon and redeploys historically durable critiques of financial speculation, for example, by equating speculative excess with sexual excess. However, the film's easy gestures toward the pervasiveness of prostitution, the visits to strip clubs charged to corporate accounts and the perverse minds of financial traders (demonstrable by MRI scans) do little to 'explain' the causes of the crisis. They merely recycle age-old gendered clichés that associate speculative excess with sexual deviance and do little to produce insights into the complex gender dynamics of Wall Street (Fisher 2012; McDowell 1994). Another durable theme of financial critique redeployed in the film is that of the distinction between value-generating 'real' labor and idle speculation or 'wind trading'. One of the more interesting critical voices in the film comes from Singapore's Prime Minister Lee Hsien Loong, who asks: 'Why should a financial engineer be paid 4–100 times more than a real engineer?' The film seems to suggest that Asian models of capitalism might form a future threat to the decaying and decadent US model, precisely because of their valuation of 'real' engineering over financial engineering. This critique originating from the non-West is an appealing part of the film, but does little to elucidate how countries like China themselves have turned to embrace the creation of speculative markets (Siu 2010).

Ultimately, however, this is a film of cause-and-effect, of good-and-bad, of perpetrator-and-victim (see also Brassett and Clarke, this volume). It pits the greedy financial traders against the pensioners of Mississippi, financial bedazzlement against displaced migrant labor. But does the film really disentangle the complex and contrasting relations between the Mississippi pensioners and financial speculation and invite critical reflection on these mutual implications? Or upon the profound implication of European pension funds in the ratcheting up of financial innovation and global investment chains? Perhaps the most interesting moments in the film are when it encounters voices that straddle the boundary between good-and-bad, sitting uneasily in between. For example, the uncomfortable interview with Frederic Mishkin – co-author of a standard textbook in financial economics and, until 2008, member of the Board of Governors of the US Federal Reserve – complicates the film's narrative of good-and-bad. Mishkin does not quite fit the portrait of greedy and amoral financial ideologue, nor, clearly, is he a victim. His academic commitment to market liberalization and financial economics, his 2008 resignation from the Federal Reserve and his relative candor in the interview – where he admits to having made mistakes in evaluating the strength of Icelandic financial regulation – exceed the boundary between perpetrator and victim and raise thorny questions concerning actual ideological commitment and the predictability of crisis.

Following van Munster and Sylvest's template (2013: 6–7), we may say that this film engages in 'saying over showing': it seeks to expose 'a deeper reality or truth' and to 'enlighten the public'. The film seeks to educate and expose in a traditional sense, and it individualizes guilt. However much they might deserve it, this parade of individual faces of 'evil' (including politicians Rubin and Summers and former Lehman chief Fuld) eventually works to underplay the systemic or discursive aspects of the constitution of financial worlds in which MBSs continue to be normal and legitimate ways of trading. The film turns on spectacular representations of financial trading as both compellingly sexy and powerful (cf. Staeheli 2013) that ultimately represent the financial crisis as a trauma and a 'meltdown'. Taken together, these representations of individual guilt and spectacular meltdown absolve the viewer of complicity and ethical responsibility for the evils of contemporary financial speculation.

The Food Speculator

The Food Speculator: Money, Grain and Revolution (2011) is a 50 minute TV documentary directed by Kees Brouwer and Maren Merckx. The film is part of a series of Dutch TV documentaries called *Tegenlicht* (*Backlight*), which has a reputation in the Netherlands for critical investigative journalism on a wide variety of issues, including the economy, the environment and security. The film pursues the central question whether food speculation played a role in driving up global food prices, so indirectly fostering the Arab Spring protests. Starting with the assertion that financial investment in natural resources has become more popular with the collapse of house prices and stock markets, the film asks what happens when foodstuffs become securitized – i.e., turned into speculative investment vehicles – and how this has a bearing on global food prices and mundane lives.

In order to pursue these questions, the filmmaker Kees Brouwer decides to become a speculator himself and invests around €1,000 in commodity derivatives. More precisely, he purchases so-called grain 'turbos' – a novel financial contract that gives the owner the right to purchase grain futures for a certain price in the future, though the rights of purchase are never exercised in practice, as turbos are used for speculative purposes only. Through buying the turbo, Brouwer places himself firmly within the frame of his documentary, thus departing from the detached or disembodied mode of documentary filmmaking critiqued by Ragazzi. Brouwer reveals the negotiations he had to undertake with his boss at the TV station to acquire permission to enter the speculative trade and details the fortunes of his investment by showing price graphs throughout the film. However, if the filmmaker becomes an active participant in his film – rather than a disembodied documenter – he is still a participant operating at the threshold of the financial world, observing it with naivety and detached bemusement from a liminal position. Akin, perhaps, to Walter Benjamin's notion of the *flâneur*, the filmmaker regards the bustling world before him with fascination for its novelty and strangeness, while resisting becoming part of it (see Figure 4.1). In Benjamin's words, the filmmaker demands 'elbow room' on the inside of financial speculation, while at the same time remaining deliberately 'out of place' (Benjamin 1973: 174). Like the *flâneur*, the filmmaker has an ambiguous relationship to the capitalist spectacle he is observing, being fascinated but distant at the same time: 'He becomes their accomplice even as he dissociate[s] himself from them' (Benjamin 1973: 174).

Positioning himself as a *flâneur* in the world of financial speculation, then, the filmmaker embarks on a quest to find out more about the logic and professional practices of food speculation, and to assess how and to what extent his turbo relates to global price developments. From his mock-naïve position, the filmmaker

Figure 4.1 A *flâneur* visits the Royal Bank of Scotland. Reprinted with permission from *Tegenlicht*.

is able to ask questions that might seem incredulous or even senseless if posed from within the logic of financial speculation. The central question concerns the relationship between the €1,000 turbo and the actual underlying stuff of grain. The filmmaker simply *refuses* to be told that his turbo 'has nothing to do' with the underlying grain trade and is entirely disembedded or fully 'virtual'. One interesting encounter in the film is with a representative from the Royal Bank of Scotland (RBS) – where the turbo was purchased – who is asked to explain how this complex derivative works. The smartly suited financial expert is filmed in his anonymous office explaining the technical workings of speculation in foodstuffs. He loses his bearings only when pressed to explain *where* the filmmaker's grain now is, and whether, indeed, the filmmaker owns any of the grain. After some hesitation, the RBS representative emphasizes that there is no relationship *whatsoever* between the turbo and the grain. He waves away the question of the impact on food prices as simply irrelevant through making an argument referring to quantity, stressing how €1,000 worth of derivatives is but a drop in the ocean of the daily global grain trade.

Despite its seeming naiveté, the question of the material embeddedness of financial speculation is an important one in the literatures on political economy. This literature is less interested in uncovering a straightforward cause-and-effect relationship between the material stuff of trade and the precise impact of the financial instrument, emphasizing instead how 'financial derivatives, abstract though they appear, are particular material configurations' (MacKenzie 2007: 357) that depend upon technical arrangements, embodied expertise and what Annelise Riles (2011) has called 'collateral knowledge'. The filmmaker's questioning thus plays on the much discussed virtuality of financial speculation and refuses to accept its profound disembeddedness from the underlying commodity.

The endeavor to reconnect the abstract turbo to the stuff of grain frames the central narrative of the film and underpins the geographical connectivities that are being pursued. The filmmaker follows the geographically distant and conceptually tenuous connections between his derivative and the global trade in grain in a manner akin to the assemblage. He moves from Tunisia, a major grain importer where prices are state-controlled and where a representative of the Ministry of Agriculture laments the rise in global grain prices since 2010 and condemns food speculation as 'immoral', to London, where speculators gather in professional seminars and praise the global commodities markets as vast and profitable opportunities, to Chicago, where the Board of Trade (CBoT) is the oldest and still perhaps the most important financial market in commodities, to the wheat-growing farmlands of the American Midwest, where farmers regard and deal with the fluctuating grain prices as a fact of life, 'like the weather'. The strength of the film lies in its drawing and pursuing of these global connectivities and distant relations, which connect Tunisian bread-buyers to American farmers, via savvy investment advisors, large grain companies, the director of the CBoT and Western speculators and their critics. Rather than demonstrating a causal relationship between grain speculation and fluctuating prices, the film depicts a distant global assemblage where elements are interconnected, though not easily linked in a causal manner, and where power and responsibility are distributed as well as increasingly dislocated.

Some of the questions and critiques in the film connect closely – if perhaps unknowingly – to important historical strands of criticism of financial markets. The moral evil of food speculation, the relationship between the 'real' work of crop cultivation and the fictitious work of speculators and the nefarious effects of speculation on its underlying trade have been themes of speculative critique since the first tentative trades in futures (de Goede 2005), with a rich history in US Populism (Ott 2011). One of the film's key findings concerns the increased lack of transparency in the global commodities markets after the move to fully electronic trading. If in open outcry markets buyers and sellers – and quantities traded – were at least partially known and openly visible, electronic trading allows players in global food speculation to remain invisible and to maintain potentially large but undisclosed positions. The film's analysis of the political ramifications of technological changes in trading systems succeeds in opening this technical domain to critical viewing.

Ultimately, however, the film reverts to a familiar template of 'good' and 'bad', of 'perpetrator' and 'victim'. Having established that large investors may have a substantial impact on the foodstuff markets and their price developments, but also that their identity remains unknown and invisible due to the new trading systems, the filmmaker tries to make an appointment with these mysterious and elusive 'bad guys' who are supposedly *behind* undue price movements. The implicit suggestion here is that 'big speculators' are ultimately to blame for excessive price movements, which in turn reduces other participants in the film (from the Tunisian ministry to the London investment advisors and CBoT operatives) to small players in the narrative. The film ends on the failure to secure an appointment with a big investor. The notion of elusive but powerful financial manipulators just beyond our reach (and just out of sight) reestablishes a conventional narrative frame of market manipulation and speculative excess. It absolves viewers from their own implications in global finance through, for example, their pensions, mortgages and student loans and discourages them from reflecting on their own responsibilities for financial politics.

Black Sea Files

Ursula Biemann's *Black Sea Files* is a self-described 'artistic documentary work' that premiered at Kunst-Werke in Berlin in 2005 and has had regular showings in European museums, including a 2006 showing at the 'World Unlimited' exhibition at the Museum for Modern Art in Arnhem in the Netherlands. It consists of ten synchronized double video files that document and visualize the local geographies surrounding the Baku-Tblissi-Ceyhan oil pipeline, contracted to bring Caspian Sea oil to European consumers and constructed during 2003 and 2004. Biemann documents the pipeline's history, tracing it from high-level political deal to material realization to the local ramifications in the landscape and the lives of the farmers, oil-workers, migrants and prostitutes who work on

Figure 4.2 The pipeline as incision in the landscape. Reprinted with permission from Ursula Biemann.

and around the pipeline. Biemann calls the pipeline a 'massive foreign incision in a fragile region' and, quite literally, renders its heavy presence in the vast landscape visible (n.d.: 70) (see Figure 4.2). The film focuses on the 'complex regional relations and local textures' brought about by the pipeline construction and what it calls the 'secondary scenes' of the lives it affects (n.d.: 64).

Similar to *The Food Speculator*, *Black Sea Files* is anchored in the *pursuit of the contract* and the objective to understand the complex connections forged through global deals and speculative contracts. In her own words, Biemann pursues and investigates the 'million small contracts and negotiations' that are behind the signing of the 'big deal' that is the Caspian Sea oil pipeline. The film digs behind announcements of the deal in global news headlines in order to visualize and interrogate the 'radically incomplete, and radically inconclusive, structures' on the contested ground of pipeline construction (Guerra n.d.: 63). Many of the video files start with news fragments announcing the pipeline deal and its route before moving to local scenes of, for example, migrant oil-workers in Azerbaijan and dispossessed Turkmen farmers in Istanbul.

As in *The Food Speculator*, the filmmaker puts herself consciously inside the narrative of the film – not through a strategy of mock-innocent involvement, but by offering the films as 'files of visual intelligence' and by inviting the viewer to participate in making sense of these complex and ambiguous political geographies. 'I arrived on the scene when long-negotiated contracts had turned the region into an open ditch', narrates the voice-over in File 1, 'and started a file which would collect visual intelligence relevant to the case'. Though this statement can be interpreted as a fairly conventional approach to documentary film as a disembodied *showing* of supposedly objective realities, it is Biemann's explicit acknowledgment of the interpretative work required to make sense of the files and the film's refusal to draw conclusions about culpability that produce an open-ended narrative. Indeed, Biemann's term is deliberately close to the notion of 'secret intelligence' and draws attention to the ways in which knowledge is subjectively organized in her film. Intelligence – as analysts themselves will readily admit – never 'speaks for itself', but requires complex and contested processes of analysis, interpretation and connection in order to become meaningful (cf. de Goede 2014). Biemann's notion of visual intelligence acknowledges this contestability and invites the viewer to partake in the interpretative analysis, which remains ultimately but unavoidably incomplete. Though perhaps not 'jolting' the viewer out of his or her comfort zone, the film at least succeeds in drawing in and rendering the viewer a participant in the process of documenting and meaning-making.

Two elements stand out in *Black Sea Files* that to some extent sets it apart from the films discussed in this chapter so far. First, the film spends a lot of time visualizing and documenting the materiality of the pipeline, its fixtures and equipment. The film offers long shots of the Baku oil-extraction zone and of the process of pipeline construction. Visual prominence is given to the machinery of oil extraction and transportation; we see drilling towers, tractors, machines, trucks (see Figure 4.3). The film 'foregrounds the gigantic investments in the infrastructures necessary for extraction' (Pendakis 2012: 2). In this film, the oil, its investment structures and extraction technologies have themselves become agents in the story, worthy of as much airtime as the human interviewees. This visual strategy connects to conceptualizations of new materialism that are now making their way into International Relations (IR) theory and that emphasize the agency of non-humans in making up political assemblages and directing their unfolding (e.g., Barry 2013; Best and Walters 2013). In line with Bennett's (2010: 10) notions of assemblage, *Black Sea Files* represents the materiality of the pipeline as 'lively and self-organizing ... rather than passive or mechanical'. As I will suggest below, attentiveness to the non-human in the financial-economic assemblages of transnational pipeline construction has a bearing on the way in which we are able to understand politics and responsibility.

Second – a related point – the film does not offer a narrative of cause-and-effect, good or bad, guilt and justice. Indeed, the film is not primarily *motivated* by a quest for culpability, as the other two films seem to be. That does not mean that it refrains from criticism or from identifying the harmful political effects of the pipeline project. The film contextualizes and critiques the pipeline as the operation of transnational power relations and the dominance of the West over the acquisition of precious global resources. In innumerable ways, the film

Figure 4.3 The materiality of oil extraction. Reprinted with permission from Ursula Biemann.

critiques the pipeline's power to force peoples to migrate, dispossess farmers, transport valuable resources away from impoverished localities and devastate the landscape. At the same time, however, the film's participants and interviewees are not easily categorized as 'victims'. Though it is clear in the film that the pipeline is capable of (environmental) damage and local violence, the oil-workers and landowners depicted in it are not simply passive. Many have profited from the pipeline's construction: local landowners became wealthy land speculators, and Colombian oil-workers were offered new transnational earning opportunities. Thus, the film refuses to assign blame. This is also enacted through its techniques of narration and editing. The film does not provide a pre-scripted narrative of what we see, and the voice-over is hesitant and careful, refraining from positing hard facts and drawing firm conclusions. The method of visual intelligence *resists* representing 'human crisis as spectacle' (Biemann n.d.: 70). As Biemann herself writes: 'In the end, hard facts always tend toward a discourse of exploitation, rarely revealing strategies of mobility, slyness and inventiveness, which are ultimately required in these geographies of survival' (n.d.: 70). Unlike *Inside Job* and, ultimately, *The Food Speculator*, this film refrains from expressing the moral outrage that allows the viewer to claim the moral high ground.

The end result is a visualization that perhaps comes quite close to what Bennett has called distributed responsibility, in which the pipeline itself is inscribed with agentic capacity, and in which responsibility for globalization's inequities are distributed widely, including the viewer as well. There is no comfortable viewing here, from cinema chair or sofa – instead, there is a participatory puzzling together of the political significance of the pipeline, its vast material presence and its complex local impacts.

Power and responsibility

Of the three films discussed here, I have suggested that *Black Sea Files* most closely connects to Bennett's notion of distributed responsibility by refusing to locate guilt or apportion blame and instead visualizing the complex interrelations of global economic deals, and detailing local shifts without reverting to a narrative of manipulation. From the point of view of IPE, which aims to develop critical purchase on political-economic power, an important question raised by Biemann's approach is whether the film ultimately renders power invisible. Does its dissembling of the big contract into a million little deals ultimately render its uneven power relations invisible? Does ascribing agentic capacity to the pipeline leave us without human actors to blame or hold accountable? Or, on the contrary, does the quest for culpability – motivating the narrative of *Inside Job* – entail a narrow sense of responsibility that is prone to easy scapegoating? Does attention to the million little contracts distribute responsibility in a manner that is closer to an ethical reading of global politics that shows us all to be complicit in the Big Deal in various, complex and sometimes contradictory ways (Amoore and Langley 2004)? If *The Food Speculator* ultimately places blame with an invisible and unnamed 'big speculator', a greedy mogul who has transgressed the boundaries of a presupposed practice of 'normal' speculation, *Black Sea Files*, in contrast, suggests that we are all complicit in, and thus in some measure responsible for, global economic assemblages. By showing the complex 'long-term strings' of events where big oil deals are connected to the displacement of workers, buyouts of farmland, local opportunities and global inequalities, *Black Sea Files* documents, connects, assembles. It raises poignant critical questions *without* judging.

A parallel example of the way in which documenting long-term strings of events (both spatially and temporally) without narrating a clear cause-and-effect or binary good-and-bad is provided in the film *Darwin's Nightmare*. Hubert Sauper's 2004 documentary film about Victoria-Lake Nile perch production and its connection to the global economies of the fish trade and arms circulation depicts the complex relations between what the film's website calls 'an army of local fishermen, World Bank agents, homeless children, African ministers, EU commissioners, Tanzanian prostitutes and Russian pilots'.[3] One poignant scene in the film documents a visit by a delegation from the European Union (EU) to the local fish factory to assess whether the factory complies with European health and safety standards, and whether consequently the fish should be allowed on to European markets. The EU delegation tours the sanitized factory in appropriate protective gear and inspects various aspects of the production process. In its closing press conference, the Head of Delegation proudly announces that the local fish production can match economic standards 'anywhere in the world' and that the fish is deemed fit for access to the European markets. However, the scene of the factory inspection is intercut with powerful but revolting images of the local destination of the fish waste. While the EU-approved fillets leave the factory's front door neatly packaged, the film's audience sees the fish heads and carcasses leaving the factory backdoor in trucks. This rotting fish waste is dumped in open-air space and is picked up by children who use it in play. In separate scenes, we see the fish heads, now teeming with maggots, being processed for further consumption by impoverished workers, who stand with bare feet in rotting waste and who suffer severe health consequences from the ammoniac fumes. 'I cannot complain. I have work', says one woman, as she busily picks up the fish carcasses and places them to dry, seemingly not being allowed to interrupt her work to answer the filmmaker's questions.

By juxtaposing the export of the fish fillets to Europe with the local destination of the fish waste, and by placing the self-congratulatory words of the European delegation into the broader context of the local immiserization and profoundly limited chances of the fish workers, this particular scene powerfully draws out the inequalities of globalization. There is no space in this chapter to offer a more in-depth reading of *Darwin's Nightmare*, but like *Black Sea Files*, it demonstrates and documents the materiality of the sometimes apocalyptic capitalist landscape, focusing the camera on the uneasy and ugly details of oil rigs and factory sites; machinery and waste; trucks, planes and corridors. In fact, like *Black Sea Files*, the film has been understood as a work of 'visual journalism': it does not use a voice-over to narrate the complex and sometimes confusing connections of global political economy, but leaves viewers to puzzle out the visual strands and draw their own conclusions (Scott 2005). Indeed, for the *New York Times*, *Darwin's Nightmare* is also a work of art:

> There are images here that have the terrifying sublimity of a painting by El Greco or Hieronymus Bosch: rows of huge, rotting fish heads sticking out of the ground; children turning garbage into makeshift toys. The beauty ... is an integral part of the movie's ethical vision, which in its tenderness and its angry sense of apocalypse seems to owe less to modern ideologies than to the prophetic rage of William Blake, who glimpsed heaven and hell at an earlier phase of capitalist development.
>
> (Scott 2005)

More broadly, *Darwin's Nightmare* produces a profound critique without easily or explicitly apportioning blame: while viewers might understand the much-valued EU health and safety standards in a more critical light, or might be repelled by the confessions of the Russian pilots that weapons are sometimes transported in their cargo planes, no single cause or invisible manipulator is suggested lurking behind the miseries depicted in the film. If *Inside Job* seeks to nail the 'ugly faces' of individual responsibility for financial deregulation and crisis to a public scaffold, *Darwin's Nightmare*, in contrast, finds that participants in an 'deadly' assemblage do not necessarily represent individual evil. As Sauper himself notes:

It seems that the individual participants within a deadly system don't have ugly faces, and for the most part, no bad intentions. These people include you and me. Some of us are 'only doing their job' ... some don't want to know, others simply fight for survival.[4]

Conclusion

This chapter has examined an eclectic selection of political-economic documentary films in order to analyze how and to what extent they create a 'critical visibility' that elicits political engagement in the context of the financial crisis (Tellmann 2009). With the help of the notion of 'assemblage', the chapter has discussed four documentary films that are comparable in their projects to trace and visualize the distant relations and global connectivities of contemporary political economies, yet radically different in their message concerning blame and political responsibility. Taken together, my reading of these films points to the variation and versatility of the documentary genre: while *Inside Job* holds up the individual 'faces of evil' to public scrutiny and seeks to call political leaders to account, *The Food Speculator* suggests that the real manipulators exist just outside our grasp and outside our field of vision. In contrast, *Black Sea Files* and *Darwin's Nightmare* deliberately refrain from offering easy answers to the questions of guilt and blame, drawing attention instead to the dispersed and complex relationships between individual agency and global constellations.

In *Black Sea Files* and *Darwin's Nightmare*, the global political economy acquires an agentic capacity that exceeds the sum of individual agency. While this renders the crafting of concrete political agendas complicated, these modes of visualization seek to break out of the moral superiority that for Vuori and Lisle too often accompanies Western viewing. What I have suggested in this chapter is that – despite the challenges this poses for enacting public accountability – seeking out individual evil is politically insufficient in the face of complex political economies, as it may lead to easy scapegoating and narrow questioning. Certainly, holding individuals and institutions to account is important. For example, trials of traders and courtroom proceedings in the wake of the financial crisis offer a platform on which complex derivatives contracts are debated and institutions are called to account. At the same time, political change may require a notion of distributed responsibility that acknowledges how we all participate in complex global economies – through pensions, mortgages or student loans – and that responsibility for inequity is distributed and dispersed. For Biemann, for example, an abstract and distant representation of the oil economy is 'yet another way to keep it firmly in the hands of market dynamics, a remote and inaccessible entity, supposedly too big and complex to grasp for the average citizen' (Pendakis 2012: 2). Rendering the crisis from a distant spectacle into a political event anchored in everyday life is important in fostering ethical and everyday responsibility – for example, in a classroom setting and in relation to students' personal experiences. Such visualizations suggest that we are all implicated in, and responsible for, the inequities of contemporary global economies, and they also acknowledge that 'we all find ourselves' in 'contradictory relationships with the global political economy' (Amoore and Langley 2004: 106).

Notes

1 Many thanks to Casper Sylvest and Rens van Munster for involving me in this project and for their detailed comments on previous versions of this chapter. I wish to thank also the participants in the 'Documenting World Politics' workshop at the Danish Institute for International Affairs for their helpful comments on this chapter, especially Mark Duffield, who suggested that the filmmaker of *The Food Speculator* could be compared to Benjamin's 'flâneur'. I gratefully acknowledge Ursula Biemann's and Kees Brouwer's permissions to use the images from their films. Financial support for this research was provided by the Dutch Council for Scientific Research (NWO), through the VIDI grant 'European Security Culture' (award number 452–09–016).
2 See also, for example, van Munster and Sylvest (this volume), Andersen and Möller (2013), Shapiro (2009), Simon (2012) and Weber (2006).
3 'Synopsis', *Darwin's Nightmare*. Available at: www.darwinsnightmare.com/darwin/html/startset.htm (accessed 27 January 2014).
4 'Director's Statement', *Darwin's Nightmare*. Available at: www.darwinsnightmare.com/darwin/html/startset.htm (accessed 27 January 2014).

Films

Black Sea Files (2005) Directed by Ursula Biemann. Switzerland. Partly available at: www.youtube.com/watch?v=bNlPZfpObMk (accessed 28 May 2014).
Darwin's Nightmare (2004) Directed by Hubert Sauper. Austria, Belgium and France, Mille et Une Productions, Coop 99 and Saga Film.
Inside Job (2010) Directed by Charles Ferguson. USA, Sony Pictures Classics.
The Food Speculator: Money, Grain and Revolution (2011) Directed by Kees Brouwer. The Netherlands, VPRO Backlight. Available at: http://tegenlicht.vpro.nl/backlight/food-speculator.html (accessed 28 May 2014).

References

Aitken, Rob (2006) 'Capital at its Fringes', *New Political Economy*, 11, 479–498.
Amoore, Louise (2006) '"There is No Great Refusal": The Ambivalent Politics of Resistance', in Marieke de Goede (ed.) *International Political Economy and Post-structural Politics*. London: Palgrave, 255–274.
Amoore, Louise and Paul Langley (2004) 'Ambiguities of Global Civil Society', *Review of International Studies*, 30, 89–110.
Andersen, Rune S. and Frank Möller (2013) 'Engaging the Limits of Visibility: Photography, Security and Surveillance', *Security Dialogue*, 44, 203–221.
Anderson, Ben and Colin McFarlane (2011) 'Assemblage and Geography', *Area*, 43, 124–227.
Atia, Mona (2007) 'In Whose Interest? Financial Surveillance and the Circuits of Exception in the War on Terror', *Environment and Planning D: Society and Space*, 25, 447–475.
Atia, Mona (2013) 'The Politics of Preemption and the War on Terrorist Finance', *Political Geography*, 32, 53–55.

Barry, Andrew (2013) 'The Translation Zone: Between Actor-Network Theory and International Relations', *Millennium: Journal of International Relations*, 41, 413–429.
Benjamin, Walter (1973) *Illuminations*. Translated by Harry Zohn. London: Fontana.
Bennett, Jane (2005) 'The Agency of Assemblages and the North American Blackout', *Public Culture*, 17, 445–465.
Bennett, Jane (2010) *Vibrant Matter: A Political Ecology of Things*. Durham, NC: Duke University Press.
Best, Jacqueline (2010) 'The Limits of Financial Risk Management: Or What We Didn't Learn from the Asian Crisis', *New Political Economy*, 15, 29–49.
Best, Jacqueline and Matthew Paterson (eds) (2009) *Cultural Political Economy*. London: Routledge.
Best, Jacqueline and William Walters (2013) 'Translating the Sociology of Translation', *International Political Sociology*, 7, 345–349.
Biemann, Ursula (n.d.) *Embedded Fieldwork and Global Oil Circulation: Black Sea Files*. Available at: www.geobodies.org/books-and-texts/texts (accessed 29 January 2014).
Brassett, James and Chris Clarke (2012) 'Performing the Sub-Prime Crisis: Trauma and the Financial Event', *International Political Sociology*, 6, 4–20.
Butler, Judith (2009) *Frames of War: When Is Live Grievable?* London: Verso.
Campbell, David (2002) 'Atrocity, Memory Photography: Imaging the Concentration Camps of Bosnia', *Journal of Human Rights*, 1, 1–33.
Campbell, David (2003) 'Salgado and the Sahel: Documentary Photography and the Imaging of Famine', in Francois Debrix and Cynthia Weber (eds) *Rituals of Mediation: International Political and Social Meaning*. Minneapolis, MN: University of Minnesota Press, 69–96.
Fisher, Melissa S. (2012) *Wall Street Women*. Durham, NC: Duke University Press.
de Goede, Marieke (2005) *Virtue, Fortune and Faith: A Genealogy of Finance*. Minneapolis, MN: University of Minnesota Press.
de Goede, Marieke (2014) 'Preemption Contested: Suspected Spaces and Preventability in the July 7 Inquest', *Political Geography*, 39, 48–57.
Guerra, Charles (n.d.) 'Introduction', *Embedded Fieldwork and Global Oil Circulation: Black Sea Files*. Available at: www.geobodies.org/books-and-texts/texts (accessed 29 January 2014).
Langley, Paul (2008) *The Everyday Life of Global Finance: Saving and Borrowing in Anglo-America*. Oxford: Oxford University Press.
Langley, Paul (2013) 'Toxic Assets, Turbulence and Biopolitical Security: Governing the Crisis of Global Financial Circulation', *Security Dialogue*, 44, 111–126.
Lenglet, Marc (2011) 'Conflicting Codes and Codings: How Algorithmic Trading is Reshaping Financial Regulation', *Theory, Culture & Society*, 28(6), 44–66.
Lisle, Debbie (2011) 'The Surprising Detritus of Leisure: Encountering the Late Photography of War', *Environment and Planning D: Society and Space*, 29, 873–890.
MacKenzie, D. (2005) 'Opening the Black Boxes of Global Finance', *Review of International Political Economy*, 12, 555–576.
MacKenzie, Donald (2007) 'The Material Production of Virtuality: Innovation, Cultural Geography and Facticity in Derivatives Markets', *Economy & Society*, 36, 355–376.
McDowell, Linda (1994) *Capital Culture: Gender at Work in the City*. London: Blackwell.
van Munster, Rens and Casper Sylvest (2013) 'Documenting International Relations: Documentary Film and the Creative Arrangement of Perceptibility', *International Studies Perspectives*, DOI: 10.1111/insp. 12062, 1–17.

Ong, Aihwa and Stephen J. Collier (eds) (2005) *Global Assemblages: Technology, Politics and Ethics as Anthropological Problems*. Malden, MA: Blackwell.

Ott, Julia (2011) *When Wall Street Met Main Street: The Quest for an Investors' Democracy*. Cambridge, MA: Harvard University Press.

Pendakis, Andrew (2012) *This Is Not A Pipeline: Ursula Biemann and the Politico-Aesthetics of Oil*. Available at: www.geobodies.org/books-and-texts/texts (accessed 17 March 2014).

Riles, Annelise (2011) *Collateral Knowledge: Legal Reasoning in the Global Financial Markets*. Chicago, IL: University of Chicago Press.

Scott, A. O. (2005) 'Feeding Europe, Starving at Home', *New York Times*, 3 August 2005. Available at: http://movies.nytimes.com/2005/08/03/movies/03darw.html?_r=0 (accessed 17 March 2014).

Shapiro, Michael J. (2009) *Cinematic Geopolitics*. London: Routledge.

Simon, Stephanie (2012) 'Suspicious Encounters: Ordinary Preemption and the Securitization of Photography', *Security Dialogue*, 43, 157–173.

Sinclair, Timothy J. (2010) 'Round Up the Usual Suspects: Blame and the Subprime Crisis', *New Political Economy*, 15, 91–107.

Siu, Lucia (2010) 'Gangs in the Markets: Network-Based Cognition in China's Futures Industry', *International Journal of China Studies*, 1, 371–389.

Staeheli, Urs (2013) *Spectacular Speculation: Thrills, the Economy and Popular Discourse*. Stanford, CA: Stanford University Press.

Tellmann, Ute (2009) 'Foucault and the Invisible Economy', *Foucault Studies*, 6, 5–24.

Weber, Cynthia (2006) *Imagining America at War: Morality, Politics and Film*. London: Routledge.

Wolfe, Tom (1987) *Bonfire of the Vanities*. New York, NY: Farrar Straus Giroux.

5 Non-linearity in the ocean documentary

Philip E. Steinberg

Fiction and fact in an emergent ocean

Few topics in International Relations (IR) are as in need of exposure through the documentary genre as the ocean, a space that is rarely understood for the complex, but essential role that it plays in global political, economic and ecological systems. Basic principles of public international law, including the fundamental notion of territorial state sovereignty, derive from Hugo Grotius' work on the law of the sea, and the sea remains an important arena for the development of institutions to regulate cross-border resources and environmental problems. Ninety-five percent of international trade travels by sea. The ocean plays a crucial role in amplifying and bringing to bear the destabilizing effects of climate change. In fact, even in its antithetical designation as a space *beyond* state territories and competencies, the ocean plays a central role in discursively reproducing modernity's foundational sociopolitical formation: the land-based, sovereign, territorial state (Steinberg 2001, 2009).

In short, the ocean binds the world together, it buttresses notions of territory and sovereignty and it generates relations of both cooperation and conflict. Yet it presents specific challenges as the subject of a cinematic documentary. In part, this is because of the ocean's relative inaccessibility. Particularly in its light-deprived depths, the ocean is a difficult place to inhabit for any length of time and an exceptionally difficult place to film. Depictions of the ocean are also limited by the blinding suppositions that are all too often adopted by scholars, journalists and artists (including filmmakers), who accept its political-legal construction as a fundamentally non-territorial space that exists simply to be crossed or to be entered solely for the purpose of extracting resources that can be brought to the territory of a developable society-state on land. This political-legal perspective, in turn, is buttressed by capital's idealization of the ocean as a friction-free, dematerialized surface whose space can be expressed simply as distance, and which then can (and should) be progressively annihilated by technologies that relentlessly accelerate the circuits of capital.

Perhaps the fundamental barrier, however, arises from the ocean's mobile, dynamic nature. As a space that is continually being reconstituted by molecules, biota, ships and ideas (ranging from those of freedom to nostalgia to effortless military projection), the ocean – quite literally a space of fluid dynamics – does not stand still long enough to be described. The ocean is always emergent, and thus fundamentally beyond representation (Anderson 2012; Peters 2012; Steinberg 2009, 2011, 2013b). Deleuze and Guattari, in their conceptualization of the world as divided into 'smooth' spaces of affect and emergence and 'striated' spaces of order, hierarchy and representation, call the ocean the 'smooth space *par excellence*' (Deleuze and Guattari 1988: 479).

The ocean is thus, on the one hand, a space that *needs* to be represented in International Relations pedagogy, while on the other hand being a space that *defies* representation, at least by means of straightforward, linear narratives (Steinberg 2008). For this reason, most documentaries that attempt to represent the ocean miss their mark. To be clear, even relatively 'traditional' ocean documentaries take on a variety of forms. From the utterly conventional *The End of the Line* (dir. Rupert Murray 2009), in which narrator Ted Danson leads the viewer through a series of interviews and encounters with fishermen, scientists and enforcement officials to document the global fisheries crisis, to the more innovative *The Cove* (dir. Louie Psihoyos 2009), a suspense-filled piece of investigative reporting that follows a team of activist-detectives as they discover the secret dolphin slaughters that regularly occur in a remote Japanese village, most ocean documentaries focus on how the over-extraction (or inhumane extraction) of marine resources is facilitated by lax regulation, corporate greed and the structural problems of resource management in a global commons. In these documentaries, the ocean itself merely forms the setting within which social and environmental issues unfold. In its liquidity, its wetness, its depth and its rhythms; in its affective properties that alternately spur ideas of danger, escape, turmoil and boredom; and also in the way that it is perpetually being remade through connections across its borders, the material ocean escapes the camera's eye. If any of these dynamics behind the social and geophysical construction of the ocean are incorporated into the narrative, they are typically reduced to metaphor or nostalgia (Steinberg 2013b).

The challenge for an ocean documentary is, then, to depict how the ocean's role in global political and economic systems is enabled by the paradoxical way in which it is simultaneously perceived as *both* a featureless surface beyond nature and society *and* a mysterious, complex and dynamic geophysical-human-animal ecological assemblage of material and emotive encounters and memories that is perpetually in formation. Traditional, linear documentaries are not up to this task. To that end, this chapter examines two films that use non-conventional narrative devices to explore the global space of the ocean: *The Forgotten Space* and *Leviathan*.

Place, space, time and the non-linear documentary

The philosopher Edward Casey expresses a prevalent, if often implicit, theme in modern thought when he declares that the fundamental corequisite of human existence is *place*: 'the limit and condition of all that exists' (Casey 2009: 15).

Places, Casey writes, are the points on the earth's surface where humans both transform nature (which is the material condition of human existence) and experience things (which is the phenomenological condition of human existence). A broad range of social theories ground themselves (literally) in this fundamental understanding of place. For instance, John Locke's (1690) understanding of social and political institutions begins by envisioning a world of points on the earth's surface. Over time, as humans cluster at these points and transform the nature around them, not only places but also social institutions develop. Eventually, these institutions evolve into states that, through the drawing of boundaries, gather points into territories. As Stuart Elden (2005) has noted, the modern notion of territory (and the territorial state) that is fundamental to International Relations theory is dependent on an underlying conception of the world as consisting of a series of places. Because these places all have their origins in substantively formless *points*, they are deemed fundamentally equivalent. Hence, the places that emerge at these points are understood as calculable in their difference, and this establishes a basis for the hierarchical ordering of the world's space.

Implicit in this place-based construction of space is a linear sense of time, exemplified in Yi-Fu Tuan's (1977: 138) definition of place as a 'pause in movement'. For Tuan, as individuals interrupt their movements through both space and time, they embed themselves in place, giving meaning to those places which, in turn, become repositories of their experiences. In the process, humans, through being in place, realize both their individual and social humanity. Thus, the development of a place and its people is associated with the forward progression of time.

This foundationalist understanding of place and its alignment with a linear sense of time impacts on how we understand the world, in a number of ways. First, because places are equated with temporal progress, and because geographical difference becomes rescripted as temporal difference (i.e., difference in levels of development), alternative trajectories based on more open-ended conceptualizations of space are deferred (Massey 2005). Second, the equation of bounded territories with the societies in which 'place' happens supports the inside/outside distinction that is central to modern notions of sovereignty and international relations (Agnew 1994; Bartelson 1995; Walker 1993). Third, and a corollary of the second point, the identification of 'society' with bounded, sovereign territories and with the points (or places) that constitute territories' 'insides' leads one to dismiss the extraterritorial ocean as necessarily beyond the (place-based) social and socio-natural processes that constitute modern political life (Steinberg 2001, 2009).

As I argue below, the films considered here challenge these presumptions by presenting alternatives to the linear construction of time that provides the rhythm for modernity. While non-linear temporal sequencing has a long history in feature films, most documentaries eschew non-linearity. After all, if social life occurs in places which, after Tuan, are 'pauses', then it would seem that temporal linearity would be necessary to give definition to these 'pauses'. Put another way, if the role of the documentary is to provide access to reality or truth, and if these social phenomena, like all such phenomena, occur in places, then it would seem that a clear delineation of the place and its contextualization within a historical trajectory would be necessary to ground a documentary's claims to authenticity. Indeed, linearity would seem to be particularly important for a documentary with an activist agenda: if a documentary seeks to inspire viewers to become involved after the film ends, then a temporal trajectory should assist viewers in connecting the 'past' and 'present' of the film with the 'future' that (hopefully) will result from their post-cinematic involvement.

'Truths' about the sea require a different approach, however, because the sea defies linear time. Neither life at sea nor the sea itself has 'pauses': the rhythms and perpetual re-formations of the sea never stop, or, to quote the poet Mary Oliver (1986: 66): 'The sea isn't a place but a fact, and a mystery/under its green and black cobbled coat that never stops moving.' This does not mean that there are *no* 'truths' to be told about the sea: Roland Barthes (1972: 112) over-states the case when he calls the ocean 'a non-signifying field [that] bears no message'. In fact, the ocean signifies loudly, but it does not signify through linear narrative. The sea needs to be narrated not as an object to be read or analyzed, but as an assemblage that is continually being remade through its geo-physical recomposition, as well as through the actions of the human and non-human beings that accrue within, and overflow, its borders (Anderson 2012; Peters 2012; Steinberg 2013b). In other words, although the sea, like anywhere else, occurs in time, it has its own temporality and its own rhythm. The sea thus requires a form of storytelling that reflects and reproduces its existence as a dynamic, ever-emergent space *and* as a space that, through a certain constant functionality, serves to bind the world together. The sea is simultaneously *in* time, *beyond* time and in its *own* time, and this puts a burden on those who seek to tell stories of the sea.

To achieve a truth-telling in ocean-time, the directors of both films discussed here employ elements of the non-linear realist documentary genre pioneered by Soviet filmmaker Dziga Vertov. Arguably one of the founders of modern documentary cinema (Hicks 2007), Vertov was, in one sense, entirely conventional in that his films and writings squarely address all four of Michael Renov's (1993: 22) criteria for a documentary: 'to record, reveal or preserve; to persuade or promote; to analyze or interrogate; and to express'. Indeed, Vertov, a committed Marxist, had particular disdain for films that simply sought to provide bourgeois diversion. However, following Marx's admonition that understanding requires one to uncover hidden social relations, Vertov held that, for a film to tell the truth, it would have to do much more than simply record the observations of daily life. For Vertov (as for Marx), common-sense observations that reproduce linear notions of time and point-based notions of place *obscure* the truth, because they reflect hegemonic ideologies. Temporal linearity obscures the truth, because it leads one to focus on the end product (e.g., the commodity), rather than the process behind it (e.g., the alienated labor). Similarly, point-based notions of place obscure the truth, because they discourage understanding of how elements of life are connected across space (e.g., how the consumption of a commodity in the city is dependent on exploitative labor relations in the countryside).

For Vertov, therefore, the task of the documentarist is to use the filmic perspective – the *kino-eye* – to rearrange space beyond points and to rearrange time beyond linear narratives. Through these manipulations, the documentary film can reveal connections that would otherwise remain unseen:

> Kino-eye is the documentary cinematic decoding of both the visible world and that which is invisible to the naked eye.
>
> Kino-eye means the conquest of space, the visual linkage of people throughout the entire world based on the continuous exchange of visible fact, of film documents as opposed to the exchange of cinematic or theatrical presentations.
>
> Kino-eye means the conquest of time (the visual linkage of phenomena separated in time). Kino-eye is the possibility of seeing life processes in any temporal order or at any speed inaccessible to the human eye.
>
> Kino-eye makes use of every possible kind of shooting technique: acceleration, microscopy, reverse action, animation, camera movement, the use of the most unexpected foreshortenings - all these we consider to be not trick effects but normal methods to be fully used.
>
> Kino-eye uses every possible means in montage, comparing and linking all points of the universe in any temporal order, breaking, when necessary, all the laws and conventions of film construction.
>
> Kino-eye plunges into the seeming chaos of life to find in life itself the response to an assigned theme. To find the resultant force amongst the million phenomena related to the given theme. To edit; to wrest, through the camera, whatever is most typical, most useful, from life; to organize the film pieces wrested from life into a meaningful rhythmic visual order, a meaningful visual phrase, an essence of 'I see.'
>
> (Vertov 1984: 87–88)

In the remainder of this chapter, I explore how these techniques are utilized in very different ways by two sets of directors to reveal an ocean that is all too often written out of the sphere of International Relations or, when it is considered, is relegated to the historic past. Both films, I suggest, use non-linear techniques to think *with* the ocean. That is, they mimic the cyclical reconfigurations, complex networks and intricate ecologies of ocean-time in order to lead the viewer to Vertov's 'essence of "I see".'

The Forgotten Space[1]

The Forgotten Space (dir. Allan Sekula and Noël Burch 2010) is a film that revolves around the sea, but it is not a film *about* the sea. Indeed, by the end of the film it is not even clear what 'the forgotten space' is: is it the sea, the ship, the port, the shipping container, the networks of mobility that power the maritime world economy or the interstices that are passed by between the webs of these networks? Although the film focuses on all of these elements – and many more – as they link the world together in networks of production, trade and consumption, relatively little attention is given to the sea that lies at the centre of these networks.

To the extent that the film has a spatial focal point, it is not the sea but the port city. Lengthy segments on four port cities (Rotterdam, Los Angeles/Long Beach, Hong Kong and Bilbao), plus an epilogue on the village of Doel, which sits adjacent to the Port of Antwerp, are separated by interludes aboard the container ship *Hanjin Budapest*. Taken together, the *Hanjin Budapest* scenes account for just twelve of the film's 113 minutes, and even in those twelve minutes the sea is barely a presence. The ship always floats on smooth waters; the crew is oblivious to the ocean's depth, its geophysical movement or its biota, except as these are mediated through computer monitors; the weather is consistently calm and pleasant; and the power of the sea is alluded to only once, indirectly, when a crew member speaks of the never-ending battle against rust.

Although each port city episode includes shots of that city's harbor, the viewer is instructed right at the beginning of the film that ports are as much entryways to land ('the hinterland, the greedy continent') as they are connected with the sea ('other ports, great harbor cities, oceans, 100,000 invisible ships, 1.5 million invisible seafarers'). Thus, during each of the port city segments, the film journeys away from the port to spaces that seem, at first glance, far removed from maritime trade: a California tent city for homeless men and women; a Dutch orchard employing Polish apple-pickers; an appliance factory in China that employs upwardly mobile young women from rural villages; and the Guggenheim Museum in Bilbao, which is decried as a misguided monument to a romanticized maritime past and a forgotten maritime present. Because the maritime economy takes place on land as well as at sea, we are all reproducing it and being reproduced by it, and this will continue whether or not we 'remember' its unifying element: the ocean.

Of course, Allan Sekula and Noël Burch, the directors of *The Forgotten Space*, want viewers to 'remember' the ocean. More specifically, they want viewers to become cognizant of the ocean's role in their lives and in the social relations of capitalism. This is a project that Sekula persued through essays, photography exhibits and films over more than two decades (e.g., Sekula 1995), although the specific aspect of the ocean in capitalism that is highlighted varied from project to project. In *The Forgotten Space*, the focus is specifically on the role of the ocean in binding the world together, as the central surface for transportation (and thus integration) in what is essentially a *maritime* world economy.

In taking on this task, however, Sekula and Burch are faced with a challenge: how can one make a film about the maritime world economy that highlights the significance of the ocean, but that is not *about* the ocean? A film *about* the ocean would run the risk of fetishizing the sea as an object that exists apart from the social relations and technologies that permeate our lives and political-economic institutions, and such a film would run counter to Sekula and Burch's ideological project. Like Vertov, Sekula and Burch understand that a film about a specific object, or that tells a specific linear story about a phenomenon or place, is as likely to obscure as to reveal underlying structural forces, leading the viewer *away* from the processes that extend beyond that space to the networks of connectivity and power that are the essence of society.

Thus, for Sekula and Burch, the authority of the documentary as a source for revealing hidden truths lies in it *not* telling a single, linear narrative about a single place or phenomenon. Instead, Sekula and Burch, like Vertov, turn to montage – the juxtaposition of images and vignettes that are discontinuous across time and space. Although the montage in *The Forgotten Space* is less frenetic than it is in, say, Vertov's films, it serves a similar purpose: to construct a non-linear, place-transcending story where the whole (in this case, the global maritime economy) is much larger and all-encompassing than the sum of the parts (the various laborers, ships, containers, gantry cranes, etc. that enable shipment across the ocean's surface).

In a manner reminiscent of actor-network theory (Latour 2005), the maritime world economy is presented in *The Forgotten Space* as neither a grand entity with its own logic, nor as a series of actions undertaken by intentional individuals. Rather, the maritime world economy is continually reenacted amidst the interactions and reconstructions performed by human and non-human actors as they shape a world that is perpetually in process. While these interactions occur at sea and in ports, they also occur at a range of settings that are far removed from the sea, but that would not exist as they do were it not for the maritime world economy.

Thus, Sekula and Burch's 'truth' is constructed not only with reference to the ship, shipping infrastructure and maritime labor, but to a cascading universe of people, places, objects and technologies, including the homeless Californian whose job has moved overseas due to containerization and the makeshift community centre beneath a Hong Kong office tower where Filipino workers gather on Sundays. Small items have magnified impacts amidst the system's complex interrelations. We learn that a pile of rusted chain heaped on an empty pier in Bilbao is crucial to the interlocking processes of the economy: 'These chains are not antiques. Without them, ships would never anchor and there would be no world trade.'

The intersection of systemic understanding (the workings of the network) with the everyday encounters between humans and technology is epitomized in the final of the five *Hanjin Budapest* interludes. In this scene, a series of shots of workers laboring on the ship's deck at night accompanies a ninety second lecture by the narrator (Sekula) on how late capitalism is characterized by rising debt, falling profit margins and impending crisis. The passage concludes by provisionally materializing the structural contradictions of capitalism in the central icon of the maritime world economy – the shipping container: 'Does the container, like capitalism in general, sow the seeds of its own destruction by allowing industry to take flight – a Trojan horse that turns on its inventors?'

Sekula and Burch's narrative is powerful and focused, but in their desire to tell a decentered story of the maritime world economy, the directors relegate the actual, material ocean to the background. This was noted indirectly by David Harvey at a 2011 forum on the film:

> I know Allan [Sekula]'s been very interested in the oceans and the seas, but the thing that really struck me here is how passive the sea had become. [...] It is imagined that you can just ride across the surface in an unruffled way and that you can just bring the world together in a unity of production and consumption.
>
> (Harvey 2011)

Although Harvey does not elaborate on this point, by decentering the ocean from their narrative, Sekula and Burch dismiss its materiality and its actorness. In reducing the ocean to a surface, they deny the ocean's existence as a *space* in the sense that Lefebvre (1991) uses the term: as a convergence of experience, power, resistance and planning, not *just* as an arena for interaction.

Sekula and Burch's decision to devote so little of their film to the sea itself is undoubtedly strategic: their point, after all, is to demonstrate that, while the ocean is a necessary component of the maritime world economy, that economy's essence lies not in any space, but in the contradictory logic of capitalism. For Sekula and Burch, the *space* of capitalism, to borrow a term used by Marxist urban sociologists, is merely 'contingent' (Saunders 1985; Sayer 1985).

Sekula and Burch thus successfully steer clear of what Lefebvre calls 'spatial fetishism' – the error of analysis that occurs when,

> instead of uncovering the social relationships (including class relationships) that are latent in space ... we fall into the trap of treating space as space 'in itself' ... and so fetishize space in a manner reminiscent of the old fetishism of commodities.
>
> (Lefebvre 1991: 90)

However, in the process of making this point, the filmmakers inadvertently reproduce capitalism's idealization of the ocean as a flat surface in which space is devoid of geophysical matter, an abstract quantity of distance that can be annihilated by technologies that enable the compression (or, better yet, the transcendence) of space-time. Although the ocean that was previously 'forgotten' is now 'remembered' by Sekula and Burch, it remains an ocean that is absent of any character. The historic 'sea of exploit and adventure' (itself a problematic romanticization) has been transformed 'into a lake of invisible drudgery'. For Sekula and Burch, containerization has turned the maritime heterotopia once applauded by Foucault (1986) into a neoliberal dystopia, a 'civilization without boats, in which dreams have dried up, espionage has taken the place of adventure, and the police have taken the place of pirates' (adapted from Foucault 1986: 27).

This literally and figuratively 'flat' portrayal of the ocean in *The Forgotten Space* is surprising, given that greater attention is given to the ocean's complex and contradictory dynamics in Sekula's other works, including *Fish Story* (Sekula 1995), the photographic exhibition/catalogue that formed the initial inspiration for *The Forgotten Space*, as well as *The Lottery of the Sea* (dir. Allan Sekula 2006), a documentary that explores the ocean as a site of risk. *Fish Story*, for instance, begins with a meditation on the 'crude materiality' of the sea (Sekula 1995: 12), and Sekula reminds the reader throughout the book that the ocean's materiality persists, despite the best intentions of capital to wish it away. Thus, for instance, we learn in *Fish Story* that

> large-scale material flows remain intractable. Acceleration is not absolute: the hydrodynamics of large-capacity hulls and the power output of diesel engines set a limit to the speed of cargo ships not far beyond that of the first quarter of [the twentieth] century.
>
> (Sekula 1995: 50)

In *Fish Story*, the ocean is a space of *contradictions* and an actant in its own right. In *The Forgotten Space*, by contrast, it is merely a contextual, contingent surface.

Human frictions on the sea likewise feature in *Fish Story*: militant seafarers, longshoremen and mutineers all make appearances in the text. In contrast, these individuals receive scant attention in *The Forgotten Space*, and much of the attention that they do receive focuses on their failings. A relatively hopeful account of union organizing in Los Angeles is paired with a story of labor's defeat in the face of automation in Rotterdam and that of a faded movement in Hong Kong, where the union hall has become a social club for retirees and their widows.

In sum, by turning away from the frictions encountered at sea, Sekula and Burch end up tacitly reproducing the very 'forgetting' of the sea promoted by capital as it subscribes to an ideology of limitless mobility. The dialectics of the ocean, which flow like an undertow beneath the surface in *Fish Story*, are missing from *The Forgotten Space*. Instead, for Sekula and Burch, *all* that remains (or that soon will remain) of the ocean is the shipping container and the various channels of infrastructure across which it moves: the world has been successfully striated and the sea tamed. The capitalist fantasy of an annihilated (or forgotten) ocean has now become a reality. Although their investigation of capitalist mobilities may have recovered the significance of the long-forgotten ocean, the ocean they have found is merely a dead background for capitalism, a striated grid of GPS coordinates and adjoining lines. It is an ocean that is hardly worth remembering.

And yet, for Deleuze and Guattari (1988), no space is completely striated. To understand the space of global capitalism, one needs to see not just the striated space of ordered, hierarchical production and exchange, but also the smooth space of chaotic dynamism that makes the ocean so much more than just a surface of lines that connect points. Although the ocean entices with promises of its own transcendence, it is simultaneously a world of chaos and depth that *limits* human conquest. As Deleuze and Guattari write, the distant, optical perspective – exemplified in *The Forgotten Space* by Sekula's omniscient narration and by a sea so distant that it is rarely captured by the camera's lens – is well suited for the depiction of striated spaces. To represent smooth spaces, however, a different sensory perspective is needed, one that relies less on distant vision and optics and more on proximate interaction and haptics. This alternative view of the ocean is provided by the second documentary considered here: *Leviathan*.

Leviathan

In many ways, *Leviathan* (dir. Lucien Castaing-Taylor and Véréna Paravel 2012) is the polar opposite of *The Forgotten Space*. At the most obvious level, *The Forgotten Space* is about shipping, while *Leviathan* is about fishing. However, the differences extend well beyond their focus on different ocean activities. Where *The Forgotten Space* features extensive narration, not a single word is spoken in *Leviathan*. Where *The Forgotten Space* produces a highly contextualized narrative – an optical 'view from above' that looks down on its subject matter to situate the sea within the striated space of the capitalist maritime economy – *Leviathan* presents an immersive, haptic view that is so close-up, so decontextualized that the encounter, although still primarily visual, is reduced to raw experience in what one might call a 'view from nowhere'. Where *The Forgotten Space* sees the ocean as a horizontal, flat and stable surface across which commodities seamlessly and laterally move, *Leviathan*'s perspective is profoundly vertical, as fishermen live in a world of ship, sea and air, all buffeted by the up and down motion of the ocean's undulating wave action and dramatically variable weather. The two films even represent opposite sides of the spectrum in reference to this chapter: *The Forgotten Space* is about global connections and power, but is only marginally about the sea; *Leviathan*, conversely, is most certainly about the sea, but – at least when the film is viewed in isolation – it is only marginally about international relations.

Leviathan, shot entirely on a New Bedford, Massachusetts-based fishing boat in the Gulf of Maine, is a profoundly *ecological* film. By 'ecological', I do not mean that it is an environmentalist film. Certainly, the footage of gutted fish and bloodied bycatch befouling the ocean could lead one to attach an environmentalist message to the documentary, but, as its directors have stated in several interviews, their intention was not to impart any specific message, but simply to portray the North Atlantic fishery in all its visceral complexity. And it is in this respect that the film is ecological, portraying the fishery ecosystem as an integrated set of processes that – much like the maritime world economy portrayed by Sekula and Burch – cannot be broken down into its constituent parts. Fish, birds, water, waves, bubbles, foam, ships, bait, rust and men (there are no women) are all portrayed in the same disorientingly intimate style by a dozen tiny cameras that are attached to structures on the ship, fishermen's helmets and the ends of sixteen foot poles dangled over the ship's sides.

Leviathan is thus a profoundly sensory film, which perhaps is not surprising, given that its directors, Lucien Castaing-Taylor and Véréna Paravel, are both associated with Harvard University's Sensory Ethnography Lab. Favoring the haptic over the optic, Castaing-Taylor explicitly distances their approach from that of directors like Sekula and Burch, who rely on the distancing representational analytics of language:

> Most documentaries' representation of the real is so attenuated and so discourse-based and language-based. We lie and we mystify ourselves with words. Words can only take us so far. I think we want to get to a much more embodied, a much more corporeal representation of reality that's almost a presentation of reality. Reality that transcends our representation, so it's not reducible to a set of statements of what commercial fishing's about.
>
> (quoted in Juzwiak 2013)

As in Vertov's films, representational techniques of narration (whether verbal or pictorial) are eschewed in favor of a mode of presentation in which elements of the 'story' being told are presented in a disjointed manner that enables the viewer to construct a whole that exceeds the limits of the frame, as well as the bounds of her or his cognitive capacities. The effect is immersive, but also disorienting. Over the course of the eighty-seven minute film, there are many points at which it is unclear what is going on; in a sense, the viewer experiences the confusion of the fish that suddenly finds itself on deck, the wave that suddenly finds its path cut by a ship or the fisherman who is trying to stay awake after working a gruelling shift. In all cases, the elements of the marine-fishery ecosystem adapt, and the ecosystem as a whole is reproduced. But each actor's knowledge of that system is partial, and each actor remains vulnerable. In addition, there is an underlying destructive element within the various actors' efforts at adaptation. One senses that the fishermen, the boat, the ocean and the fishery are all being pushed to the limit, and that the overstimulating, mind-numbing confluence of elements is as tiring for the fisherman (and the fish) as it is for the viewer. Although this point is never made explicitly in the film, this bird's-eye (and fish's-eye, and fisherman's-eye) view of desperate adaptation amid chaos mirrors the state of North Atlantic fisheries and New England fishing communities, which are frequently understood as being on the brink of collapse. Explicit contextual references, however, are pointedly avoided by the filmmakers. Just as Sekula and Burch steer their narrative away from the sea in order to keep the focus on the globe-spanning processes of the maritime world economy, Castaing-Taylor and Paravel studiously avoid any references to contextual factors that cannot be captured by their cameras so as to ensure that nothing interferes with the viewer's sensual immersion in the human and non-human experiences and rhythms of the North Atlantic fishery.

The one contextual reference that *is* sustained throughout the film is the concept of Leviathan. This is, in fact, a triple reference, as there are three noted expositions on the concept: the Bible (specifically, the Book of Job), Thomas Hobbes' (1651) *Leviathan* and Herman Melville's (1851) *Moby Dick*. The biblical reference is the most explicit, as the film begins with an epigraph from Job 41:

> Can you pull in Leviathan with a fishhook
> Or tie down its tongue with a rope?
> Can you put a cord through its nose
> Or pierce its jaw with a hook?

In Job, Leviathan is a fearsome creature that, in its awesome, totalising force, defies representational description (as well as physical capture). Although Leviathan is a sea creature, it is also an ecology that incorporates those who attempt its capture. This is a theme developed further in Hobbes' book, where Leviathan is an integrated body held together not by any underlying moral imperative, but by relations of desperate, agonistic interdependence and mutual suspicion, tinged with respect for the power of the Other. Leviathan is thus a force that encompasses life, but is also larger than life, the most profound form of Gothic terror.

While Job is directly referenced in the film and there are clear links with Hobbes' *Leviathan*, it was Melville's *Moby Dick* that provided the film's direct inspiration. Castaing-Taylor and Paravel's original project was to use a portrayal of the New Bedford fishing community to reflect on *Moby Dick*, the opening scenes of which are set in New Bedford. Subsequently, as they began filming in New Bedford, interaction with fishers and an invitation to document a locally based fishing vessel at sea led them to reorient the project. Even on the ship, however, Castaing-Taylor and Paravel spent their leisure time reading selections from *Moby Dick* out loud to each other (Lim 2012).

As C. L. R. James (1978) elaborates in his analysis of *Moby Dick*, Melville's Leviathan is not just the whale, but also the society aboard the *Pequod* and, more apocalyptically, the fate of modern civilization. Of particular relevance for our understanding of the film is James' observation that the submission of the individual to the whole that occurs in Melville's (and Hobbes') Leviathan is inseparable from a submission of humanity to nature:

> This is modern man, one with Nature, master of technology, all personal individuality freely subordinated to the excitement of achieving a common goal. They have reached it at last by the complete integration of the ship and the wind and the sea and their own activity.
>
> (James 1978: 74)

James goes on to describe this integration less as a stable coherence than as a terror-filled relationship of mutual dependence and attempted adaptation amidst a sensory immersion that defies representation:

> [In Melville,] the sense of fear is annihilated in the unutterable sights that fill all the eye, and the sounds that fill all the ear. You become identified with the tempest; your insignificance is lost in the riot of the stormy universe around.... Nature is not a background to men's activity or something to be conquered and used. It is a part of man, at every turn physically, intellectually and emotionally, and man is a part of it. And if

man does not integrate his daily life with his natural surroundings and his technical achievements, they will turn on him and destroy him.

(James 1978: 100–101)

It is difficult to imagine a view of the ocean-society relationship more different than that proffered by Sekula and Burch. In *Leviathan*, the nature of the sea, rather than being transcended, subsumes all the ocean's elements, including any humans who dare to cross it. Taming the sea is not an option. Therefore, the appropriate way to approach an understanding of the sea is not through distanced linguistic discourse that assumes a (false) position of omniscient, objective observation – the equivalent of the stylized whale drawings derided by Melville at the beginning of *Moby Dick* – but through sensual immersion.

And yet, for all their differences, *The Forgotten Space* and *Leviathan* share a critique of the mainstream, linear ocean documentary. This is perhaps most evident in how the two films incorporate the concept of *place*. At first glance, this would appear to be another area of difference between the films. *Leviathan* appears to be about a single place – the fishing boat – and, indeed, the entire film was shot there, in contrast with *The Forgotten Space*, which is pointedly *not* about the ocean. However, it would be a mistake to consider the fishing boat in *Leviathan* as a 'place' in the sense raised by Tuan or Casey. That is, the fishing boat bears little resemblance to a human 'pause', where the known and experienced is contrasted with an external, unexperienced context. Rather, as in *The Forgotten Space*, the world of *Leviathan* is an unstable maritime network where elements from beyond the screen continually enter, make their presence known and exit, bringing about a bit of drama that stresses, but does not truly challenge, the system. In both films, the notion of 'place' is replaced with a notion of the dynamic, open-ended, multi-actor network.

Just as *Leviathan*, like *The Forgotten Space*, complicates notions of place so as to better depict the complex instability and irreducibility of the maritime world, the two films share a commitment to working outside the notion of linear time. *Leviathan*'s non-linear temporality is described in a *Cinema Scope* cover story on the film:

[In *Leviathan*,] all the narrative we normally hang on to [is] torn away, leaving us with only our senses to follow in the dark. It's that lack of narrative that makes it seem ridiculous to call this something like 'a documentary on commercial fishing in the North Atlantic off the coast of New Bedford.' Rather, *Leviathan* takes on the shape of the system it describes, a circular flow, choppy like those cold waves, that moves neither forward nor backward but simply works and accumulates (fish, footage) without ever linking to a history, an endgame ...

[In *Leviathan*,] sensual time has replaced historical time. This is ultimately a more profound dislocation from narrative than the absence of characters or dialogue, and the base on which it builds this world [is] removed from the mechanics of the market, the great historical marker of our young century. It would make no sense to follow these fishermen back to the sale of their haul, because at no point does the film acknowledge the sort of time that renders an event complete. Sensual time links actions into an ongoing stream: rays are caught; they are butchered; the undesirable parts are tossed overboard; blood flows into the sea; gulls are attracted to the floating carcasses; they dive into the waves to eat; the waves rock the boat; men shower amidst the rocking; they return to work.... And so it goes.

(Coldiron 2012)

The structuring of space to achieve non-linearity is accomplished in a completely different way in *Leviathan* than in *The Forgotten Space*. Whereas *The Forgotten Space* wanders almost aimlessly to the 'forgotten' interstices of the maritime world economy as it seeks comprehensive analysis, *Leviathan* maintains an obsessive focus on a corner of the maritime world economy that is so small that, although sense is enhanced, analysis is impossible. Nonetheless, the effect is much the same: through a refusal to portray the ocean in a grammar inherited from land, the viewer is led to think differently not just about the sea, but also about the ways in which time, space and connections across distances, species and forms of matter are constructed.

It is in these respects that *Leviathan*, like *The Forgotten Space*, uses a maritime perspective to challenge mainstream International Relations thinking. Both films use the ocean – a space that has always held an awkward position within the fixed territories of the state system – to question the global ontology that underpins, among other things, state-centrism. States are not insignificant in either narrative. In *The Forgotten Space*, states invest in port infrastructure to support both economic development and homeland security (although Sekula and Burch question whether these investments can ever achieve their stated goals). In *Leviathan*, there are (despite, perhaps, the title) no direct references to the state, but clearly the fishing vessel is supported by a land-based network, which includes state-imposed safety regulations, marketing networks, etc. For both films, however, the *essence* of the maritime ecology/economy being presented is not the state, but the connections and processes that occur in and across the seas. These connections involve humans and their institutions, but they also involve non-human objects and forces, from fish and water molecules to gantry cranes and corrugated steel boxes. Thus, both films, though in very different ways, use the ocean to encourage a reconceptualization of both the space and substance of international relations. When the two films are taken together, the starting point for international relations is the smooth space of chaotic natures, immanent objects, emergent mobilities and circuits of connection without beginning or end, not the striated space of bounded territories, stable places and bureaucratized social institutions.

Conclusion

Modern narratives of the ocean tend to emphasize one of two perspectives, both of which construct the ocean as beyond society. Either the ocean is seen as an empty transportation surface which ships need to cross with as few distractions as possible in order to get to the other side, or it is seen as a nature-rich space into which ships venture in order to gather resources that can be brought back home to enhance the development of land-based societies. In either case, the apparent implication for International Relations scholars is that the ocean can and should be rationally managed by the community of states, whether to preserve its functionality as a transport surface or to steward and allocate its resources efficiently (or equitably).

At a superficial level, *The Forgotten Space* appears to reproduce the first of these imaginaries, while *Leviathan* reproduces the second. However, as I have shown throughout this chapter, both sets of directors utilize a Vertovian approach to go beyond these simplistic understandings, turning away from linear and place-based narratives to depict the ocean as a complex space that is continually being remade by the social and ecological processes that overflow its borders.

Each film certainly has its gaps. Because it fails to account for the materiality of the ocean, *The Forgotten Space* presents an excessively stable perspective on the 'striated' space of the maritime capitalist economy, notwithstanding the film's emphasis on the dialectical nature of capitalism. Conversely, *Leviathan*, by eschewing any reference to context, fails to appreciate how the 'smooth' marine ecosystem of the present around which the film revolves is connected to larger human (and non-human) economies, ecologies and histories.

The power of the films is fully realized when they are paired together, taking to another level Vertov's call for the juxtaposition of asynchronous elements and perspectives so as to reveal underlying connections and contradictions. Viewed together, the films successfully reveal the dynamic and multidimensional constructions of what appear at first to be coherent 'smooth' ocean ecologies and 'striated' maritime economies. Taken together, the films reveal that no space is truly 'smooth' or 'striated,' but rather that the smooth and the striated exist in a (dis-)unity of ongoing tension and re-formulation. Although employing radically different techniques and aesthetic sensibilities, the films use their maritime perspectives to reveal the limits of mainstream International Relations thinking, in which fixed territories ('nations') are understood to 'relate' to each other across empty, intervening fields of distance. Instead, *The Forgotten Space* and *Leviathan* harness the destabilizing nature of the ocean to foster an understanding of how global spaces, ecological systems, labor relations and social norms are continually reconstituted amidst the flux and flow of international political economy.

Note

1 Parts of this section are derived from Steinberg (2013a).

Films

Leviathan (2012) Directed by Lucien Castaing-Taylor and Véréna Paravel. France, UK and USA, Arrête Ton Cinéma and Le Bureau.

The Cove (2009) Directed by Louie Psihoyos. USA, Diamond Docs, Fish Films, Oceanic Preservation Society, Participant Media and Quickfire Films.
The End of the Line (2009) Directed by Rupert Murray. UK, Arcane Pictures, Calm Productions, Dartmouth Films and Fish Films.
The Forgotten Space (2010) Directed by Allan Sekula and Noel Burch. The Netherlands and Austria, Doc.Eye Film and WILDart Film.
The Lottery of the Sea (2006) Directed by Allan Sekula. USA.

References

Agnew, John (1994) 'The Territorial Trap: The Geographical Assumptions of International Relations Theory', *Review of International Political Economy*, 1(1), 53–80.
Anderson, Jon (2012) 'Relational Places: The Surfed Wave as Assemblage and Convergence', *Environment and Planning D: Society & Space*, 30(4), 570–587.
Bartelson, Jens (1995) *A Genealogy of Sovereignty*. Cambridge: Cambridge University Press.
Barthes, Roland (1972) *Mythologies*, edited and translated by Annette Lavers. New York, NY: Hill & Wang.
Casey, Edward S. (2009) *Getting Back into Place (second edn)*. Bloomington, IN: Indiana University Press.
Coldiron, Phil (2012) 'Blood and Thunder: Enter the *Leviathan*', *Cinema Scope*, 52. Available at: http://cinema-scope.com/features/blood-and-thunder-enter-the-leviathan/ (accessed October 18, 2014).
Deleuze, Gilles and Félix Guatarri (1988) *A Thousand Plateaus: Capitalism and Schizophrenia*. London: Athlone.
Elden, Stuart (2005) 'Missing the Point: Globalization, Deterritorialization, and the Space of the World', *Transactions of the Institute of British Geographers*, 30(1), 8–19.
Foucault, Michel (1986) 'Of Other Spaces', *Diacritics*, 16(1), 22–27.
Harvey, David (2011) 'Remarks at "Forgotten Spaces" Symposium', Cooper Union, New York, 15 May. Available at: http://vimeo.com/24394711 (accessed October 18, 2014).
Hicks, Jeremy (2007) *Dziga Vertov: Defining Documentary Film*. London: I. B. Tauris.
Hobbes, Thomas (1651) *Leviathan* (numerous reprint edns).
James, C. L. R. (1978) *Mariners, Renegades & Castaways: The Story of Herman Melville and the World We Live In (second edn)*. Detroit: Bewick.
Juzwiak, Rich (2013) '*Leviathan*: A Documentary Made by People Who Hate Documentaries', *Gawker*, 1 March. Available at: http://gawker.com/5987966/leviathan-a-documentary-made-by-people-who-hate-documentaries (accessed October 18, 2014).
Latour, Bruno (2005) *Reassembling the Social: An Introduction to Actor-Network Theory*. Oxford: Oxford University Press.
Lefebvre, Henri (1991) *The Production of Space*. Oxford: Blackwell.
Lim, Dennis (2012) 'The Merger of Academia and Art House: Harvard Filmmakers' Messy World', *New York Times*, 31 August. Available at: www.nytimes.com/2012/09/02/movies/harvard-filmmakers-messy-world.html?_r=1&pagewanted=all (accessed October 18, 2014).
Locke, John (1690) *Second Treatise on Government* (numerous reprint edns).
Massey, Doreen (2005) *For Space*. London: Sage.
Melville, Herman (1851) *Moby Dick; or, the Whale* (numerous reprint edns).
Oliver, Mary (1986) 'The Waves', in Mary Oliver, *Dream Work*. Boston, MA: Atlantic Monthly Press, 66–67.

Peters, Kimberley (2012) 'Manipulating Material Hydro-Worlds: Rethinking Human and More-Than-Human Relationality through Offshore Radio Piracy', *Environment and Planning A*, 44(5), 1241–1254.

Renov, Michael (1993) 'Toward a Poetics of Documentary', in M. Renov (ed.) *Theorizing Documentary*. New York, NY: Routledge, 12–36.

Saunders, Peter (1985) 'Space, the City and Urban Sociology', in D. Gregory and J. Urry (eds) *Social Relations and Spatial Structures*. London: Macmillan, 67–89.

Sayer, Andrew (1985) 'The Difference that Space Makes', in D. Gregory and J. Urry (eds), *Social Relations and Spatial Structures*. London: Macmillan, 49–66.

Sekula, Allan (1995) *Fish Story*. Düsseldorf: Richter.

Steinberg, Philip E. (2001) *The Social Construction of the Ocean*. Cambridge: Cambridge University Press.

Steinberg, Philip E. (2008) 'It's So Easy Being Green: Overuse, Underexposure, and the Marine Environmentalist Consensus', *Geography Compass*, 2(6), 2080–2096.

Steinberg, Philip E. (2009) 'Sovereignty, Territory, and the Mapping of Mobility: A View from the Outside', *Annals of the Association of American Geographers*, 99(3), 467–495.

Steinberg, Philip E. (2011) 'Free Sea', in S. Legg (ed.) *Sovereignty, Spatiality, and Carl Schmitt: Geographies of the Nomos*. London: Routledge, 268–275.

Steinberg, Philip E. (2013a) 'Film Review: Allan Sekula and Noël Burch, *The Forgotten Space*', *Environment and Planning D: Society & Space*. Available at: http://societyandspace.com/reviews/film-reviews/sekula/ (accessed October 18, 2014).

Steinberg, Philip E. (2013b) 'Of Other Seas: Metaphors and Materialities in Maritime Regions', *Atlantic Studies*, 10(2), 156–169.

Tuan, Yi-Fu (1977) *Space and Place: The Perspective of Experience*. Minneapolis, MN: University of Minnesota Press.

Vertov, Dziga (1984) *Kino-Eye: The Writings of Dziga Vertov*, edited by Annette Michelson, translated by Kevin O'Brien. London: Pluto.

Walker, R. B. J. (1993) *Inside/Outside: International Relations as Political Theory*. Cambridge: Cambridge University Press.

6 Shots of ambivalence

Nuclear weapons in documentary film

Casper Sylvest

> The film is the art form that is in keeping with the increased threat to his life which modern man has to face. Man's need to expose himself to shock effects is his adjustment to the dangers threatening him.
>
> (Benjamin 1936: 250)

Introduction

The atomic bomb is a fetish of modernity. As Gabrielle Hecht has elegantly put it: 'The atom bomb has become the ultimate fetish of our times. Salvation and apocalypse, sacred and profane, sex and death: the bomb contains it all' (Hecht 2007: 100; see also Harrington de Santana 2009). A crucial part of the concept of the fetish concerns how an object is presented as something else or more than what it also or really is. Fetishism is therefore intimately bound up with representation and reproduction. But as Hecht's observation about the 'ultimate' nature of the nuclear fetish suggests, the imagery and vocabulary we deploy to represent nuclear weapons harbor radical dualisms that constantly deny full closure. Perhaps the theme of life and death is the most plentiful and historically significant in our representation of nuclear weapons – a trait related to the sheer power of these weapons, as well as to their association with both triumph and ruin since the dawn of the nuclear age – but many forms of dissonance surrounding these weapons have been subjected to scrutiny in cultural history and related disciplines.[1] Ambiguity even extends to modern notions of the technological sublime, where awe, pleasure and pride in nature and technology are undermined by the central role of human creation.[2]

In this as in many other instances, ambiguity and importance go hand in hand. It is not uncommon in nuclear weapons discourse to find otherwise divergent viewpoints agreeing on the significant role of these weapons in producing the political order(s) we inhabit. In the opening decades of the nuclear age, there was no shortage of positive, often visually driven narratives about the technology produced by successive US administrations and government agencies like the Atomic Energy Commission (AEC) or the Federal Civil Defense Administration (FCDA). However, the increasing, and increasingly unfathomable, destructiveness of the bomb, as well as its centrality in a tense ideological conflict between the superpowers, could hardly be ignored. Conversely, struggles against nuclear weapons and militarism and their wide-ranging detrimental effects have repeatedly been driven to exploit, if not idolize, the imagery of the nuclear detonation. The relative strength of these tropes continues to shape our reactions to nuclear weapons, including the thinking that governs their (non-)use and the risks with which they are associated.

Film has played a crucial role in political argument about nuclear weapons. This is due to the momentous destructiveness that they embody *and* the fact that they lend themselves more to *representation* than to *experience*. In Derrida's words, nuclear war is a '*fabulously* textual' phenomenon that can only be 'the signified referent, never the real referent (present or past) of a discourse or text' (1984: 23). Although this fantasy or fable of nuclear war is different from the 'massive "reality" of nuclear weaponry' (Derrida 1984: 23), the opposition is far from clear-cut. Nuclear weapons also possess an element of hyper-textuality, at least for the general public. They exist *alongside* us, but most living persons – excluding the *hibakusha* of Hiroshima and Nagasaki and victims of nuclear testing – have little or no direct experience *of* them. So while it is a truism that representation matters, in the realm of nuclear politics representation arguably matters most. Moreover, filmic representation is the nuclear document *par excellence* and therefore of considerable political and cultural significance. But what politics is involved in the representation of nuclear weapons on film? What are the political implications of (re)producing the awe-inspiring imagery associated with these weapons? Traditionally, representations of the bomb in fiction and fiction feature films have attracted much attention (Sontag 1964; Broderick 1991; Evans 1998; Shapiro 2002; see also Dowling 1987). However, due to the nature of nuclear weapons and the forms of statehood and political practice with which they are associated – and given the close association between filmic representation and political authority in general (Tagg 1985) – the documentary is especially promising in the analysis of nuclear politics. As a genre defined above all by a claim to authenticity, the documentary provides fascinating insights into the historical development and deep ambivalences of this site of political (de-)contestation.

In this chapter, therefore, I use documentaries as a prism on nuclear politics. I show how such films reflect nuclear politics, but also how they frame and provide access to a deeply political but increasingly virtual phenomenon, thereby sustaining or creating particular kinds of politics. Various modes of documentary make the political visible and actionable in different ways; they involve, in short, different 'arrangements of perceptibility' (Introduction, *infra*; van Munster and Sylvest 2013). Documentary films can, then, be read as parables that reinforce, disrupt or expose a range of assumptions and value judgments about nuclear politics. In three sections, I examine how the 'technoaesthetic spectacle' of nuclear weapons (Masco 2004) has appeared in documentary film at three crucial junctures of the nuclear age: its early, formative period, the years bracketing the pinnacle of the nuclear disarmament movement in the 1980s and the post-9/11 period. By focusing on the representations and understandings of the bomb in selected documentary films, I show that the political import of the nuclear documentary is not straightforward.[3] The subject, authors, sponsors, audiences, intentions, reception and circulation and the context into which they are injected are just some of the aspects of filmmaking that, apart from filmic technique and narration, matter a great deal. The expository documentary, concerned with positing or revealing the (or a deeper) truth about nuclear weapons, is dominant, but as I shall argue, more reflexive films that play on irony, doubt and dissonance have a distinct political efficacy in the realm of nuclear politics. What unites these films, however, is the central role played by the deep ambivalences surrounding nuclear weapons.

Domesticating the bomb in the early nuclear age

It is hard to fathom just how much of our shared visual imagery of nuclear weapons derives from US Government activity in the early nuclear age.[4] Most striking, perhaps, is the recurrence of certain iconic clips, including blast pictures of heat and shock waves from nuclear weapons running over almost any conceivable artifact or natural object familiar to modern civilization. Noting this ubiquity, one scholar has argued that documentary films and footage of the early nuclear age 'show the high-water mark of the militarization of American culture' (Mielke 2005: 35), while another has claimed that the early post-war decades – saturated as they were with notions of nuclear war fighting, civil defense and weapons science – 'not only engineered the US nuclear arsenal but ... also produced and fixed American visual understandings of the technology on film' (Masco 2010: 10; also Masco 2008b). While far-reaching, these claims are not implausible, particularly because the US Cold War state, shrouded in secrecy and lavishly funding a wide range of research related to nuclear technology, came to enjoy a virtual monopoly on the production of and access to footage of nuclear weapons tests. This 'politics of (controlled) visibility' (Kirsch 1997: 247) invoked both the militarization of society and a particular, paradoxical aestheticization of the bomb. After all, no other object, artifact or phenomenon was so successfully securitized as nuclear weapons, which, in turn, legitimized their exception from conventional political practices and procedures.

Apart from the atomic weapons used on Japan in August 1945, the US conducted 1,054 nuclear tests in the period 1945–1992. Roughly 20 percent of these tests were above ground and took place before 1963. As part of the scientific and military development of nuclear weapons capabilities, various civil and military government agencies invested huge sums in documenting nuclear weapons tests and associated activities on film. The 1352nd Photographic Group of Lookout Mountain Air Force Station, California, a clandestine film studio, produced an astonishing 6,500 documentary clips and films between 1947 and 1969. Lookout Mountain productions were often of high quality, since the studio was not short of funding and equipment.[5] A great deal of declassified footage, although merely a fraction of the total production, bears the imprint of Lookout Mountain and has been crucial in producing a culturally shared imagery and imagination of nuclear weapons. Other branches of the US Government were also deeply involved in the production of educational and informational films that were intended to govern sections of the population (for example, military personnel) or the population as a whole. The US military and agencies like the FCDA placed great emphasis on these educational initiatives.[6] While initially successful in achieving their objectives, inescapable ambivalence is a constitutive feature of many of these films.

If we turn first to educational and information films made by the US military for internal or wider public use, it is true, as Bob Mielke (2005) has pointed out, that they are nothing extraordinary from the filmic point of view. Arguably their most interesting aspect is the strategies deployed to deal with the paradoxes that follow from the total nature of nuclear weapons. Indeed, the governing binary of their narratives is between representations of nuclear (weapons) technology as a harbinger of civilizational destruction or as their representing a scientific advance heralding a peaceful world. This is typically brought out in the way in which the spectacle of the nuclear blast is impressed on the audience. As the 'voice of God' argues in *Operation Buster Jangle* (1951), a Department of Defense documentary preparing (it appears) US military personnel for a new kind of warfare:

> Today, whatever you are, whatever you do, wherever you may go, you are a part of atomic warfare. It involves you – personally. In laboratories and in the field, in little known places and ways, units of the defense establishment of the United States are learning to work with atomic weapons. Learning to strike. Learning defense against the effects of atomic weapons. Blast. Heat. Light. Radiation.

Putting the individual viewer center stage confers responsibility. At the same time, the inexorable is uneasily conjoined with the conscious harnessing of great, overwhelming power. The incompatibility of these narratives is as obvious as it is discomforting. Similarly, many of these productions tread softly around questions of radiation, safety and war. Production teams appear to want to reassure their audiences, but the nature of the subject and the secrecy surrounding nuclear weapons facilities means that, while little is said, much is implied. The political strategy was, in the words of one government memorandum of 1950, 'to make the atom routine in the continental United States and make the public feel at home with atomic blasts and radiation hazards' (quoted in Kirsch 1997: 231). In this quest, scientific authority and technical expertise were deployed to confer legitimacy on US nuclear weapons programs (O'Gorman and Hamilton 2011). And yet, while messages of seriousness, loyalty and sacrifice are clearly conveyed in government films, they are also constantly undermined by the prospective destruction involved in nuclear war. To take just one example, a Department of Defense film about the Bikini tests of 1946 warned that '[a]lthough a beautiful sight, this swirling, boiling mushroom cloud is certain death to any living thing which approaches too close to its edge'.[7]

A consistent theme running through the productions of this period concerns safety and survivability. Again, documentaries precariously balance messages of deep anxiety, optimistic postulates about the possibility of surviving nuclear war and the obligations of citizens that followed from these postulates. Educational films for use within the military stress that the safety of military personnel is a prime concern and that the testing and use of nuclear weapons is feasible if handled by the appropriate scientific and military authorities. Civil defense films deploy a particular arrangement of perceptibility that brings out these tendencies. The FCDA film *Let's Face It* (produced by Lookout Mountain) begins with a chilling description of the thermonuclear threat, before urging its audience to 'face it': 'Let's face it. Your life. The fate of your community and the fate of your nation depend on what you do when enemy bombers head for our cities. And that is why civil defense was organized.' This is consistent with the central message of 'all government civil defense materials' – namely, that 'you could survive an atomic attack if you learned the prepatory steps and took the correct actions' (Jacobs 2010: 26). But the dissonance and ambivalence is hard to gloss over, since a positing of existential fear is the essential action-inducing ingredient that threatens to make all civil defense measures redundant. Messages of reassurance and specific recommendations for minimizing physical harm – epitomized in the legendary *Duck and Cover* film of 1952 – coexist, then, with the practice of nuclear weapons testing as attempts to 'nationalize nuclear fear and install a new civic understanding via the contemplation of mass destruction and death' (Masco 2008a: 376). In this sense, civil defense was a mixture of collective emotion management and a form of nation-building (Masco 2008a).

Despite the contradictions and instability at the root of such projects, US Government documentaries were politically powerful, since they formed part of a larger and chiefly successful attempt to simultaneously rationalize, normalize *and* securitize nuclear weapons, which, in turn, also helped (re)produce a vision of American society complete with values, fears, (gendered) roles and (conforming) conduct. These deadly devices required far-reaching processes of militarization and the extension of state authority, but this was made possible by domesticating the extraordinary, revolutionary technology on which they were based. The secrecy and unchecked exercise of authority involved in this quest severely challenged civil liberties and exposed many citizens and non-citizens at atomic test sites and beyond to physical danger. This is just one testament to how the lives of people were transformed by the highly invasive nature of the military-industrial complexes that fought the Cold War. While it is naturally difficult to discern the precise impact of educational and informational films produced during these years, watching them, it is hard to deny that, with varying degrees of subtlety, they provided an ideological rationale for such encroachments. The US Government has since issued apologies and paid reparations to some victims, but residues of this ideology are still discernible in the current administration of filmic material from the early decades of the nuclear age. Thus, the 'Nuclear Weapons Film Declassification Project', under the Department of Energy's (DoE) openness initiative, aims to make publicly available (some) films about US nuclear weapons programs. Presenting the project, the DoE argues that

> [i]n hindsight, the AEC and the DoD made many mistakes in the testing program, such as underestimating the effects of fallout and deploying troops in areas of excessive radiation. Despite the errors in the early testing efforts, the U.S. surged ahead of all other nations in nuclear weapons capabilities and gained the expertise which now sets the standard for what is 'safe'.[8]

The scare quotes ('safe') constitute an admission of the inherent risks involved in producing, testing and using these weapons, but they can also be seen as the remnants of the culture of reassurance that was, in part, engineered and installed by early nuclear weapons documentaries.

Advocacy as irony: exposing ambivalence

The Limited Test Ban Treaty of 1963 can be seen as the beginning of the end of the period of fallout worry and extreme Cold War anxiety (Boyer 1998). Détente and arms control efforts came to dominate the political agenda. Clearly, there was a lag in popular politics, and many important oppositional voices and products emerged in the 1960s, including, most famously Stanley Kubrick's fiction feature *Dr. Strangelove* (1964) (Bliddal 2013). Documentaries produced independently of government agencies were mainly of an informational nature and did not at this stage play a significant role in politics.[9] The resurgence of the nuclear disarmament movement occurred as détente faltered and the Cold War intensified during the early 1980s with the hard-line nuclear policy of President Reagan's first term. An important precondition for this revitalization was a new level of critical awareness of nuclear weapons technology and its actual and potential consequences. This emerged, for example, from debates about nuclear winter and Reagan's Strategic Defense Initiative or in the wake of the abolition of the AEC in the mid-1970s that saw numerous skeletons tumbling out of the nuclear-state closet (e.g., Wittner 2009: Ch. 6–7).

In this context, documentaries (and arguably popular culture more widely) came to play a new role. While it is not possible in the context of this short chapter to do justice to all documentary films on nuclear weapons produced in the decade from the late 1970s, some important trends deserve notice. Although the majority of these films had informational or educational objectives, they almost invariably had an anti-nuclear bent (see Nicholls 1986 for a filmography; see also Barnouw 1993: 306–314). From being a prerogative of the government, the documentary became an important weapon of the governed in the latter's persistent questioning of nuclear policy and its implications. However, as a result of the underground test regime, the films of this period were constrained by the availability of footage, which meant that they often meditated on 'found' or recently declassified government material.[10] Films that combine these traits and arguably illustrate and epitomize the dynamics and spirit of (anti-)nuclear politics of the period are *The Atomic Café* (dir. J. Loader, K. Rafferty and P. Rafferty 1982) and *Radio Bikini* (dir. Robert Stone 1988). What is most distinctive about these movies is a deliberate play on irony, ridicule, revelation and shock through the use of government footage.[11]

The Atomic Café and *Radio Bikini* fed off and contributed to a radically different *Zeitgeist*. What used to signal authority, authenticity and public obligation became sources of tragicomedy, disbelief and a sarcastic, resigned form of political opposition (see also McEnteer 2006: 38–40). One example is the narration in early advocacy films made by the US Government. Official interviews or voice-overs in these productions involved a preposterous positing of authority and truth that, transported to this new context, communicated the exact opposite of what was originally intended. Thus, when *The Atomic Café* features a statement by AEC Chairman Lewis L. Strauss explaining what went wrong during the disastrous Bravo test in 1954,[12] the editing, in conjunction with the altered context, issues in an unmasking of authority that feeds reflection, suspicion and critique. Similarly, a clip of a US colonel impressing on native inhabitants the rationale of the test program (and the reason for their evacuation) – namely, to turn a 'great destructive force' into 'something good for mankind' – is immediately followed by a radio news host explaining that the natives are a nomadic group and that they are 'well pleased that the yanks are going to add a little variety to their lives' (15 mins). The editing also produces such effects – for

Figure 6.1 *The Atomic Café*, theatrical release poster, 1982. Reprinted with permission from Pierce Rafferty.

example, when *The Atomic Café* reproduces but also distorts original clips and music from *Duck and Cover*, either by sampling the soundtrack or by interspersing images of major figures of the nuclear age (including Eisenhower, Nixon, (a young) Reagan, Einstein and Oppenheimer) (65 mins).

Robert Stone's *Radio Bikini,* produced six years later when the Cold War had thawed somewhat under Reagan and Gorbachev, deals with the impact of the 1946 Bikini atmospheric tests on the Marshall Islands population and US military personnel and makes use of similar filmic and political tactics (Koppes 1995). In this case, however, irony competes with the use of cinematic shock techniques. Like many other nuclear documentaries of the period, the general drift is opposition to nuclear weapons and their consequences. Indeed, the final clip of the film is of Bernard Baruch, US representative to the United Nations Atomic Energy Commission and author of the Baruch Plan for the international control of atomic energy, making the Manichean argument that 'we must select world peace or world destruction'. Although there is little by way of direct calls to action in the film, the material is clearly organized in a way that aims at particular effects on its audience: reflection, critique and outrage. In the climactic scene of the film, an interview with Bikini-test veteran John Smitherman is played alongside images from the time. A sudden cut directs the attention of the audience towards a normal looking, middle-aged Smitherman, now appearing on the screen as he begins to speak of his physical disabilities, particularly swelling, produced by his participation in the tests. When the camera zooms out, the rolling images reveal the veteran's enormously swollen and hideously disproportional left hand. Only gradually does it dawn on the viewer that the veteran is also in a wheelchair and has lost both his legs due to his exposure to radiation. The plight of the interviewee is truly shocking when set against footage of people smiling innocently to the camera on-board a vessel off Bikini Atoll.

The satire, irony and shock in films like *The Atomic Café* and *Radio Bikini* is achieved by editing – occasionally at reduced pace – found footage that has a particular political drift (typically in favor of government policies or institutions) or by combining such footage with new or old oppositional viewpoints or facts. What Mielke (2005: 30–31) has argued was 'a relentlessly cheery use of smiles and metaphors to naturalize the uncanniness of these weapons and their testing' in the era of government propaganda films is not merely a matter of spent energy in the 1980s; the smiles and metaphors are now the weapons of anti-nuclear campaigners. The political impact of these films were, therefore, at least twofold. First, they inaugurated a form of oppositional, subversive nukespeak during the 1980s. Paul Chilton used the term 'nukespeak' to refer to the existence of a 'specialized vocabulary for talking about nuclear weapons and war with habitual metaphors' (1982: 95) that undergirded the existing nuclear culture and had political implications for how people formed opinions about the subject. Second, by exposing the hyper-textual, visual nukespeak of official documentaries, *The Atomic Café* and *Radio Bikini* offered resistance to the idea of the domesticated bomb. The point of this exercise was to question and re-politicize nuclear weapons technology and the wide range of political institutions and social practices that governed their existence. *The Atomic Café* and *Radio Bikini* had some success in reintroducing these questions to a revitalized and more receptive public sphere.

Zealous advocacy

Although the 1990s witnessed the release of important and acclaimed documentaries – in particular, Peter Kuran's *Trinity and Beyond* (1995), *The Atomic Filmmakers* (1998) and *Atomic Journeys* (1999) – they arguably contributed more to historical understanding than political debate. This is hardly surprising, since in 'the 1990s Cold War-level fears of a global nuclear Holocaust almost entirely disappeared' (Booth 1999: 2). While new anxieties associated with the risks of the proliferation of nuclear weapons emerged towards the end of the decade, the 1990s was the least politically intense decade of the nuclear age (if one of the more successful in terms of international cooperation, as the 1995 decision to indefinitely extend the Nuclear Non-Proliferation Treaty demonstrated). In this section, I shall, accordingly, focus on more recent nuclear documentaries that explicitly seek to mobilize, once again, the nuclear disarmament movement. In these productions, historical footage continues to figure prominently, and while it evokes a certain familiarity and a sense of Cold War futility, it also – alongside the filmic style and political emphases – confines the potentially radical messages of these films.

Before proceeding, a few remarks on recent trends in documentary film and the salience of nuclear issues in this genre are appropriate. Generally, the post-Cold War period has witnessed a marked increase in the production and circulation of documentaries. The simultaneous commercialization and popularization of documentary film – as well as the proliferation of filmmaking technology – means that there is greater variation in nuclear documentaries than I can do justice to here. First, recent years have witnessed new documentaries about the bombings of Hiroshima and Nagasaki produced by major broadcasters like the BBC and HBO (e.g., *White Light, Black Rain* 2007). Second, as documentary filmmaking has increasingly become a medium for critically examining global political problems, sophisticated new films have appeared, including the Nuclear World Project's ambitious, educational *In My Lifetime* (2011) or Michael Madsen's film about nuclear waste, *Into Eternity* (2010).[13] Finally, historical documentaries on Cold War security politics have also focused on the dangers, absurdity and existential questions raised by nuclear weapons and nuclear weapons technology. One of the most powerful and imaginative films of recent years – Errol Morris' Academy Award-winning *The Fog of War* (2003) – gave voice to former US Secretary of Defense Robert S. McNamara's (1916–2009) deep concerns about nuclear weapons.[14]

McNamara's *volte face* on the rationale and risks of nuclear weapons is part of a wider pattern in US politics, in which former US statesmen of the Cold War period have spearheaded a campaign for universal nuclear disarmament. The intellectual lead is provided by the so-called 'four horsemen of the apocalypse' –

George P. Schultz, William J. Perry, Henry A. Kissinger and Sam Nunn – and the idea has received support from the US President. While the views behind this push for 'nuclear zero' are clearly not all idealistic – is it not, after all, in the interests of a waning superpower in a world plagued by proliferation? – and while there are divergent personal reasons and rationales behind such campaigning, the movement has once again achieved a distinctive voice in the public sphere. In documentary films this is reflected in the release of two prominent productions: *Countdown to Zero* (2010) and *Nuclear Tipping Point* (2010). Below, I shall argue that these films reproduce some of the more salient features of contemporary nuclear and security politics and that, viewed as ideological interventions, they evince powerful, if short-lived, rhetoric, but also some deeper problems associated with the nature of campaigning on these issues. Three themes are particularly important in this context.

First, *Countdown to Zero* and *Nuclear Tipping Point* differ somewhat from earlier productions sympathetic to the cause of nuclear disarmament by virtue of their strong institutional backing from the nuclear disarmament movement and through their explicit association with the subgenre of advocacy and exposure. *Nuclear Tipping Point* is a high-profile production narrated by Hollywood actor Michael Douglas and produced by the Nuclear Security Project (NSP), the institutional home of the joint efforts of Schultz, Perry, Kissinger and Nunn. NSP is, in turn, backed by the Nuclear Threat Initiative (NTI) and the Hoover Institution. *Countdown to Zero*, a film produced by Participant Media[15] and the team behind *An Inconvenient Truth* led by Lawrence Bender, is a cog in a wider advocacy campaign run from websites like globalzero.org and takepart.com. At the time of its release, *Countdown to Zero* had some impact in mainstream US media and was screened for the then Secretary of State, Hillary Clinton. Both films end by explicitly encouraging their viewers to take part in the campaign by donating, distributing the films or contacting their political representatives.

Second, the arrangements of perceptibility, including the imagery and the narrative structure of these films, allude strongly to contemporary security discourse. On the one hand, the planetary iconography that today (and certainly after *An Inconvenient Truth*) has almost become synonymous with the fight to stem climate change is heavily invoked. This amalgamation of imagery and vocabulary is intriguing, since the rapid development of the earth sciences in the US context was partly an 'unintended by-product' of the Cold War nuclear project (Masco 2010: 7). The planetary imagery produced by the space race and accorded scientific meaning through the earth sciences in the latter part of the twentieth century produced a post-Cold War rivalry for political attention. In the commercial packaging of *Countdown to Zero*, these competing discourses are visually merged: the core of an atom pictogram is a blue marble photo of the planet accompanied by the traditional 'WARNING' (see Figure 6.2). In the case of the NSP production, the use of the term 'tipping point' evokes the climate change discourse which enjoys (at the time of production, at least) more political attention.

Nuclear weapons in documentary film 105

Figure 6.2 Countdown to Zero, theatrical release poster, 2010. Reprinted with permission from Dogwoof.

Similarly, both films, but in particular *Nuclear Tipping Point*, base their strongest claim to attention on making the threat of nuclear terrorism a central point of reference. Due to the enormous and disproportionate hold that the terrorist threat has had on Western and particularly American security discourses since 9/11, this obviously attracts attention. Following an endorsement from former Secretary of State Colin Powell, *Nuclear Tipping Point* opens with footage of terrorist attacks on the World Trade Center (1993), the USS *Cole* (2000), New York and Washington (2001), Bali (2002), Madrid (2004), Beslan (2004), London (2005) and Mumbai (2006, 2008).[16] Set to dramatic music, the film immediately asks: 'What if they get a Nuclear Weapon?' Moreover, both in the film and on its front cover, *Nuclear Tipping Point* makes use of a statement from the 9/11 Commission Report: 'Al Qaeda has been seeking nuclear weapons for 10 years.' Indeed, it can be argued that the center of gravity of nuclear politics in the post-Cold War period has, indeed, been the fear of nuclear terrorism and/or the proliferation of nuclear weapons to 'rogues' (who earn this moniker through an association with terror). In the contemporary public mind, nuclear terrorism and its associated imagery contains 'a special emotional power' and 'does trump all'.[17]

Finally, as a result of this mode of narration, the messages of these advocacy films are confined within a matrix of familiar, irreducible ambivalences that extend to a craving for unfolding worst-case scenarios in order to mobilize support for political action. Partly this relates to the format and the recurrent use of fear-inducing blast footage. In *Countdown to Zero* similar shots open and close the movie, and viewers are presented with a series of terrifying facts about the near-supernatural powers of nuclear weapons. After examining the dangers of nuclear terrorism, accidents and miscalculation, the film calls for substantial reductions in American and Russian stockpiles (which make up more than roughly 96 percent of all nuclear weapons). Still, the film is short on specific policy recommendations or discussions of the problems associated with a dramatic reduction in the numbers of nuclear weapons. Given the downright *reasonableness* of the argument for nuclear disarmament, it is striking that the film virtually ignores the intransigence of the political context that has so far rendered the argument ineffective.

A series of further dissonances marks *Countdown to Zero*. The film balances a view of nuclear weapons that is primarily Western (if not American) in its portrayal of, in particular, the threat of nuclear terrorism and a cosmopolitan, universal ambition. This gap between political subjectivities is exposed towards the end of the film, when a closing call for (local American) political action sits uneasily with the cosmopolitan narrative that explicitly seeks to reclaim nuclear politics for citizens of the world. A similar tension concerns images of time and political action invoked in the film. On the one hand, the film calls for and trusts in human volition and political action. On the other hand, it represents nuclear weapons as crypto-natural phenomena on a teleological track to elimination or Apocalypse. Perhaps as a result of these conflicting narratives, difficult and technical questions about a continued journey towards nuclear zero – the potential design of verification systems, fuel banks and the political enigma of getting from, say, 100 to zero nuclear weapons, to name but a few – receive scant attention. Instead, the film employs the metaphor of the mechanical and unstoppable clock (i.e., countdown). But what is perhaps most disturbing is that the representation of nuclear weapons as awe-inspiring, catastrophic and superhuman somehow produces a smaller political yield than intended. It is as if the uncanny fluctuation of government propaganda between fear and normalcy, between intention and effect, is reproduced in a new form. Blast footage presents a spectacle, certainly, but it is a relic from the Cold War that appears only faintly real in the context of terrorism.

Nuclear Tipping Point is plagued by constraints of a more overtly political nature. The film comes close to willfully ignoring *the* central political problem in contemporary nuclear politics: the broken bargain at the heart of the non-proliferation regime (NPT), by which the nuclear 'haves', in return for horizontal non-proliferation, commit themselves to disarmament (vertical non-proliferation) (Price 2007). Henry Kissinger's appearance in *Nuclear Tipping Point* is particularly illustrative in this respect. According to Kissinger, the logic of the NSP is that the US cannot 'keep asking other societies to restrain their participation in the nuclear field if we [are] not prepared to accept limits to our own activities'. There is, then, a need for concrete steps. And yet these are anything but specific:

a call for 'reducing substantially the size of nuclear forces in all states that possess them' is unlikely to convince nuclear weapons-seeking have-nots (24 mins). Crucially, Kissinger and his fellow Cold Warriors-turned-disarmers also equivocate on the interests that such a step would serve. They mention both US national security interests and the interests of humanity at large, and before long Douglas' voice of God argues that, because the process is long, 'the US must have nuclear weapons as long as any other state or group possesses them' (26 mins). In this sense, *Nuclear Tipping Point* can be seen as forming part of the 'nuclear proliferation complex' that has recently been criticized for clinging to zero as a mere mantra – 'like a hare at a dog track' – while contributing to a suspicion among the have-nots that this kind of anti-nuclear politics is 'just a cover to allow the nuclear powers to perpetuate their advantage' (Craig and Ruzicka 2012: 37–38).

What is, then, the political significance of these films? While apparently successful in attracting attention, their quest to posit nuclear weapons as a global security problem and return them to a reasonable and democratically legitimate form of political decision-making – that is, to re-politicize these artifacts and rob them of the aura of exceptionality in which they are shrouded – is less successful. Indeed, *Countdown to Zero* and *Nuclear Tipping Point* are blunted by their parochialism, by a visual strategy that, to some extent, reifies nuclear weapons as extraordinary objects of awe and by (unconvincing) attempts to latch the risks of nuclear weapons on to threats like terrorism or climate change that obscure vital differences in their character and political dynamics.

Conclusion

Documentary film has been an instructive prism on the nature and logics of nuclear politics since 1945. I have illustrated not only how such documentaries frame and provide access to these weapons, but also how and to what extent they reflect, sustain and shape nuclear politics. I examined films at three junctures in the nuclear age. In the first period, documentaries were characterized by government-sponsored propaganda, education or information about the technical aspects of nuclear weapons and the impact of blasts on humans, society and nature – a project that reflected the ongoing militarization and expansion of the US state apparatus. Many of these films were classified, but those that circulated in the public domain ultimately furthered the simultaneous domestication *and* securitization of nuclear weapons. In the second period, critical documentary films reflected the revitalization of the nuclear disarmament campaign. The aim of the reflexive films of this period was to repoliticize nuclear weapons, nuclear technology and their consequences. In this, they were relatively successful, not least because they deployed an effective arrangement of perceptibility that suited the theme and the new political context. Finally, among contemporary documentary films on nuclear weapons, campaign films seeking to breathe new life into the political project of nuclear non-proliferation and disarmament are prominent. Against the backdrop of a crisis-ridden nuclear non-proliferation regime, nuclear weapons dropping off the political and cultural radar of the 1990s, a new planetary awareness and the fear of terrorism in the wake of 9/11, these films latch on to the dominant contemporary security discourses in order to undergird the project of nuclear zero. Such films are successful in attracting attention, but their political import is blunted by their rhetorical and visual strategies, which reproduce the familiar ambivalences (necessity/contingency, stability/instability, normalcy/exceptionalism) of nuclear politics.

The analysis raises an interesting question about the staying power of iconic images and the role of documentation in nuclear politics. Dissonance seems integral to the nuclear fetish of modernity, but so is the constant visual reproduction of nuclear blast footage. Indeed, despite their wildly different aims, endless replays of blast footage appear to be a *sine qua non* of nuclear weapons documentaries. The limited access to this footage and its close association with the context of a hostile early Cold War climate produce further dilemmas. Recent documentaries arguably face the problem of turning what is perceived to be an unlikely catastrophe into actionable political reality. But what role can blast footage play here? Does it still represent something 'real'? Does it have contemporary political resonance, or is it merely of historical interest? Does it represent an existential threat to humanity, or is merely an awe-inspiring, even entertaining spectacle? And does its constant reproduction help decide such questions? Or, perhaps most worryingly, does nuclear-aesthetics risk becoming nuclear-anesthetics, to paraphrase Susan Buck-Morss (1992)? If, indeed, a hidden ideologization of iconic images is taking place, this is of considerable importance for how the politics of nuclear weapons can attract and sustain political attention.

At a time when nuclear weapons are once again on the political agenda, two visual strategies seem particularly promising in the attempt to communicate a deeper understanding of nuclear weapons and the threats they pose. First, 'naked' photographic documentation can be a politically effective strategy, by serving to remind us of the fact that nuclear weapons are *real* 'in an everyday, familiar, undeniable way'.[18] In the borderland between art and documentation, these photos are revealing in more than one sense: they unmask and disturb. Second, and perhaps more pertinent for documentary film, the difficulty is to avoid old mindsets and familiar pitfalls. Perhaps the most constructive role that documentary films can play is to take the dissonance of 'the nuclear' as their starting point. Instead of shunning or hopelessly trying to eradicate the ambivalences at the root of our modern fetish, documentaries that move their audiences to reflect on its absurdities, paradoxes and inconsistencies hold political potential befitting the nuclear age in which we still live.

Notes

1 J. Robert Oppenheimer's recital of the *Baghvad Gita* following the Trinity Test of July 1945 – 'I have become Death, the Destroyer of Worlds' – is the iconic illustration of this idea. Dissonances expressed (to take just a few examples) in intellectual or political denial, in heavily gendered or racialized discourses, attempts to co-opt the

weapon into existing practices or war and strategy, near-religious hopes for technological salvation and the frantic rhetoric of impending doom are analyzed in Kaplan (1984 [1983]), Boyer (1985), Cohn (1987), Gusterson (1999) and Masco (2008a).
2 See, especially, Nye (1994: 225). Whereas classic Burkean and Kantian concepts of the sublime were primarily related to direct sensory experience of natural phenomena, according to Nye a modern, technological sublime is, especially in the US, tied to technology and the identification of man and machine.
3 I make no claim to comprehensiveness, but I believe that the films selected demonstrate important traits and trends in nuclear politics.
4 Government films dominate this era. There is, however, one fascinating exception that I cannot deal with here – namely, the nuclear horror documentary *One World or None* (1946), produced by the National Committee on Atomic Information in association with the Federation of American Scientists (www.youtube.com/watch?v=u6ORe_tHYXU, accessed 6 September 2013).
5 *The Atomic Filmmakers Behind the Scenes* (dir. P. Kuran 1999).
6 See, for example, some of FCDA's annual reports issued in the mid- to late 1950s (e.g., 1956–1958, available at: http://training.fema.gov/EMIWeb/edu/ (accessed 23 January 2014)). Cf. also Homeland Security National Preparedness Task Force (2006).
7 Available at: www.youtube.com/watch?v=4wWSTVaHIZo (accessed 23 January 2014), at 3:15.
8 Available at: www.nv.doe.gov/library/films/fulltext/0800000.aspx (accessed 13 September 2013).
9 Two important exceptions deserve mention: Peter Watkins' award-winning and horrifying *The War Game* (1965), which investigated the social and physical consequences of a nuclear attack on Britain; and the eye-opening *Hiroshima-Nagasaki, August 1945* (1970), which circulated new footage about the human effects of the bombings (Barnouw 1988).
10 One important, but more intentionally apolitical precursor here was *Hiroshima-Nagasaki, August 1945* (Barnouw 1988).
11 A television documentary entitled *Clouds of Doubt* aired by KUTV in Salt Lake City in 1979 apparently pioneered this ironic use of 'found' footage (Nicholls 1986: 2, 14).
12 The Castle Bravo test was plagued by a series of problems, including, fatally, the fact that the test was two to three times more powerful than expected and that meteorological forecasts used to predict fallout patterns were inaccurate. The test was 'the worst radiological disaster in U.S. history' (Light 2003: n. 99) and spurred considerable anti-nuclear activism.
13 For a discussion of Madsen's movie, see also Vuori's chapter in this volume. Information about *In My Lifetime* is available at: http://nuclearwordguide.com/the-documentary/ (accessed 23 January 2014). Finally, *Radio Bikini* director Robert Stone's latest pro-nuclear energy film, *Pandora's Promise*, deserves mention in this context. The film's advocacy of nuclear energy and its attempt to dissociate it from the stigma of nuclear weapons in a quest to stem climate change have sparked intense debate among environmentalists and anti-nuclear campaigners. See, for example, http://dotearth.blogs.nytimes.com/2013/06/13/a-film-presses-the-climate-and-security-case-for-nuclear-energy/ (accessed 23 January 2014). A wide variety of documentary films about nuclear energy and nuclear weapons have been produced in these years, many of them part of the Uranium Film Festival: www.uraniumfilmfestival.org/index.php/en/ (accessed 6 February 2014).
14 For a more detailed analysis of this film and its importance for the study of International Relations, see Sylvest (2013). More sarcastic treatments of nuclear weapons in documentary film are also still appearing. Using 'found recordings', the 2009 documentary feature on Daniel Ellsberg and the Pentagon Papers, *The Most Dangerous*

Man in America, featured this conversation between Nixon and Kissinger at the time of the Vietnam War to drive home the absurdity of the Cold War security imagination:

> *President*: See, the attack in the North that we have in mind, power plants, whatever's left - POL [petroleum], the docks. And, I still think we ought to take the dikes out now. Will that drown people? *Kissinger*: About two hundred thousand people. *President*: No, no, no, I'd rather use the nuclear bomb. Have you got that, Henry? *Kissinger*: That, I think, would just be too much. *President*: The nuclear bomb, does that bother you?… I just want you to think big, Henry, for Christsakes.

15 This company is run by Jeff Skoll, one of the founders of the internet auction website eBay. For insight into his vision of activist filmmaking, see www.ted.com/talks/jeff_skoll_makes_movies_that_make_change.html (accessed 23 January 2014).
16 *Countdown to Zero* opens in a similar fashion, but is more rounded in its treatment of other risks, including dangers arising from miscalculation and the failure of nuclear weapons safeguards.
17 Weart (2010: 251, 256) – a text that includes a fine analysis of the shifting meanings and connotations of nuclear terrorism.
18 Shambroom (2003: Prologue). Alongside Robert Del Tredici, Paul Shambroom is one of the most skillful exponents of this tradition of naked nuclear photography. See also the reflections in Gallagher (2013).

Films

An Inconvenient Truth (2006) Directed by Davis Guggenheim. USA, Lawrence Bender Productions and Participant Media.
Atomic Journeys (1999) Directed by Peter Kuran. USA, Visual Concepts Entertainment.
Countdown to Zero (2010) Directed by Lucy Walker. USA, Lawrence Bender Productions, Nuclear Disarmament Documentary and Participant Media.
Dr. Strangelove (1964) Directed by Stanley Kubrick. USA and UK, Columbia Pictures Corporation and Hawk Films.
Duck and Cover (1952) Directed by Anthony Rizzo. USA, Archer Productions and Federal Civil Defense Administration.
Hiroshima-Nagasaki, August 1945 (1970) [No director credited]. USA, Eric Barnouw.
In My Lifetime (2011) Directed by Robert E. Frye. USA, Austria, Iceland, Czech Republic, Norway, Japan, France and UK.
Into Eternity (2010) Directed by Michael Madsen. Denmark, Finland, Sweden and Italy, Atmo Media Network, Film i Väst, Global HDTV, Magic Hour Films ApS, Mouka Filmi Oy, Sveriges Television and Yleisradio.
Let's Face It (1954) [No director credited]. USA, United States Air Force (Lookout Mountain Laboratory).
Nuclear Tipping Point (2010) Directed by Ben Goddard. USA, Nuclear Security Project.
One World or None (1946) Directed by Philip Ragan. USA, National Committee on Atomic Information and Federation of American Scientists.
Operation Buster Jangle (1951) [No director credited]. USA, Department of Defense and United States Air Force (Lookout Mountain Laboratory).
Pandora's Promise (2013) Directed by Robert Stone. USA, Robert Stone Productions.
Radio Bikini (1988) Directed by Robert Stone. USA, Crossroads, Robert Stone Productions, Spark Media and WGBH.

The Atomic Café (1982) Directed by Jayne Loader, Kevin Rafferty and Pierce Rafferty. USA, The Archives Project.
The Atomic Filmmakers Behind the Scenes (1999) Directed by Peter Kuran. USA, Visual Concept Entertainment.
The Fog of War (2003) Directed by Errol Morris. USA, Sony Pictures Classics, Radical Media and SenArt Films.
The Most Dangerous Man in America (2009) Directed by Judith Ehrlich and Rick Goldsmith. USA, Kovno Communications.
The War Game (1965) Directed by Peter Watkins. UK, BBC.
Trinity and Beyond (1995) Directed by Peter Kuran. USA, Visual Concept Entertainment and Documentary Film Works.
White Light, Black Rain (2007) Directed by Steven Okazaki. USA, Farallon Films.

References

Barnouw, Eric (1988) '*Hiroshima-Nagasaki*: The Case of the A-bomb Footage', in A Rosenthal (ed.) *New Challenges for Documentary*. Berkeley, CA: University of California Press, 581–591.
Barnouw, Eric (1993) *Documentary: A History of the Non-Fiction Film (second rev. edn)*. Oxford: Oxford University Press.
Benjamin, Walter (2007 [1936]) 'The Work of Art in the Age of Mechanical Reproduction', in W. Benjamin, *Illuminations*, edited by H. Arendt. New York, NY: Schocken Books, 217–242.
Bliddal, Henrik (2013) 'The Joke's on You: International Relations and Stanley Kubrick's *Dr. Strangelove*', in H. Bliddal, P. Wilson and C. Sylvest (eds) *Classics of International Relations: Essays in Criticism and Appreciation*. London: Routledge, 118–127.
Booth, Ken (1999) 'Nuclearism, Human Rights and Constructions of Security (Part I)', *International Journal of Human Rights*, 3, 1–24.
Boyer, Paul (1985) *By the Bomb's Early Light: American Thought and Culture at the Dawn of the Atomic Age*. New York, NY: Pantheon.
Boyer, Paul (1998) *Fallout: A Historian Reflects on America's Half-Century Encounter with Nuclear Weapons*. Columbus, OH: Ohio State University Press.
Broderick, Mick (1991) *Nuclear Movies: A Critical Analysis and Filmography of International Feature Length Films Dealing with Experimentation, Aliens, Terrorism, Holocaust and Other Disaster Scenarios, 1914–1989*. London: McFarland.
Buck-Morss, S. (1992) 'Aesthetics and Anasthetics: Walter Benjamin's Artwork Essay Reconsidered', *October*, 62, 3–41.
Chilton, Paul (1982) 'Nukespeak: Nuclear Language, Culture and Propaganda', in G. Aubrey (ed.) *Nukespeak: The Media and the Bomb*. London: Comedia, 94–112.
Cohn, Carol (1987) 'Sex and Death in the Rational World of Defense Intellectuals', *Signs*, 12, 687–718.
Craig, Campbell and Jan Ruzicka (2012) 'Who's In, Who's Out?', *London Review of Books*, 23 February 2012, 37–38.
Derrida, Jacques (1984) 'No Apocalypse, Not Now (Full Speed Ahead, Seven Missiles, Seven Missives)', *Diacritics*, 14, 20–31.
Dowling, David (1987) *Fictions of Nuclear Disaster*. London: Macmillan.
Evans, Joyce A. (1998) *Celluloid Mushrooms: Hollywood and the Atomic Bomb*. Boulder, CO: Westview Press.

Gallagher, Carole (2013) 'Nuclear Photography: Making the Invisible Visible', *Bulletin of the Atomic Scientists*, 69, 42–46.

Gusterson, Hugh (1999) 'Nuclear Weapons and the Other in the Western Imagination', *Cultural Anthropology*, 14, 111–143.

Harrington de Santana, Anne (2009) 'Nuclear Weapons as the Currency of Power', *The Nonproliferation Review*, 16, 325–345.

Hecht, Gabrielle (2007) 'A Cosmogram for Nuclear Things', *Isis*, 98, 100–108.

Homeland Security National Preparedness Task Force (2006) *Civil Defense and Homeland Security: A Short History of National Preparedness Efforts*. US Department of Homeland Security. Available at: https://training.fema.gov/emiweb/edu/docs/DHS%20Civil%20Defense-HS%20-%20Short%20History.pdf (accessed 23 January 2014).

Jacobs, Bo (2010) '*Atomic Kids: Duck and Cover* and *Atomic Alert* Teach American Children How to Survive Atomic Attack', *Film & History*, 40, 24–44.

Kaplan, Fred (1984 [1983]) *The Wizards of Armageddon*. New York, NY: Touchstone.

Kirsch, Scott (1997) 'Watching the Bombs Go Off: Photography, Nuclear Landscapes, and Spectator Democracy', *Antipode*, 29, 227–255.

Koppes, Clayton R. (1995) '*Radio Bikini*: Making and Unmaking Nuclear Mythology', in Robert A. Rosenstone (ed.) *Revisioning History: Film and the Construction of a New Past*. Princeton, NJ: Princeton University Press, 128–136.

Light, Michael (2003) *100 Suns, 1945–1962*. London: Jonathan Cape.

Masco, Joseph (2004) 'Nuclear Technoaesthetics: Sensory Politics from Trinity to the Virtual Bomb in Los Alamos', *American Ethnologist*, 31, 349–373.

Masco, Joseph (2008a) ' "Survival is Your Business": Engineering Ruins and Affect in Nuclear America', *Cultural Anthropology*, 23, 361–398.

Masco, Joseph (2008b) 'Target Audience', *Bulletin of the Atomic Scientists*, 64, 22–31.

Masco, Joseph (2010) 'Bad Weather: On Planetary Crisis', *Social Studies of Science*, 40, 7–40.

McEnteer, J. (2006) *Shooting the Truth: The Rise of American Political Documentaries*. Westport, MA: Greenwood Publishing.

Mielke, Bob (2005) 'Rhetoric and Ideology in Nuclear Test Documentary', *Film Quarterly*, 58, 28–37.

van Munster, Rens and Casper Sylvest (2013) 'Documenting International Relations: Documentary Film and the Creative Arrangement of Perceptibility', *International Studies Perspectives*, DOI: 10.1111/insp. 12062.

Nicholls, Leanne (1986) *Nukes and Anti-Nukes: A Selective Filmography on Nuclear Weaponry and the Anti-Nuclear Movement*. Melbourne: publisher unknown.

Nye, David (1994) *American Technological Sublime*. Cambridge, MA: MIT Press.

O'Gorman, Ned and Kevin Hamilton (2011) 'At the Interface: The Loaded Rhetoric of Nuclear Legitimacy and Illegitimacy', *Communication and Critical/Cultural Studies*, 8, 41–66.

Price, Richard (2007) 'Nuclear Weapons Don't Kill People, Rogues Do', *International Politics*, 44, 232–249.

Shambroom, Paul (2003) *Face to Face with the Bomb: Nuclear Reality After the Cold War*. Baltimore, MD: Johns Hopkins University Press.

Shapiro, Jerome F. (2002) *Atomic Bomb Cinema: The Apocalyptic Imagination on Film*. London: Routledge.

Sontag, Susan (1994 [1965]) 'The Imagination of Disaster', in Susan Sontag, *Against Interpretation and Other Essays*. New York, NY: Vintage, 209–225.

Sylvest, Casper (2013) 'Interrogating the Subject: Errol Morris' *The Fog of War*', in H. Bliddal, P. Wilson and C. Sylvest (eds) *Classics of International Relations: Essays in Criticism and Appreciation*. London: Routledge, 240–249.

Tagg, John (1985) *The Burden of Representation: Essays on Photographies and Histories*. Minneapolis, MN: University of Minnesota Press.

Weart, Spencer (2010) 'Nuclear Fear 1987-2077: Has Anything Changed? Has Everything Changed?' in R. Jacobs (ed.) *Filling the Hole in the Nuclear Future*. Lanham, MD: Lexington Books, 229–265.

Wittner, Lawrence S. (2009) *Confronting the Bomb: A Short History of the World Nuclear Disarmament Movement*. Stanford, CA: Stanford University Press.

7 Inside war

Counterinsurgency and the visualization of violence

Rens van Munster

[I]f we see ourselves merely as photographers, we are failing our duty. It isn't good enough anymore just to be a witness.

(Tim Hetherington, in Kamber 2010)

Introduction

In International Relations (IR) theory, war is often studied as a set of policy decisions and battles that take place at specific times and in specific places. From a broader cultural perspective, however, war is also about the dominant ways of seeing that shape how we understand war, ourselves and our enemies, as well as others. Particularly in today's highly mediatized and technological landscape, cinematic aestheticizations have become an important element in how we understand the nature and purpose of war.[1] Although this applies to popular culture in general, it takes on particular urgency for the documentary genre, which historically has had strong ties to war and political ideology. Particularly in (the run-up to) the Second World War, documentary film served as an instrument of propaganda for mobilizing the public behind the war effort. Probably the most pertinent example is Leni Riefenstahl's *Triumph of the Will* (1935), which chronicles the 1934 Nuremberg Congress of the Nazi Party and served to fuse Hitler's aspirations with those of the German state and people.

Yet the use of documentary film for propaganda purposes in times of war is by no means a sole prerogative of totalitarian regimes. *Why We Fight* (1942–1945) is a series of seven documentaries justifying US participation in the Second World War. According to director Frank Capra, who in 1945 was awarded the Distinguished Service Medal for his efforts by US Army Chief of Staff General George C. Marshall, the series presents 'a general picture of two worlds; the slave and the free, and the rise of totalitarian militarism from Japan's conquest of Manchuria to Mussolini's conquest of Ethiopia' (Capra 1971: 335). In an attempt to justify the Global War on Terror and the US war in Afghanistan, *Operation Enduring Freedom: America Fights Back* (2002) is a recent piece of film propaganda that repeats this binary world view of freedom posited against oppression. With the waning of government monopolies on social truth, many recent documentaries about war have turned on war propaganda. To take just one example, Eugene Jaracki's *Why We Fight* (2005) – a deliberate reference to Capra's propaganda movies – seeks to expose the official 'lie' that we fight for freedom by uncovering what war is 'really' about: the military-industrial-political complex's insatiable quest for profit. Other documentaries, such as Errol Morris' Oscar-winning portrait of McNamara, *The Fog of War* (2003), in turn perform their critical role through more subtle artistic arrangements.[2]

War continues to capture the imagination of documentary filmmakers, but as the nature of war changes, war documentaries change with it. Particularly, current counterinsurgency (COIN) operations in Iraq and Afghanistan have given rise to a range of observational documentaries that seek to place contemporary war under the microscope. This chapter seeks to interrogate the relationship between documentary and COIN by zooming in on two of the most popular and widely circulated films on the war in Afghanistan: *Armadillo* (2009) and *Restrepo* (2010).[3] *Restrepo*, jointly directed by Sebastian Junger and Tim Hetherington (who died in 2011, while reporting from Libya), is a feature-length documentary that follows the deployment of a US platoon in the Korengal Valley, north-eastern Afghanistan, over the course of ten months. Providing an unmatched insight into the highs and lows of experiencing war, the film was awarded the Sundance Grand Jury Prize and was nominated for an Academy Award for Best Non-fiction Feature Film. Although the film did not win, its nomination was arguably instrumental in drawing attention to the war in Afghanistan. *Armadillo* has a similar approach to *Restrepo*, as film director Janus Metz closely follows a platoon of Danish soldiers in the Afghanistan province of Helmand for a period of six months. Like the outpost Restrepo, Camp Armadillo is located close to enemy positions in an attempt to bring law and security to the area. In Denmark, the film sold more than 100,000 Danish theatre tickets, and a quarter of the Danish adult population watched the shorter TV version. Receiving the Critics' Week Grand Prix at the 2010 Cannes Film Festival, as well as four Emmy nominations in 2012 (of which it won one), *Armadillo* was also widely circulated internationally.

The micro-cosmos of combat and soldier life is a particularly fruitful starting point for interrogating how the doctrine of counterinsurgency – with its focus on decentralized command, constant adaptation and winning the hearts and minds of the local population – makes and unmakes social and political realities on the ground. The concept of counterinsurgency has been heralded as a culturally sensitive attempt to establish stability and peace by winning the hearts and minds of local populations (US Army/Marine Corps 2007). Yet, both films provide a much more messy perspective on such efforts – indeed, their line of sight can be seen as X-raying counterinsurgency and inspiring audiences to ask macro-questions about the nature and purpose of war.

This chapter consists of four sections. First, I briefly compare and contrast the 'embedded documentaries' of *Armadillo* and *Restrepo* with the genre of embedded journalism, which has emerged as the dominant form of war reporting over the past decade. Whereas the journalistic act of witnessing is often repackaged as dramatized scripts of 'militainment' intended for global consumption, I suggest that *Restrepo* and especially *Armadillo* enable a more critical stance to be adopted towards counterinsurgency. The following section further unpacks this claim and argues that a close-up of the soldier's life can expose the tensions, contradictions and paradoxes at the heart of counterinsurgency. Despite their merits, it is also necessary to point to some of the in-built limitations of the two films. To this end, the next section provides a more critical reading of them both. The chapter closes with a brief conclusion.

A grunt's-eye view

Media productions actively compel the adoption of an interpretative frame for warfare. On a most general level, the turn towards embedded media represents a point of view that focuses on the marines – or 'grunts' – engaged in battle, rather than the perspectives of generals or decision-makers. Embedding allows journalists, photographers and filmmakers to get close to combat and fighting, activities that might otherwise remain off-limits and out of sight. However, different forms of embedded media exist, each operating under different professional conditions, codes and production criteria. As a result, embedded media render the experience of war (in)visible in a variety of ways.

The most prominent form of embedded media is that of embedded journalism, as we have come to know it since the 2003 Iraq War.[4] Embedded reporting is the most recent attempt to balance the ambiguous and often tense relationship between the media and the military. On the one hand, reporters have historically surrendered objective reporting for propaganda reasons, including sustaining public support, misleading the enemy or selling papers. As Bill Katovsky, journalist and co-editor of *Embedded: The Media at War in Iraq*, wryly observes: 'It's an American tradition for the pen to ally itself with the sword' (2003: xv). On the other hand, critical war reporting has also been considered one of the potentially most damaging factors in maintaining domestic support. During the Vietnam War in particular, reporters were accused of standing in the way of victory. Most notoriously, the popular CBS news anchor Walter Cronkite, who during the 1968 Tet Offensive told the American public that the Vietnam War was unwinnable, has been identified as the journalist who single-handedly tipped public opinion against the war. Although the idea that the war could have been won had it not been for negative reporting by journalists is a myth (Barkawi 2004), it has played an important role in press-military relations ever since. In the decades following the end of the Vietnam War, including the military operations in Grenada and Panama in the 1980s and the first Gulf War in the 1990s, the US military has sought to keep the media on a short leash.[5] The press, as Secretary of State Dick Cheney famously remarked in the run-up to operation Desert Storm, is not an asset but a problem to be managed.[6]

Although censorship and control have been the norm since the Vietnam War, the military opted for a new strategy during the Iraq War. Born out of a desire to minimize the negative effects of media presence on the one hand and to optimize its potentially positive effects on the other, embedded journalism emerged as a carefully designed program to manage the military-media relationship in wartime. The program is a response to the availability of new technologies, such as digital media, satellite communication and the internet. From the perspective of the Pentagon, these cheap forms of transmission created a problem of how to channel flows of information in ways that would not compromise missions or undermine public support. These new, advanced technologies of reporting took on additional relevance in light of the shift from public and national media to commercial broadcasting intended for global consumption. Particularly, the rise of Al-Jazeera and other non-Western cable networks that framed the war in terms unfavorable to the Pentagon version of events emerged as a cause of concern. In this context, the use of embedded journalists made it possible not only to verify or correct enemy propaganda or amateur footage, but also to encourage journalistic reporting that was more favorable to the war effort. The program of embedded journalism presented an opportunity, as one Pentagon Public Affairs Officer put it, 'to get the word out by using the media to tell the story'.[7]

The framework of embedded journalism has been regarded as a considerable improvement in comparison to earlier, more intrusive attempts to control and censor the media in wartime since the Vietnam War. Generally, however, embedded journalism has failed to deliver on its promise to provide different angles of perception. First, the practice has significantly limited the scope and outlook of news in space and time, often reducing it to the individual unit, while neglecting the larger social and political context, including the perspectives of other relevant actors, such as victims, enemies and other people affected by the war (Lewis *et al.* 2006). Second, many journalists or editors consciously presented a sanitized version of war, as it was deemed 'indecent' or 'bad taste' to show domestic audiences images of civilian casualties, American casualties or other gruesome scenes of war. Embedded journalists sometimes also toned down the culture of martial masculinity, which in turn made it easier for audiences to identify or even develop an affective relationship with the soldiers (see, for example, Katovsky and Carlson 2003).[8]

Most importantly, perhaps, the sanitization of war also made possible its dramatic aestheticization, with embedded journalists playing a lead role. Rather than an objective eyewitness asking difficult questions about the nature and purpose of war, the journalist turned into a heroic, sometimes openly patriotic protagonist willing to sacrifice her or his life for the sake of bringing us the latest news from the front (Liebes and Kampf 2009). Evan Wright probably most explicitly embodies the close relationship between the practice of embedded journalism and entertainment. He created the popular TV miniseries *Generation Kill* (2008). Based on his book of the same name and his reporting for *Rolling Stone* magazine, the series follows a *Rolling Stone* reporter during the Iraq War and relies on the same gritty, realist aesthetics of authenticity as embedded journalism. Furthermore, the emphasis on soldiers' personal histories – their pre-war interests, reasons for joining the war and their mundane, everyday routines in the midst of war – privileged a way of seeing that made it easy for audiences to connect and identify with soldiers ('this could be me!'). Although not all embedded journalists subscribed to this mode, the majority of war accounts were nonetheless narrated through dramatic storylines that focused on the triumph of humanity in the midst of war. For example, journalists started to follow wounded soldiers home and focused on their attempts at overcoming the 'physical and psychological aftermath of war'. Although this focus on casualties could provide an important counterpoint to the Pentagon perspective, it rather shifted the focus from the nature and purpose of warfare to a hospital drama invested with humor, pathos and the desire for life: 'Our loose idea was "St. Elsewhere" in wartime' (Hull 2004).[9] As a result, the camera eye turns away from distant civilians or enemies who were killed and instead zooms in on the soldiers as the victims suffering from physical and psychological trauma.

However, there is more to embedded media than embedded journalism. Over the last few years, the embedded war documentary has emerged as an interesting alternative that enacts a new form of cinematic aestheticization. Unlike embedded journalists, documentary filmmakers are often (but not always) independent filmmakers without affiliation to highly capitalized broadcasting corporations or news production companies. This means that, from the moment of shooting to the final editing decisions, they are in control of all creative and productive phases (cf. Zimmerman 2000). Of course, not all such documentaries present a different angle of perception. *The Battle for Marjah* (dir. Ben Anderson 2010) and *Occupation: Dreamland* (dir. Ian Olds and Garrett Scott 2005) may be more critical than most embedded journalism, but they nonetheless largely repeat its basic formula.[10] *Armadillo* and *Restrepo*, however, stand out in important ways. First, neither film attempts to establish an affective relationship between director and audience. Opting for a more observational position of showing, the filmmaker does not appear on screen as an interpreter or narrator, let alone as the protagonist of a war drama. As one of the directors of *Restrepo* explains on the website that accompanies the film:

> We were not interested in the political dimensions of the war, only the experience of the soldiers.... It was that principle that excluded Tim and me from the movie as well ... and prevented us from using an outside narrator.[11]

The second major difference is that the embedded documentary is not constrained by the criterion of 'immediacy' that characterizes the production of news. *Armadillo* and *Restrepo* were both filmed in 2007, but were not released until 2009 and 2010, respectively. Whereas reporters and filmmakers are usually embedded for a few days or weeks, the directors of these productions spent prolonged periods of time with the platoon they filmed. The filmmakers considered this a central precondition for being able to tell stories that went beyond the standard narratives found in embedded reporting. For Metz, the embedded program, where journalists and filmmakers are allowed to follow a platoon for a few weeks, constitutes a 'borderline propaganda machine' (Sim 2011: 18), while

Hetherington points out that in a three-week period 'you're not able to get under the veneer very much.... [W]e embraced the embed system beyond what it was designed for. The military didn't expect us to get that amount of time with a group of soldiers.'[12] Finally, the absence of immediacy as a conditioning factor also meant that filmmakers could use a different format of showing. *Armadillo* and *Restrepo* are both full feature-length films, which stand in sharp contrast to the much shorter footage presented in news updates or live reportage. The feature-length format allows filmmakers to go beyond what happens in the here and now and allows them to ruminate on the nature and experiences of war in a way that goes beyond the immediacy of the moment. In an interview with *Film Quarterly*, Janus Metz points out:

> what's important to me is, through a *poetic appropriation of reality*, to get closer to some of the things that are not necessarily immediate – to see some of the hyperreal structures or mythological implications of the moment. And I think often, there is a more profound or severe truth to be uncovered than what the immediacy of realism tries to tell audiences. I don't really believe in direct mimicry of reality through the camera to an audience. I see myself as someone who's trying to *create* something authentic and sincere.
>
> (Sim 2011: 20 [emphasis added])

This statement comes close to Grierson's classic definition of documentary as the creative treatment of actuality. The objective is not to cover a conflict from all perspectives, but to show and intervene in reality. Editing (in) reality is fraught with difficulty, particularly because the objective of the chosen aesthetic form is to capture, to make tangible, the experience of war as closely as possible. Metz is well aware that a deviation from the pure observational mode as we know it from embedded reporting is 'easily politicized into not being real documentary or a fictionalized version of reality' (Ward 2011), but he maintains that editing, in departing from reality, may in fact appropriate that reality in a more authentic way. In that sense, *Armadillo*, in particular, may share less with the genre of embedded reporting than with more literary renderings of war, such as Sebastian Junger's *War* (2010) or Karl Marlantes' *Matterhorn* (2010), and cinematic aestheticizations, such as *The Deer Hunter* (dir. Michael Cimino 1978), *Apocalypse Now* (dir. Francis Ford Coppola 1979) and *The Hurt Locker* (dir. Kathryn Bigelow 2008). Through camera techniques and the creative arrangement of sound, music, color and images, the filmmaker can communicate a reality that reaches beyond the picture created by the camera.

A close-up of counterinsurgency

The documentaries also provide a unique perspective on counterinsurgency that is often ignored in authoritative narratives of war. Sociologist James William Gibson (1986; see also Barkawi and Brighton 2011) has pointed out that 'warrior knowledge' often is subjugated to the accounts of intellectuals, generals, politicians and academics. This certainly holds true for counterinsurgency: while the official doctrine of counterinsurgency has been widely discussed, Keith Brown and Catherine Lutz (2007) point out that the voices of the 'participant-observers of empire' have been conspicuously absent from our attempts to make sense of these conflicts. Although they can hardly be argued to be representative of all perspectives or sentiments, *Armadillo* and *Restrepo* go some way towards filling this gap in knowledge.

The turn towards counterinsurgency as the most prominent war fighting doctrine for the US was marked by the publication of the US Army/Marine Corps *Counterinsurgency Field Manual* (US Army/Marine Corps 2007).[13] Despite its unimpressive title, the manual is a central document that weaves together an impressive range of practices, materials and fields of scientific expertise and military know-how. It extensively draws on historical writings on counterinsurgency and anthropological knowledge to develop a doctrine for how to defeat insurgent networks and incorporate local populations into stable political structures.[14] The manual was widely circulated: it was downloaded more than 1.5 million times after its initial publication in December 2006, made it to the top 100 bestseller list on amazon.com after its republication with Chicago University Press in 2007 and has been widely reviewed in academic journals, as well as other media outlets.[15] According to counterinsurgency expert Lt. Colonel John A. Nagl (2007: xvii), the manual has been a topic of debate on jihadist websites, while copies have been found in Taliban training camps in Pakistan. The manual reflects the generally shared wisdom that wars in the twenty-first century will be 'small', 'asymmetric', 'guerilla' or 'networked' and that superior military force and firepower are less decisive for victory than the capacity to win the hearts and minds of the local population, upon whose infrastructural support insurgents are said to depend:

> [The] task is to build trusted networks. This is the true meaning of the phrase 'hearts and minds'.... Over time, successful trusted networks grow like roots into the populace. Military success is dependent on producing positive attitudes, perceptions and emotions towards the counterinsurgent force. The manual condenses the strategy of winning hearts and minds into a set of so-called 'counterinsurgency paradoxes', including 'Some of the Best Weapons of Counterinsurgency Do Not Shoot', 'Sometimes, the More Force Is Used, the Less Effective It Is', or 'Sometimes Doing Nothing Is the Best Reaction'.
>
> (US Army/Marine Corps 2007: 48, 49)

COIN, then, is a form of population-centered warfare that attempts to administer the lives and perceptions of a population through a total and simultaneous mobilization of military and non-military tools (Anderson 2011). The possibility of taking life goes hand in hand with the biopolitical duty of maintaining life logistically in an attempt to out-compete insurgents for local support.

By focusing on soldiers' everyday lives, *Armadillo* and *Restrepo* offer an opportunity to watch how the winning of hearts and minds unfolds in practice. To a large degree, the visual perspective *of Armadillo* and *Restrepo* provides what critical geographer Gearóid Ó'Tuathail (1996) in a different context has referred to as an 'anti-geopolitical eye' – a way of seeing that transgresses the dominant ideological gaze of foreign policy and military strategy. According to the latter, COIN is a culturally sensitive strategy that, in the aftermath of controversies about Guantanamo, Abu Ghraib and the Global War on Terror more generally,[16] emphasizes that war is not won in battle, but by building trust and offering Afghans the hope of a better future. It expects soldiers to be at least as much nation-builders as warriors (Petraeus and Amos 2007: xlvi). The grunt's-eye view of the embedded documentary puts this dominant framing into perspective and lays bare a fundamental gap between the near experience of fighting a counterinsurgency war on the one hand and the more distant codification of such historical experiences into military doctrine on the other. In *Armadillo* and *Restrepo*, counterinsurgency appears not as a humanitarian operation to build trust, but as an unpredictable, contingent and highly violent affair shot through with mistrust and miscommunication between soldiers and the local population. As such, the experiential mode of *Armadillo* and *Restrepo* casts severe doubt on COIN's commitment to a form of intervention that has more in common with development than war.

In contrast to the focus on the survival of human values in times of war that is characteristic of the genre of embedded journalism, these films show the naked brutality of war. From a grunt's-eye view, counterinsurgency appears as a confusing and highly emotional affair, where military protocols, bodies and hearts are persistently broken (in one scene in *Armadillo*, a soldier explains how he spent six hours collecting the body parts of a dead colleague), and soldiers and civilians, including women and children, die as a result of poor (if complex) decisions on the ground. *Restrepo* performs this function mainly by confronting its audience with the addictive rush of war and killing. *Armadillo* also shows the seductive powers of war, but reflects more on the meaningless horror of violence through the use of war-weary tropes about the US experience in Vietnam. These include the use of iconic images of helicopters taking off (think *Apocalypse Now*) or the shot of a soldier who, after stumbling in a pool of water, murmurs 'Welcome to Nam'. In particular, the scene where soldiers put on camouflage paint captures Metz' poetic truth of war as a retreat from civilization. The scene is visually pre-mediated in Coppola's *Apocalypse Now*, where Lance B. Johnson's camouflage paint signifies a similar transformation of humanity into barbarism, which in turn is a filmic rendition of Joseph Conrad's 1899 novel *Heart of Darkness* (itself a mediated account of Conrad's experiences in King Leopold's Congo). This plot is beautifully captured in a camera shot of a wounded Danish soldier whose wide-open eyes (possibly induced by emergency treatment) vividly express the horror of war.[17]

The documentaries also undermine the strategy of counterinsurgency in other ways. Whereas the official doctrine calls on soldiers to perform a multitude of

Figure 7.1 A Danish soldier in shock after battle. Film still from *Armadillo*, dir. Janus Metz Pedersen. Reprinted with permission from Fridthjof Film. Photographer: Lars Skree.

military and non-military tasks, the reality on the ground – such as the Taliban's use of improvised explosive devices (IEDs) and roadside bombs – often prevents the military from establishing contact with the local population in the areas in which they operate. Moreover, Armadillo and Restrepo are both isolated outposts: 'What you see in *Restrepo* is counterinsurgency on the cheap.... It's like camping with guns. The military wanted the department of defense to know what was happening in Afghanistan. We certainly raised eyebrows when people started to see the film.'[18] Second, the films show the imminent difficulties of operating in an environment where every individual is a potential enemy. Although the objective of counterinsurgency is to build trust, such operations function against a structural background of mistrust, where today's friend could be tomorrow's enemy. As local populations can be part of the enemy's support base, every individual posits a risk. The line that divides friend from enemy is unclear and requires constant monitoring. In the extra material, Specialist Kyle Steiner, one of the main characters in *Restrepo*, offers the following reflections on winning hearts and minds:

> This whole going there acting like we're friends thing doesn't work.... Or the guy that comes, you know, shakes our hand, takes the ten bags of rice we give him for his family, and the school supplies, and the coats. And immediately walks up the mountain and shoots a RPG [Rocket Propelled

Inside war: counterinsurgency and violence 123

Grenade] at us. And walks back down and smiles at us next morning as he's walking his goats. Fuck his heart. Fuck his mind.[19]

Steiner's comment is not only revealing of the neocolonial framing of the Other as someone who should be grateful for the presence of an occupying force, it also captures the central impossibility at the heart of COIN of distinguishing between life that should be cared for (civilians) and life that can be legitimately extinguished (enemies).

Third, the counterinsurgency doctrine gives the impression of a military apparatus that privileges cultural understanding and dialogue over the use of force. In contrast, the documentaries are replete with scenes that show how efforts to make progress on the human terrain, the winning of the hearts and minds of the local population, are incredibly difficult, as local trust is hard-won and easily lost when military efforts result in the killing of children and the destruction of property and livelihoods. The distance between the soldiers and the local population is ever-present. Sunglasses, checkpoints, camp walls, body armor, guns and linguistic problems all stand in the way of free dialogue and communication. In *Restrepo*, this distance is nicely captured in a shot of Afghan elders yawning absently as an American Marine is lecturing them about the purpose of the war after the American soldiers mistakenly kill some civilians in the nearby village.

Finally, despite the 'cultural turn' in the US military and an emphasis on sensitivity and compassion towards the Other, the documentaries portray the military as an institution that remains dominated by a martial culture of hyper-masculinity. In

Figure 7.2 Captain Dan Kearney of Battle Company, 173rd US Airborne, meets with local Afghan elders in the Korengal Valley, Kunar Province, Afghanistan, 2008. Film still from *Restrepo*, dir. Tim Hetherington and Sebastian Junger. Image: © Outpost Films.

Steiner's words: 'we are not well trained in hearts and minds … We're grunts. We're loud. We're obnoxious. We're obscene, immature at times.'[20] Moreover, such male-bonding practices – the films show scenes of soldiers enjoying a strip show, watching porn, playing video games, getting matching tattoos and dancing, drinking and play-fighting together – are essential for group cohesion and military success. According to Hetherington, if you want to understand war, you need to understand the hyper-masculinity at its essence:

> It is a huge part of the war machine…. Why war exists, is because men figured out: if you take 15 men and put them together, that group, the number in a platoon, is the perfect number, the perfect group. It is like a hard-wired genetic code: if you bring a small group of men together and make them dependent on each other, they will kill for each other.
> (Kamber 2010)

In sum, the micro-universe of soldiers raises macro-level questions about the politics of counterinsurgency and the nature of war. Although the films are explicitly marketed as apolitical, the reality they show can spur larger and broader critical reflections about war. Both films manage to bring to light a world that largely remains out of sight in embedded news reporting and portrayals of war as clean, efficient, rational and victimless. They show that counterinsurgency as a topic for theorizing and military codification is different from counterinsurgency as praxis, which is often fraught with immanent difficulties and contradictions.

A loss of perspective?

The absence of a clear guiding narrative in embedded documentary means that the spectator plays a more active role in interpreting the visual material. As James Der Derian has rightfully argued: 'cinematic aestheticisation of violence can glorify as well as vilify war, depending on how the spectator identifies with the protagonist and the investigator with the informant' (2010: 181). For Hetherington, the observational mode creates an intimate space with the potential for critical reflection. In his view, it is only when audiences identify, laugh and cry with the protagonists that it becomes possible to raise larger questions about why and how the war is being fought (Kamber 2010).

Still, zooming in on the embedded unit also necessarily involves a loss of perspective, in the sense that it offers audiences a spatially and temporally restricted view of counterinsurgency. For documentaries, this need not constitute a problem to the same extent as it does for journalism. Whereas the criterion of objectivity in journalism means that an event has to be covered from more than one angle, the more poetic nature of the documentary genre means that directors simply can choose to leave out some aspects for practical or dramatic reasons. Nevertheless, at times the visualization of war through images of combat soldiers in remote places produces a particular relationship between sight and site that risks undermining the critical potential of embedded documentaries.

Inside war: counterinsurgency and violence   125

Most obviously, the exclusive focus on the military unit largely leaves the viewpoints of other relevant actors out of sight. This is defensible in as far as the directors did not intend to make a movie about Afghanistan; their primary aim was to chronicle the everyday lives of soldiers. However, since the encounter with the Other offers a significant site for debating questions of responsibility, ethics and politics (Campbell 2007; Bondebjerg 2009), it is not wholly unproblematic that in *Restrepo* locals mainly appear from a distance through binoculars or the barrel of a gun (or as passive listeners to a lecture). As a consequence, the motivations, ambitions, struggles and understandings of the local population remain invisible – and hence unintelligible for audiences.[21]

Armadillo is more reflective about this absence, in so far as the sense of isolation and cultural distance is constantly brought into view, for example, through repeated demonstrations of the difficulty, if not futility, of civil-military cooperation in improving the lives of the local population or through scenes of soldiers discussing what may await them in the world beyond the relatively comfortable confinements of the camp. In a particularly powerful scene, Metz shows soldiers playing a combat video game. As the camera slowly continues to zoom in on the TV screen, the film suddenly cuts to a real battle scene, which has a similar aesthetic feel to that gleaned from the video game. This scene not only brings out the fact that the experience of war is always 'already informed by

Figure 7.3 Specialist Misha Pemble-Belkin (l.) and fellow soldiers from Battle Company, 173rd US Airborne, during a firefight at Outpost Restrepo during combat in Afghanistan's Korengal Valley, Afghanistan, Kunar Province, 2008. Film still from *Restrepo*, dir. Tim Hetherington and Sebastian Junger. Photograph: © Tim Hetherington.

mediated experiences of Hollywood movies and computer games' (Ward 2011), it can also be seen as a reflection on the fact that the Other only appears as a distant, somewhat unreal target. Still, audiences need not pick up this point and instead may well be drawn to the adrenalin rush experienced in combat and revel in the aestheticization of war-as-video game, rather than questioning its nature or purpose.[22] The marketing strategy behind *Armadillo* and *Restrepo* further reinforces this ambivalence. On the one hand, the films are presented as documentaries; on the other hand, they are promoted as war movies that are just as exciting and action-packed as fiction features, only more real.

In addition, the exclusive focus on a small group of soldiers operating in remote outposts runs the risk of replaying the familiar trope of Western soldiers overrun and outgunned by a hostile and largely invisible enemy (Barkawi 2004). Even if such framings capture the grunt's-eye view, they leave out the fact that the West relies on superior firepower, not least through complete aerial dominance. Again, *Armadillo* appears to be more reflective than *Restrepo* in this respect. In *Armadillo*, the central scene around which the drama evolves concerns the killing of five Taliban fighters by the Danish platoon. The scene confronts audiences with witnessing the killing of foreigners, which in turn may lead them to ask questions about the role Denmark is playing in Afghanistan. By contrast, the central scene in *Restrepo* is one where the platoon is ambushed and attacked by the Taliban. As such, *Restrepo* is arguably more easily incorporated in a frame where Western soldiers are victims rather than perpetrators.[23]

Although *Restrepo* shows soldiers calling in air support several times, the dramatization of the ambush involves a triple framing: of soldiers as victims, of air support as the last resort of an outgunned unit and of civilian casualties as collateral damage. This framing, in turn, leaves out the fact that air strikes and military raids have been an integral part of counterinsurgency operations in Afghanistan (indeed, around 70 percent of all American bombs were dropped in the Korengal Valley, where the outpost of *Restrepo* was located). In 2010, after General McChrystal took command and emphasized that the war could only be won by winning over the population, air strikes reached a peak of 1,000 strikes during the month of October.[24] Although these raids are said to involve fewer civilian casualties than previously, McChrystal also commenced a strategy of nightly raids alongside official population-centric counterinsurgency initiatives. Executed by elite Special Forces and the CIA, these killing missions focused not just on high-profile enemy targets, but concentrated on anyone contributing to the Taliban war effort. When McChrystal was replaced by General Petraeus, the godfather of COIN, the number of these raids further increased from 250 to an astounding 600 raids per month (Niva 2013). Hence, a broader focus on the war effort would paint a more nuanced picture that complicates the image of young men caught in isolated outposts willing to sacrifice themselves to save the population from the Taliban.

Finally, the anti-geopolitical eye of the embedded filmmaker risks being absorbed into the authoritative gaze of counterinsurgency knowledge. Even if *Armadillo* and *Restrepo*, as well as other documentaries on counterinsurgency such as *The Battle for Marjah* or *Operation Dreamland*, show that *particular* counterinsurgency operations are largely unsuccessful, they do not necessarily question the *concept* of counterinsurgency. Paradoxically, the failure of local operations can become a condition for the continued success of the concept. Indeed, it is the very failure of previous counterinsurgency operations, most notably in Vietnam, that constitute the basis for the current COIN doctrine. When failures are codified and reinscribed as 'lessons learnt', the COIN doctrine is no longer viewed as riddled with unsolvable tensions and contradictions, but as an imperfect doctrine that can nonetheless be improved if we learn from our past mistakes.

Ultimately, therefore, an effective, radical critique of counterinsurgency must also be articulated on a global level. As Joseph Masco (2010: 198; see also Luke 2007) has insightfully argued: 'counterinsurgency theory today says much more about the fantasy of US military power and official desires to realize US hegemony than it does about expert knowledge of politics on the ground'. The embedded viewpoint may provide an invaluable close-up view of counterinsurgency, but in the current situation it is also increasingly important to understand the longer histories and greater geographies of Western interaction with other parts of the world. In the Oscar-nominated film *Dirty Wars* (2013), which is based on a book by the same title, investigative journalist Jeremy Scahill explicitly seeks to show the other, more global side of COIN. For him, the question is not one of zooming in on individual battles and combat situations, but of connecting the dots between US military operations in, among other places, Afghanistan, Somalia and Yemen. What emerges in his film is a chilling picture of counterinsurgency as a global (targeted) killing machine that operates in over 100 countries (Scahill 2013). One should be careful, however, to draw too sharp a distinction between the global and the local: the two perspectives complement and require each other. If Scahill's *Dirty Wars* urges audiences to see the counterinsurgency operations at local sites as elements in a larger, global effort, the value of *Armadillo* and *Restrepo* is that they allow us to see how this global fantasy of military power takes shape and is contested on the local level.

Conclusion

War is a central object of analysis in IR. Yet, actual combat often remains black-boxed, as analyses tend rather to focus on the political economy of conflict. *Armadillo* and *Restrepo* show that experiences on the ground should be taken seriously. These 'grunt' views and voices lay bare the brutal ontology of fighting and show how the uncertainty of the battlefield unsettles established truths about COIN. As such, these documentaries may prove a useful point of departure for thinking more critically about war. At the same time, I have also shown how embedded documentaries may nonetheless fall short of realizing this potential. Although *Armadillo* in particular seeks to complicate and prevent the complete identification of the audience with the film's protagonists, *Restrepo*'s aim of bringing to light the 'thrill of war' may end up reinforcing dominant frames of the West as an outgunned force of good in a world of evil. Embedded documentaries are thus both sites of power and resistance. When audiences primarily regard these documentaries as entertainment, there is a risk that they reinforce the authority of the COIN complex. A more nuanced reading suggests that they also have scope to subvert or at least contest dominant narratives about war in media and official government discourses. Popular culture, then, is another crucial battleground in the war for hearts and minds.

Notes

1 The shifting representations of the Vietnam War in popular culture can be seen as attempts to inscribe the memory and meaning of that war for US identity and politics. After a first wave of war-critical films, the production of *Rambo: First Blood* (dir. George P. Costamos 1985) and similar films in the 1980s cannot be seen in isolation from the remilitarization of American society and the reliance on covert military actions in Central America that marked Reagan's presidency (Jeffords 1989; Gregg 1998).
2 For in-depth analyses of *The Fog of War* in IR, see Shapiro (2005) and Sylvest (2013).
3 Some parts of the analysis were first presented in van Munster and Sylvest (2013).
4 The presence of war reporters and journalists at the frontline or fighting theatre is not a new phenomenon. In a somewhat anachronistic fashion, the emergence of the 'embedded journalist' can be traced back to the US Civil War, when reporters often traveled with the troops on whom they were reporting (Knightley 2004 [1975]; Smith 2004). This, in turn, was made possible by the technological invention of the telegraph, which allowed reporters to transmit their stories to the press in a matter of moments. On the role of foreign correspondents in World War I, see Farish (2001).
5 Media control can take different forms, including direct censorship, pooling (where the military takes a selected group of journalists on a tour of preselected and relatively safe battle sites) or press conferences (where journalists are unable to double check the military newsfeed).
6 Compare this to his later statement, this time as Secretary of Defense, on the eve of the Iraq War: 'Having people around who are honest and professional see these things [happening on the ground] and be aware of that is useful. So I consider it not just the right thing to do but also a helpful thing' (Katovsky 2003: xiii).
7 See Katovsky and Carlson (2003: 270), 'Making the Media Feel at Home', interview with Sergeant Major Carol Sobel, Public Affairs Officer.
8 Katovsky and Carlson have collected and chronicled the experiences of embedded journalists during the 2003 Iraq War. Many of them, including *Orange County Register* columnist Gordon Dillow and CNN correspondent Martin Savidge, note that (self-)sanitization was an important element of reporting.
9 *St. Elsewhere* (1982–1988) was a realistic medical drama series about doctors having to make critical medical and life decisions. The show was produced by Steven Bocho, who also created the lifelike cop series *Hill Street Blues* (1981–1987) and the Iraq drama series *Over There* (2005). Debrix (2006: 774) has suggested that these series condition their viewers to the basic ideological truth that 'boils down to finding ways of being human in the face of horrendous struggles for survival'.
10 *The Battle for Marjah* is a miniseries produced for HBO that chronicles the counterinsurgency operation in southern Afghanistan in 2010. *Operation: Dreamland* is a movie about the 2004 counterinsurgency operation in Fallujah, Iraq.
11 See http://restrepothemovie.com/downloads/RESTREPO%20press%20notes6.14.pdf (accessed 10 February 2014).

12 Tim Hetherington, interview with Matt Kettmann, 'Grunt's-Eye View of Afghanistan', *The Santa Barbara Independent*, 10 August 2010. Available at: www.independent.com/news/2010/aug/10/grunts-eye-view-afghanistan/ (accessed 23 July 2013). Hetherington adds: 'We just kind of slipped out of the bureaucratic control of the military. We were far from Bagram. We were far from Jalalabad. Once we passed through those places, they forgot about us.'
13 Until then, military strategy had been based on the so-called 'Powell doctrine', named after Colin Powell, who, in his function as the chairman of the Joint Chiefs of Staff, outlined his vision for efficient and decisive military action on the eve of the first Gulf War in 1991. Although never codified as official US military doctrine, the Powell doctrine states that military action should be used only as a last resort and only if there is a clear risk to the national interest; that force, when used, should be overwhelming and disproportionate to the force used by the enemy ('shock and awe'); that strong support for the campaign should exist amongst the general public; and that there must be a clear exit strategy from the conflict in which the military is engaged.
14 For insightful accounts of the cultural turn in war, see Anderson (2011), Gusterson (2010), Gregory (2008) and Gonzalez (2007). In 2009, the Network of Concerned Anthropologists published the *Counter-Counterinsurgency Manual*. The ethical and intellectual conflicts of the Pentagon's Human Terrain System are also the topic of the insightful documentary film *Human Terrain* (dir. James Der Derian, David Udris and Michael Udris 2010).
15 See, for example, the review symposium on the manual in *Perspectives on Politics* (2006).
16 The systematic torturing of prisoners at Abu Ghraib has been the subject of various documentary films, including *Ghosts of Abu Ghraib* (dir. Rory Kennedy 2007), *Taxi to the Dark Side* (dir. Alex Gibney 2007) and *Standard Operating Procedure* (dir. Errol Morris 2008).
17 In their review of seven works written by American soldiers in the Iraq War, Brown and Lutz (2007: 326) identify 'a bottom-up saturation of Vietnam imagery', including *Apocalypse Now* (dir. Francis Ford Coppola 1979) and *Full Metal Jacket* (dir. Stanley Kubrick 1987).
18 Tim Hetherington, cited in Matt Kettmann (2010) 'Grunt's-Eye View of Afghanistan', Santa Barbara Independent, 22 August 2010. Available at: www.independent.com/news/2010/aug/10/grunts-eye-view-afghanistan/ (accessed 23 July 2013).
19 See www.youtube.com/watch?v=ik9dVd5IutM (accessed 10 February 2014).
20 See 'Specialist Kyle Steiner on "Hearts and Minds".' Available at: www.youtube.com/watch?v=ik9dVd5IutM (accessed 10 February 2014)
21 In making *Armadillo*, Metz has drawn inspiration from the Israeli war movie *Beaufort* (dir. Joseph Cedar 2007), where Israeli forces are under constant attack from Lebanese forces that appear to emerge out of nowhere.
22 One of the soldiers in *Armadillo* compares war to a football match, the real thing that cannot be likened to experiences gained during training and exercise. In 2009, IR scholar David Campbell and (the late) *Restrepo* co-director Hetherington debated this and other issues related to the practice of embedding journalists with US military forces. Available at: www.david-campbell.org/2009/05/22/embedded-in-afghanistan/ (accessed 27 July 2013).
23 I would like to thank Janus Metz for pointing out this important difference in dramatic narrative.
24 See http://abcnews.go.com/blogs/politics/2010/11/number-of-afghan-air-strikes-highest-ever/ (accessed 27 July 2013).

Films

Apocalypse Now (1979) Directed by Francis Ford Coppola. USA, Zoetrope Studios.

Armadillo (2010) Directed by Janus Metz Pedersen. Denmark, Fridthjof Film.

Beaufort (2007) Directed by Joseph Cedar. Israel, United King Films, Metro Communications, Movie Plus, Yehoshua Rabinowits Foundation, Cinema Project, Keshet Broadcasting, Yes-DBD Satellite Services, CDI and Cinema Industry Association in Israel.

Dirty Wars (2013) Directed by Rick Rowley. USA, Big Noise Films and Civic Bakery.

Full Metal Jacket (1987) Directed by Stanley Kubrick. UK and USA, Natant, Stanley Kubrick Productions and Warner Bros.

Generation Kill (2008) Directed by Susanna White and Simon Cellan Jones. UK and USA, Boom, Blown Deadline Productions, Company Pictures and HBO Films.

Ghosts of Abu Ghraib (2007) Directed by Rory Kennedy. USA, HBO Documentary Films and Moxie Firecracker Films.

Hill Street Blues (1981–1987, TV series) Created by Steven Bochco and Michael Kozoll. USA, MTM Enterprises and National Broadcasting Company.

Human Terrain (2010) Directed by James Der Derian, David Udris and Michael Udris. USA, Udris Film, Global Media Project and Oxyopia Films.

Occupation: Dreamland (2005) Directed by Ian Olds and Garrett Scott. USA, GreenHouse Pictures and Subdivision Productions.

Operation Enduring Freedom: America Fights Back (2002) Directed by Robert D. Kline. USA, MEDEACOM Productions.

Over There (2005–, TV series) Created by Steven Bochco and Chris Gerolmo. USA, 20th Century Fox Television and Steven Bochco Productions.

Rambo: First Blood (1985) Directed by George P. Cosmatos. USA, Anabasis N.V.

Restrepo (2010) Directed by Tim Hetherington and Sebastian Junger. USA, Outpost Films and Virgil Films and Entertainment.

Standard Operating Procedure (2008) Directed by Errol Morris. USA, Participant Media.

St. Elsewhere (1982–1988) Created by Joshua Brand and John Falsey. USA, MTM Productions and National Broadcasting Company.

Taxi to the Dark Side (2007) Directed by Alex Gibney. USA, Jigsaw Productions and Tall Woods.

The Battle for Marjah (2010) Directed by Anthony Wonke. USA, HBO Documentary Films.

The Deer Hunter (1978) Directed by Michael Cimino. UK and USA, EMI Films and Universal Pictures.

The Fog of War (2003) Directed by Errol Morris. USA, Sony Pictures Classics, Radical Media and SenArt Films.

The Hurt Locker (2008) Directed by Kathryn Bigelow. USA, Voltage Pictures, First Light Production and Kingsgate Films.

Triumph of the Will (1935) Directed by Leni Riefenstahl. Germany, Leni Riefenstahl-Produktion and Reischspropagandaleitunf der NSDAP.

Why We Fight (series) (1942–1945) Directed by Frank Capra, Anatole Litvak and Anthony Veiller. USA, Signal Services (US Army) and Signal Corps Army Pictorial Service.

Why We Fight (2005) Directed by Eugene Jarecki. USA, Sony Pictures Classic.

References

Anderson, Ben (2011) 'Population and Affective Perception: Biopolitics and Anticipatory Action in US Counterinsurgency Doctrine', *Antipode*, 43(2), 205–236.

Barkawi, Tarak (2004) 'Globalization, Culture, and War. On the Popular Mediation of "Small Wars"', *Cultural Critique*, 58, 115–147.

Barkawi, Tarak and Shane Brighton (2011) 'Powers of War: Fighting, Knowledge and Critique', *International Political Sociology*, 5(2), 126–143.

Bondebjerg, Ib (2009) 'Behind the Headlines: Documentaries, the War on Terror and Everyday Life', *Studies in Documentary Film*, 3(3), 219–231.

Brown, Keith and Catherine Lutz (2007) 'Grunt Lit: The Participant-Observers of Empire', *American Ethnologist*, 34(2), 322–328.

Campbell, David (2007) 'Geopolitics and Visuality: Sighting the Darfur Conflict', *Political Geography*, 26(1), 357–382.

Capra, Frank (1971) *The Name Above the Title: An Autobiography*. New York, NY: Macmillan.

Debrix, Francois (2006) 'The Sublime Spectatorship of War: The Erasure of the Event in America's Politics of Terror and Aesthetics of Violence', *Millennium*, 34(3), 767–791.

Der Derian, James (2010) '"Now We Are All Avatars"', *Millennium*, 39(1), 181–186.

Farish, Matthew (2001) 'Modern Witnesses: Foreign Correspondents, Geopolitical Vision, and the First World War', *Transactions of the Institute of British Geographers*, 26(3), 273–287.

Gibson, James William (1986) *The Perfect War: TechnoWar in Vietnam*. New York, NY: Atlantic Monthly Press.

Gonzalez, Roberto J. (2007) 'Towards Mercenary Anthropology? The New US Army Counterinsurgency Manual FM 3-24 and the Military-Anthropology Complex', *Anthropology Today*, 23(3), 14–19.

Gregg, Robert W. (1998) *International Relations on Film*. Boulder, CO: Lynne Rienner.

Gregory, Derek (2008) '"The Rush to the Intimate": Counterinsurgency and the Cultural Turn', *Radical Philosophy*, 150, 8–23.

Gusterson, Hugh (2010) 'The Cultural Turn in the War on Terror', in John D. Kelly, Beatrice Jauregui, Sean T. Mitchell and Jeremy Walton (eds) *Anthropology and Global Counterinsurgency*. Chicago, IL: The University of Chicago Press, 279–296.

Hull, Anne (2004) 'Proposing a Variation on Embedded Reporting', Nieman Foundation for Journalism, Harvard. Available at: www.nieman.harvard.edu/reports/article/100784/Proposing-a-Variation-on-Embedded-Reporting.aspx (accessed 12 February 2014).

Jeffords, Susan (1989) *The Remasculinization of America: Gender and the Vietnam War*. Bloomington, IN: Indiana University Press.

Junger, Sebastian (2010) *War*. New York, NY: Twelve.

Kamber, Michael (2010) '"Restrepo" and the Imagery of War', *New York Times*. Available at: http://lens.blogs.nytimes.com/2010/06/22/behind-44/?_r=0 (accessed 10 February 2014).

Katovsky, Bill (2003) 'Introduction', in Bill Katovsky and Timothy Carlson (eds) *Embedded. The Media at War in Iraq*. Guilford: Lyons Press, xi–xix.

Katovsky, Bill and Timothy Carlson (eds) (2003) *Embedded. The Media at War in Iraq*. Guilford: Lyons Press.

Knightley, Phillip (2004 [1975]) *The First Casualty: The War Correspondent as Hero and Myth-Maker from Crimea to Iraq*. Baltimore, MD: Johns Hopkins University Press.

Lewis, Justin, Rod Brookes, Nick Mosdell and Terry Threadgold (2006) *Shoot First and Ask Questions Later. Media Coverage of the 2003 Iraq War*. New York, NY: Peter Lang.

Liebes, Tamar and Zohar Kampf (2009) 'Performance Journalism: The Case of Media's Coverage of War and Terror', *The Communication Review*, 12(3), 239–249.

Luke, Timothy (2007) 'The Insurgency of Global Empire and the Counterinsurgency of Local Resistance: New World Order in an Era of Civilian Provisional Authority', *Third World Quarterly*, 28(2), 419–434.

Marlantes, Karl (2010) *Matterhorn. A Novel of the Vietnam War*. New York, NY: Atlantic Monthly Press.

Masco, Joseph (2010) 'Counterinsurgency, *The Spook*, and Blowback', in John D. Kelly, Beatrice Jauregui, Sean T. Mitchell and Jeremy Walton (eds) *Anthropology and Global Counterinsurgency*. Chicago, IL: University of Chicago Press, 193–207.

van Munster, Rens and Casper Sylvest (2013) 'Documenting International Relations: Documentary Film and the Creative Arrangement of Perceptibility', *International Studies Perspectives*.

Nagl, John A. (2007) 'Foreword to the University of Chicago Press Edition', in US Army/ Marine Corps, *Counterinsurgency Field Manual*. Chicago, IL: University of Chicago Press, xiii–xx.

Network of Concerned Anthropologists (2009) *The Counter-Counterinsurgency Manual*. Chicago, IL: Prickly Paradigm Press.

Niva, Steve (2013) 'Disappearing Violence: JSOC and the Pentagon's New Cartography of Networked Warfare', *Security Dialogue*, 44(3), 185–202.

Ó'Tuathail, Gearóid (1996) 'An Anti-geopolitical Eye: Maggie O'Kane in Bosnia, 1992–93', *Gender, Place and Culture – A Journal of Feminist Geography*, 3(2), 171–186.

Petraeus, David F. and James H. Amos (2007) 'Foreword', in US Army/Marine Corps, *Counterinsurgency Field Manual*. Chicago, IL: University of Chicago Press, xlv–xlvi.

Scahill, Jeremy (2013) *Dirty Wars. The World is a Battlefield*. New York, NY: Nation Books.

Shapiro, Michael J. (2005) 'Review Essay: "The Fog of War"', *Security Dialogue*, 36(2), 233–246.

Sim, Gerald (2011) 'A Gray Zone between Documentary and Fiction: An Interview with Janus Metz', *Film Quarterly*, 65(1), 17–24.

Smith, Kevin A. (2004) 'The Media at the Tip of the Spear', *Michigan Law Review*, 102(6), 1329–1372.

Sylvest, Casper (2013) 'Interrogating the Subject: Errol Morris' *The Fog of War*', in Henrik Bliddal, Peter Wilson and Casper Sylvest (eds) *Classics of International Relations: Essays in Criticism and Appreciation*. Abingdon: Routledge, 240–249.

US Army/Marine Corps (2007) *Counterinsurgency Field Manual*. Chicago, IL: University of Chicago Press.

Ward, Vernon (2011) 'Exclusive: Interview with Janus Metz, on Armadillo', *Culture Compass*. Available at: www.culturecompass.co.uk/2011/04/28/exclusive-interview-with-janus-metz-on-armadillo/ (accessed 10 February 2014).

Zimmerman, Patricia R. (2000) *States of Emergency: Documentaries, Wars, Democracies*. Minneapolis, MN: University of Minnesota Press.

8 The reflexivity of tears

Documentaries of sexual military assault

Robin May Schott[1]

Introduction

'Photography has kept company with death ever since cameras were invented, in 1839' (Sontag 2003: 21). As war is mass-produced death, photography has produced iconic images of the major war-time conflicts of the twentieth century, including the pictures of Bergen-Belsen, Buchenwald and Dachau after the camps were liberated in 1945, the photographs taken following the incineration of the populations of Hiroshima and Nagasaki, and the photographs of executions and napalm bombings during the Vietnam War. Another close companion of war, though not in broad public view through the lens of the camera until the last two decades, is sexual violence.[2]

My focus in this chapter is on documentaries of military sexual assault. The documentary genre has been closely related to issues of the state; since their origin, documentaries have affirmed or contested state power or more recently provided revisions of conceptions of power and subjectivities (Nichols 2001: 582, 609). An underexamined issue in this field has been the role of the state in relation to sexual violence. In discussing documentaries of military sexual assault, I bring together the themes of war and the state, as sexual assault occurs in the context of both war – fought by, against, or within a state – and of the military as an institution of the state – a war within its own ranks.

Concretely, I discuss the companionship between film and sexual violence in two films, *The Invisible War* (2012) and *Operation Fine Girl: Rape Used as a Weapon of War in Sierra Leone* (2001).[3] *The Invisible War* and *Operation Fine Girl* are examples of films dealing with ongoing or recent issues of conflict. It is instructive to discuss these films together for a number of reasons. First, both films address the phenomena of sexual violence in relation to military activities with an activist agenda. The objective is to 'do justice' to victims by enabling them to tell their stories and by encouraging viewers to engage in activities that fight injustice.

In an interview on PBS News Hour, Kirby Dick, director of *The Invisible War*, characterized his role as a documentary filmmaker in terms of the role formerly held by investigative journalists. As resources for investigative journalists have been drastically reduced, there are greater opportunities for documentary films to have an impact. Dick emphasized that the goal of the film is not to educate, but to change.[4] *Operation Fine Girl* is a forty-five minute documentary directed by Lilibet Foster, released in 2001 by WITNESS – a nonprofit and activist human rights organization. WITNESS was founded in 1988 by musician and activist Peter Gabriel. Its original focus was to 'give cameras to human rights activists around the world'.[5] Since then, it has developed into a comprehensive training approach focusing on video advocacy – the use of video as a tool in human rights campaigns.

A second reason to discuss these films together is to avoid easy misinterpretations. The national, social, and political contexts of these two films are quite different. *The Invisible War* addresses sexual violence at the heart of one of the mightiest institutions in one of the most powerful countries of the world. *Operation Fine Girl* is a story of abduction, rape, and murder committed against civilians in Sierra Leone, one of the poorest countries in the world, by rebel forces whose only authority was their drug-enhanced brutal violence. As *The Invisible War* is concerned with internal conditions within the US military, with a form of 'friendly fire' when soldiers are wounded by their own side, one can easily lose sight of the sexual violence committed by the US military in war.[6] And yet such violence has played a central role during both US wars and occupations, such as the sexual torture in Abu Ghraib.[7] While *Operation Fine Girl* puts the issue of military sexual assault during conflict brutally in view, a politically self-conscious viewer might worry that it reinforces the presumption that sexual violence is an issue for the African, black, colonial 'other' and not for a superpower like the US. Thinking about these films together pushes one to consider how sexual violence within military institutions is linked to sexual violence in conflict, and to recognize that sexual violence is not just a concern for the 'Global South', but also for 'Western' countries.

A third reason to pair these documentaries is that following the trace of tears in the films allows one to unpack the connection between gender, sexual violence, suffering, and community. I argue that these tears are linked to feminist political projects and contribute to political reflexivity by making visible the cracks in the frame of justice. Nonetheless, there are significant differences in the ways in which tears are wept in these two films – a distinction that turns on the crucial difference between living life with an expectation of justice and living life as suffering. Before I follow the trace of the sociality of tears in these two films, the next section first provides some background about the difficult history of the relationship between feminism and the genre of documentary film.

Feminism, documentaries, and sexual violence: background to the issues

There are many challenges posed to writing on a topic which bridges two different fields: the study of sexual violence and the study of documentaries. Whereas film studies scholars have expertise in film history and theory, providing them with greater insight into the genre of documentary than into the phenomenon about which the film is made, scholars in International Relations (IR) – or in my case in philosophy, with a focus on ethical and political issues of war – often have greater knowledge of the phenomenon than of film.

This difficulty in bridging two fields of scholarship is magnified by the fraught relationship between documentaries and feminist theory. As Janet Walker and Diane Waldman have argued, although the 1970s witnessed an explosion of both documentary studies and feminist film criticism, the relationship of 'documentaries to feminist concerns was primarily one of omission' (Walker and Waldman 1999: 4). Early work on documentaries neglected both the representation of women in classic documentaries and the contributions of women to the documentary form, including women's roles as cinematographers, editors, sound persons, fund-raisers, organizers of festivals, writers, and lecturers (Walker and Waldman 1999: 4; Mayne 1985: 95). With the introduction of more easily accessible and portable equipment, the surge of women filmmakers in the 1970s drew attention to explicitly feminist work, but did not otherwise impact studies of documentaries. From their side, feminists also contributed to this absence of dialogue. Feminist film theorists were occupied with a critique of realism, arguing that it failed to challenge the depiction of reality, promoting a passive subjectivity at the expense of analysis. Claire Johnston noted that film is mediation, not a neutral record of reality, and the truth of oppression cannot be 'captured', but must be 'constructed/manufactured'. In this theoretical tradition, feminists who wrote on cinema were highly critical of *cinéma vérité* techniques, which 'largely depict images of women talking to camera about their experiences, with little or no intervention by the film-maker' (Johnston 1973: 214–215, cited in Waldman and Walker 1999: 7). The alliance of feminist film theory with the avant-garde, as in Laura Mulvey's work from 1975, further contributed to an anti-realism that left thinking about documentaries a neglected area in feminist film theory. But this neglect is unfortunate, as documentaries 'frequently represent subjects and struggles that indicate the messy imbrication of gender, race, class, nation, and sexuality ...' (Waldman and Walker 1999: 19).

Although the conversation about documentaries and feminist theory has been overdue, a range of emotional and ideological stumbling blocks echo the gap between genre and phenomenon mentioned above. On the one hand, for someone like myself who has worked for years with issues of sexual and gender-based violence, viewing films that frame victims of sexual violence telling their story carries a kind of moral imperative about the urgency of these issues, which have received increasing public attention. An example of recent high-profile interest is the Global Summit to End Sexual Violence in Conflict, initiated by UK Foreign Secretary William Hague and Angelina Jolie, Special Envoy for the UN High Commissioner for Refugees, which was held in London on 10–13 June 2014. For many of us working with issues of war and conflict, it may be hard to explain why sexual violence has become so central, as there are many horrific forms of violence and suffering which are non-sexual. Perhaps reading and viewing material on sexual violence sexualizes and violates us as readers and viewers, as the brutality reaches into our own embodied existence. And yet such responses are not universal. In viewing *The Invisible War* on YouTube, one can follow other people's reactions as well, and I cite two: 'on a scale of 1–10 on the world's most important issues list, sexual assault is ranked 0'; another viewer wrote: 'Unfortunately A LOT of reported cases are false. And that hurts the real cases that need to be investigated.'

On the other hand, issues of representation bring different entanglements. Both film theory and IR have been highly influenced by poststructuralist approaches (see Introduction, this volume). While these two documentaries address the moral imperative to respond to sexual violence, are they reflexive in calling attention to the filmmaking process as linked to a critical awareness of the making of reality? And if these films were not to live up to the demands of reflexivity, would that risk undermining their moral content? Moreover, if a scholar insists on the films' moral weight over formal considerations, does she risk jeopardizing her attention to theorizing issues of subjectivity, power, representation, and framing?

In addition to these troublesome issues, there also has been a great deal of controversy amongst feminists over how to address issues of sexual violence. Whereas philosopher Linda Martín Alcoff notes that we are living in a 'continuing global epidemic of sexual violence....' (Alcoff 2012: 273), controversies amongst feminist theorists with respect to understanding the subjective and objective components of sexual violence may have had 'a deflationary set of effects' (Alcoff 2012: 274). Feminist theorists working from poststructuralist positions and with theories of intersectionality have criticized second-wave feminist discussions of rape and pornography as oversimplified and decontextualized, and as failing to address issues of race, gender, and colonial regimes of power. For example, Sharon Marcus criticizes Susan Brownmiller's *Against our Will* (1975) for treating female sexuality as an inner space which is invaded and violated by rape. Marcus argues that such an approach entails 'a complete identification of a vulnerable, sexualized body with the self' and excludes 'women's will, agency, and capacity for violence' (Marcus 1992: 394, 395). But attempts to render analyses of sexual violence more sophisticated philosophically have also contributed to a kind of uncertainty about how to think about the nature and scope of sexual violence, from the accusations against Julian Assange of WikiLeaks, to the gang rapes in India, to understanding an individual's own complex 'gray' experiences (Alcoff 2012: 273–274).

I argue that both *The Invisible War* and *Operation Fine Girl* are politically reflexive, following Nichols' use of the term, in that they give the subjectivity of victims its due. Nichols discusses reflexivity in terms of the maturation of the genre of documentary films, but notes that reflexivity need not be purely formal; 'it can also be pointedly political' (Nichols 1991: 64). Filmmaker and theorist Julia Lesage argued in 1978 that '[f]eminist documentary filmmaking is a cinematic genre congruent with a political movement, the contemporary women's movement' (Lesage 1978: 507). In this article, Lesage argues that films that show a woman telling her story are 'an artistic analogue' of the structure of the women's movement, with an emphasis on a collective awareness of the power of knowledge and an attempt to create new knowledge which challenges viewers' expectations (Lesage 1978: 515, 519). Nichols echoes her insights, noting that, even though she did not treat feminist documentaries as formally innovative, in so far as feminism 'instigated a radical reconceptualization of subjectivity and politics', such films are linked with a process of political engagement – what in Brechtian terms one would call an alienation effect (Nichols 1991: 65).

As the reflexive mode of representation makes the familiar strange, these films, too, draw attention to the strangeness of military practices in which sexual violence is routine. Both films are framed primarily by the narratives of victims, interspersed with interviews by psychologists, lawyers, human rights activists, medical doctors, and writers. In this respect, both films are very different from *The Reckoning* (2009), which Wouter Werner criticizes for its glorification of the prosecutors at the International Criminal Court (ICC) at the expense of victims, who are depicted as 'suffering bodies, with hardly any voice of their own' (see Werner's chapter, this volume). By giving subjectivity its due, these films provide counter-narratives to reigning myths, for example, about the US military as a protector. Providing counter-narratives or counter-histories is one feature of feminist historical documentaries (and other committed documentaries), as they include those who speak from the margins, inform the world about their conditions and the urgent need for social change, and show the political contingency of agency (Waldman and Walker 1999: 18, 21).

The trace of tears

It would be wrong to contrast having a voice with being a suffering body, as Werner's formulation might suggest. These films not only provide an opportunity to give subjectivity its due, they also highlight *how* victims tell their stories, *how they grieve*. Grief has troubled a great many discussions of wrongs suffered and of justice due. One common response is that the image of a crying victim reinforces the view that victims are pathetic, in contrast to survivors, who display agency and future-orientation. Diana Meyers criticizes this 'pathetic victim paradigm' that is so common in discussions of those who have suffered grave harms, and notes that both the pathetic victim paradigm and the heroic victim paradigm are 'at odds with normal human impurity of motivation' (Meyers 2011: 267). The *Oxford English Dictionary* defines 'pathetic' as arousing pity, especially through vulnerability or sadness, and the accompanying example is: 'she looked so pathetic that I bent down to comfort her'.[8] If she is pathetic, then I am outside the circle of harm, in a position to bow down from a higher position to her lower position to provide comfort. And I can be sure that her harm results from her misfortune or poor judgment, though not from a systematic harm, which would enclose me within its circle. In both of these documentaries, however, harms are systematic, as they are perpetrated widely and as perpetrators experience impunity.

Moreover, tears seem to disturb what is appropriate to a legal framework of justice. The documentary *I Came to Testify* (part of the *Women, War and Peace* series) touches on this issue in an interview with Peggy Kuo, one of the prosecutors in the Foca rape case tried before the International Criminal Tribunal for the former Yugoslavia (ICTY).[9] Kuo said:

> I had heard that in Nuremberg there was a discussion about whether to bring up the subject of rape, because a lot of rapes had occurred during and after the war, and somebody made a comment that we don't want a bunch of crying women in the courtroom.[10]

Tears fare little better in ethical appeals, as they are subject to the criticism of sentimentality. As Susan Sontag has noted, it is not necessarily better to be moved than not moved by the suffering of another human being, as sentimentality is entirely compatible with a taste for brutality, and sympathy 'proclaims our innocence as well as our impotence' (Sontag 2003: 91). Elizabeth V. Spelman also draws a sharp distinction between 'the use of images of suffering for the sake not of the sufferer but the presenter or viewer' (Spelman 1997: 11), and notes that compassion may also 'reinforce the very patterns of economic and political subordination responsible for such suffering' (Spelman 1997: 7).

To this litany of objections to a focus on tears, one might also note the way tears and gender are represented in political images. Images of crying women have populated the media for decades. According to an international study by the Global Media Monitoring Project in Canada in the 1990s, 29 percent of women interviewed in TV newscasts were victims of catastrophes, calamities, or violent crimes, compared with only 10 percent of interviewed men (Halonen 1996: 14). Halonen argues that the image of grieving women symbolizes the catastrophe of a nation, as with the photojournalism in Bosnia depicting the emotions of aged, destitute, and suffering women (Halonen 1996: 7). In such images, women appear as anonymous, functioning as mythic figures who can grieve for the nation in a way that is impossible for heroic masculine soldiers. Women appear as the bearers of grief for the destruction of domestic life. This view is echoed in journalist Douglas Ferris's comments in *War Redefined* (also part of the *Women, War and Peace* series) when he speaks about the new wars, which destroy 'ways of life, ways of thinking, educational processes and traditional role modelling. It is women who are the keepers of what survives in the conflict.'[11]

Although these objections about tears as pathetic, as having a problematic role in legal and ethical judgments, and as representing standard tropes about gender and nation make this discussion a treacherous journey, I turn to the trace of tears to see how they contribute to the political reflexivity of these films. Tears are not just private and individual; they are a social phenomenon. The sociality of the tears reveals the fissures in the frames which claim to provide justice.

The Invisible War

The opening scenes of *The Invisible War* draw on all the propaganda elements at the disposal of the US military: the reveille bugle wake-up call, black-and-white film clips of women being inducted into the army (women became a permanent part of military service in the US in 1948 and were allowed into military academies in 1976), and voice-overs of army advertisements: 'It doesn't matter whether you are a man or a woman, only that you are good.' And the jingle, familiar to those who have grown up in the US: 'Be all that you can be, because we need you in the army.' Despite the rush of patriotism and pride that these images might induce, it soon becomes clear that they belong to childhood fantasies and that the motto 'there is a right way, a wrong way, and the army way' is a disturbing premonition of the military position regarding justice for sexual assault within its ranks.

The Invisible War tells the story of the pervasiveness of sexual assault within the US military. The ubiquity of this phenomenon is one reason, according to the filmmakers, that it is invisible. Twenty percent of women in the US military have been raped, meaning that about a half million women have been sexually assaulted in the military. When one woman reported rape, she was met with the response: 'Is this a joke? You are the third woman to report rape this week.' Instead of reports of sexual assault being pursued vigorously, women find that they have to report to their commanding officer, who himself may be the assailant. Although these women joined the military with the dream of serving their country as their fathers and brothers may have done, it becomes neither a successful career path nor earns them a medal of honor. Women who have been raped in the military have higher levels of post-traumatic stress disorder (PTSD) than women who have been in combat, and 40 percent of homeless women veterans were raped while in service. Men, too, are raped in the military. Although the percentage of men who are raped is lower than that of women, because of the greater numbers of men in the military the absolute figures are much higher, with an estimated 20,000 sexual assaults against men per year.

The film focuses on a handful of stories amongst women and men, interspersed with clips from interviews with a great many other victims.[12] Following the trace of tears is one heuristic device for interpreting this complex body of material. The victims cry when telling their stories of rape, although the camera also captures a father – himself a sergeant in the US Army – breaking down when he tells the story of his daughter's telephone call: 'Dad, I am no longer a virgin.' (He replied: 'Hannah, you are still a virgin, because he took something from you that you didn't give.') The filmmakers also interview the husband of another rape victim – himself a captain in the Marine Corps – crying while he describes how he rummaged for his wife's suicide note while calling for an ambulance.

The film pieces together the narratives of physical and sexual violence by interspersing clips of interviews from several of the victims. The film highlights the story of Kori Cioca, who had enlisted in the coastguard and was assaulted and raped after twenty-two months of service. Nonetheless, the rape narratives are embedded within each other. One person's narrative is interspersed with a cut from another victim's narrative, weaving together stories of assault in the Navy, the Air Force, and the Marine Corps. One effect of this splicing of stories is that the viewer is drawn away from any presumption that the victims suffer from bad luck or poor judgment. Instead, these intertwined narratives weave a fabric of structural sexual violence in the military. At the same time, the film shows that this structural violence becomes invisible as files are lost or closed without investigation. Often, cases are dismissed against married perpetrators and then initiated against their unmarried female victims for adultery and conduct unbecoming an officer. It is the military's making violence invisible that becomes a secondary and more corrosive form of violence.

In allowing the perpetration of violence within its own ranks, this invisible war gives the lie to the notion that the military, as one military father said to his daughter, will take care of you. This notion of the military as a protective family calls to mind Susan Rae Peterson's (1977) earlier analysis of the state's relation to women as a protection racket, with the 'good' woman being protected, while protection is withheld from autonomous women (Young 2007: 303). But what the military seems to be protecting is its chain of command, its independence from civilian law, and its lack of transparency. It is not protecting the women and men who are victims in this invisible war, and who are caught in the kind of Catch 22 experienced by Kori Cioco, who left the service after twenty-two months because of her assault and rape. Her claim for medical treatment and compensation for injuries sustained during her assault was denied by the Veterans Administration (VA) on the grounds that she had served two months less than the minimum active duty required to receive disability compensation.

Following the trace of tears in this film reveals that tears have a sociality – they trace social dynamics – in four senses. First, the interspersing of the narratives of sexual assault provides evidence that this is an experience that in its repetitiveness is shared in common amongst a great many women and men. Hence, the tears that accompany the rape narratives are not an expression of a strictly private experience – although sexual assault is a trespass of individuals' boundaries of bodily integrity and intimacy. The intermingling of tears points to the way in which these violations are not isolated incidents, but examples amidst many others. Second, the sociality of the tears points to the systematic nature of the violence to which tears respond. This violence is systematic in that it is widespread – including both men and women – and implicitly condoned by the system of military command and justice, where impunity for perpetrators enables assaults to continue.

Third, the sociality of the tears points out the social relations in which sexual assault flourishes. Russell Strand, Chief of the Family Advocacy Law Enforcement Training Division of the US Army, notes that the ad campaigns of the army attract men who are 'very, very heavily masculine'. While the very heavily masculinity in the theaters of violence can be viewed in a positive light,[13] it has a less beautiful form, evident in the sexual violence that colors both the language and practices of military masculinity. For example, at Marine Corps Headquarters in Washington, DC, the showcase ceremonial unit that is responsible for security at the White House, former Marine officer Ariana Klay recounts how one senior officer said to her: 'Female marines here are nothing but objects for the marines to fuck.' After she was, indeed, fucked, her husband (a Marine Corps captain) spoke with tears about the army's view of his wife's assault: 'Yes they called you a whore, yes they called you a slut, yes they called you a walking mattress ... but you deserved it and when you complained about it you were welcoming it.' Male homo-social bonding is acted out in sexual violence against men as well. Strand estimates that 1 percent of all men in the US military are raped. Male-male rape should not be construed as an implicit acceptance of homosexuality. When male on male rape occurs, it 'taints' the victim as homosexual, although it does not taint the rapist, for whom it serves as a sign of power and dominance (Sivakumaran 2005: 1274). The vulnerability of raped men was reinforced by the explicit and implicit prohibition against homosexuality in the US military, until the 'Don't Ask, Don't Tell' (DADT) policy was repealed on September 20, 2011. Under this policy, which was signed into law in 1993, 14,500 service members were thrown out of the US military (Dunham 2011).

There is a fourth sense in which one can understand the sociality of tears, in pointing to the basis of community. In the *Republic*, Socrates said in his reply to Thrasymachus that 'a community of pleasure and pain' when 'all the citizens rejoice and grieve alike' is crucial to the existence of a unitary, non-fragmented community. As Elizabeth Spelman notes, Socrates' view implies that 'occasions for grief should be shared if a community is to have any hopes of unity' (Spelman 1997: 24, 28). *The Invisible War* depicts family relations as offering one such community of grieving, as the interviews with victims are interspersed with interviews with a father, husband, or wife crying with them. In these scenes, the camera provides representations of family members and fellow victims grieving alike. But the camera is also potentially intrusive, as when Kori reads the letter from the VA denying her claim for treatment, and she denies the camera her tears. With a voyeuristic disappointment in being cheated of her tears, the viewer is jarred into questioning his or her own relationship to this community of grieving.

The questions of who grieves with and for whom calls to mind Judith Butler's reflections on how different frames – photography, political policies, decisions, or debates – frame the differential distribution of grievability and precariousness.[14] In Butler's analytic vocabulary, grief is a response to a life that has ended. She introduces the term grievability 'as a condition of life's emergence and sustenance ... the presupposition of a grievable life ... means that this will be a life that can be regarded as a life...' (Butler 2009: 15). I would dispute her claim that grief emerges only in relation to a life that will have ended (the future anterior tense), as if only death – and not other forms of suffering – points to the conditions of what can be regarded as a life. But her insights into how frames set the conditions for what one takes for granted and what affect accompanies our quotidian acceptance of violence are crucial, not least because she also draws attention to how frames can be exposed, resulting in a critical apprehension of received renditions of reality. Butler asks: 'What would it mean to understand this "breaking out" and "breaking from" ... as the very function of the frame?' (Butler 2009: 10) In *The Invisible War*, the framing of the sociality of tears is also a framing of the failure of justice. Legal counsel for the victims' lawsuit called the military judicial system 'broken' when it comes to these cases. The film captures this broken system – the denial of victim's claims for medical compensation, the dismissal by the court of the survivors' lawsuit, the limitations of governmental policy – as the frame of national honor and service are also displayed as the frame of violence and injustice.

Operation Fine Girl: Rape Used as a Weapon of War in Sierra Leone

The opening scenes of *Operation Fine Girl* immediately cast the viewer into the chaos of war, with women relating stories of abduction, burning, and rape. There are none of the pleasurable appeals to the imagination about military adventures that opened *The Invisible War*. The film does not contrast the ideology of the military with the reality of sexual violence, but gives a sense of the omnipresence of violence, interspersed with scenes of people walking through a cemetery and chanting 'We shall overcome'. The opening of the film prepares the viewer that it is not through institutional responses but through human responses that there is a way forward.

Operation Fine Girl is based on interviews with young women and teenage girls who speak about their abduction, their lives as 'rebel wives', their escape, and their after-lives. The film also includes interviews with a former child soldier. In contrast to *The Invisible War*, where the women who were sexually assaulted had voluntarily enlisted in the military, these women were civilians who knew nothing of the war before it invaded their homes. And in contrast to *The Invisible War*, where women and men experienced the humiliation of rape and injustice, these women also carry the contamination of having been 'rebel wives', making them outcasts in their own communities. Many families did not accept their daughters – who were now often mothers – after their escape from the rebels, and the former child soldier had made no attempt to see whether his parents were alive or dead. *The Invisible War* punctures the myth of the US military as a protective family and shows the emotional consequences of this myth in comparing military rape with incest. Nonetheless, images of family are central in the film. By contrast, *Operation Fine Girl* shows the destruction of families. No parents or spouses are present within the frame of the film, only their children born of rape.

In tracing the tears in *Operation Fine Girl*, I will discuss one particular scene: an interview with a young girl called 'Mabel' at a school and rehabilitation center in Freetown. In this three minute segment, Mabel tells of her traumatic experience of being abducted, raped, finding herself pregnant, and finally escaping, as well as her sense of becoming a pariah through her association with the rebels. One nurse, she relates, said that if it were up to her, she would not let any rebel wives be treated at the hospital. As the English voice-over translation of Mabel's narrative begins, the camera shows the schoolroom in which she is sitting, the teacher at the blackboard, the room full of teenage girls, and the young child playing by her legs. This frame reminds the viewer that Mabel is herself not much more than a child, though a mother by rape. Only then does the camera move closer to catch her face as she tells her story. Sometimes she sits in class and cries, she says, and her friends ask her why she is crying. She says 'nothing', and as she says 'nothing' the tears begin to well up in her eyes and overflow, spilling over onto her cheek without her bothering to wipe them away. This spilling over of tears calls to mind Simone Weil's comments on the slave's tears in her beautiful essay 'The Iliad, or the Poem of Force', written during the Occupation of France in World War II. Reflecting on the passage in *The Iliad* describing the slave weeping at his master's misfortune, Weil notes: 'his situation keeps tears on tap for him' (Weil 1965: 10). For Mabel, too, suffering is omnipresent and tears are on tap – and 'nothing' is an occasion for them to spill over. The camera films training activities at the school, and when the camera returns to her face, it is still streaked with tears.

As Mabel concludes her story, she says that if she completes the course and is able to get a job and support her child and her parents, then she will not be anyone's laughing stock, because she knows 'people are watching to see how my life is unfolding'. We, as viewers, are also watching to see how her life unfolds, and in watching we are at a distance from her. But as listeners to her story, we might expect that those closest to her would not be watching, but would be by her side, or at least on her side. This discomfiture for the viewer of being at a distance in a way that aligns us with those who are wrongly at a distance from her raises the question of the sociality of tears within the frame of this interview. As with *The Invisible War*, the tears are social in the first sense in that they are shared by all the women who relate their stories of abduction, rape, escape, and motherhood. The sociality of tears is also evident in the second sense, as these harms are widespread and systematically committed against a large number of women – as there were neither racial, ethnic, nor religious demarcations of women who were raped.[15] Yet this form of systematic violence in Sierra Leone is different from the sexual violence in the US military, as the violence did not occur within the framework of an institution – though it was most widespread amongst the rebel soldiers – but overflowed the boundaries of institutions. As violence was not contained within the framework of an institution, neither can the sense of injustice be contained by institutional failure. Mabel's grief also points to the sociality of tears in a third sense, in that it points to the social dynamics in which violence has flourished amongst rebels.[16] But the answer to the question of the sociality of tears in the fourth sense, as providing the basis of community, requires some explication.

Mabel and the other girls at the school refer to each other as sisters, as they help each other dress for a night of prostitution. These young women have been able to create small communities, even though their distance from family and neighbors suggests an absence of a community of grieving over the same things. As these girls and young women have been contaminated by their fate as rebel wives, they are not easily accepted back into the national community. In the face of the difficulties of establishing familial, local, and national communities, the transnational video activism of the film makes an appeal to an international human community that is not disgusted by their contamination as rebel wives. Yet the emotional responses made available to this larger community are highly limited. On the film's website, viewers are asked to check off their response, choosing from: 'incredible, enlightening, fresh, informative, motivating, captivating, heartwarming, beautiful, humorous, thought-provoking, lacking'. Not one single response was made available for the negative emotions that might circulate in the viewers' body, such as horror, rage, disgust, or fury. This exclusion of negative emotions seems to be part of a strategy in which the community of viewers can be accessed and consolidated only through positive emotions, echoing the half-smiles and encouraging words at the end of the film about the women of Sierra Leone coming together and rebuilding the country in the future.

Despite the failure of the film to do justice to the negative emotions of viewers, the spilling over of tears gives a clue to the nature of affective community based on the pull of these tears. What is striking in this interview with Mabel, as in other interviews in the film, is the everydayness of the tears, which almost calls for no notice. In narrating their stories of sexual assault and the failure of institutional justice in *The Invisible War*, victims are overcome and interrupted by an explosion of tears. This is the kind of weeping we are more familiar with, we with an everyday life amidst social relations that present both hard times and good times. But the kind of weeping in *Operation Fine Girl* has another character, another form of omnipresence, as it is not contained by the boundaries of recollection or institutions. Andrew Jefferson writes in his study of Liberian refugees in Sierra Leone how the refugees experience the self as a sufferer: 'Suffering is not a form of life, a choice among many. Suffering for them is life' (Jefferson 2014: 235). The tears in this film convey this sense of suffering as life. In this context, common questions of film analysis about whether the camera 'sentimentalizes' the emotion, making it more attractive or interesting than it is, seem out of place. (What is the 'right' amount or 'exaggerated' emotion in response to teenage girls who have had their lives derailed?)[17] And yet, despite the human pull of the tears, the sense of a transnational community is fractured by this realization of the difference between tears as interruption and tears as spilling over – between the expectation of ordinary life and suffering as life. Hence, the sociality of tears in this fourth sense of a community that grieves and rejoices together is ambivalent. There is a strong appeal to a human community in the tears that mark the overflowing of a suffering and injustice that will not be contained or delimited, but only at the very best can be left behind. And yet the activist appeal to only the positive emotions of the viewer reinforces the expectation that the transnational community will fail, as the familial, local, and national communities seem to have done.

Conclusion

I have used the trace of tears as a heuristic device to unpack the connection between gender, sexual violence, suffering, and community. The trace of tears in these documentaries contributes to a politically reflexive project, which shows cracks in the frame of justice.

Documentaries about atrocities often imbibe a view of moral triumph, as exemplified in the narration in *The Rape of Nanking* (1999). The narrator concludes the tales of rape, bayonetting, beheading, and the boiling of fetuses cut from their mothers' wombs with the following sentiments: 'Out of even the greatest tragedies comes inspiration. At Nanking it was the deathless Chinese spirit ... (which) endured to rebuild.' In this standard approach, the structure of the documentary presents the background, the battle, the atrocities, the aftermath, and the justice. Although both *The Invisible War* and *Operation Fine Girl* have an activist agenda and 'do justice' to their victims, neither buys into this myth of redemptive justice. Despite the objections that tears are pathetic, have no proper role in legal or ethical judgments, and represent standard topes about gender and notion, I have argued that tears trace out complex aspects of social dynamics. Their sociality points to the shared nature of harm when it is distributed over a large group of victims; to the systematic production of harm when it is embedded in institutions; to the social relations, including military masculinity, in which such violence flourishes; and to the possibility of a community that rejoices and grieves alike.

Both films are politically reflexive, as in framing of issues of sexual violence they make visible the failure of institutions and societies to provide legal, political, medical, or economic justice. But their reflexivity is not just 'an artistic analogue' of the structure of a political movement, such as the women's movement, as Lesage wrote of earlier feminist documentaries. Although neither of these films market themselves as distinctly feminist, the films exemplify that it is still significant who is doing the talking, as Lesage noted earlier. But the filming of the tears also becomes an important element in the reflexive process, as the films trouble the standard ideas about the relation between individual and community, women and nation, and cinematically about the distinction between emotional absorption and reflexivity. In *The Invisible War*, the explosion, interruption, and disruption of the narratives by tears indicates an expectation of a life that is other than suffering, an expectation of justice and a rage at its failure, even though it is an ongoing struggle to reestablish a sense of ordinary life. This form of crying is linked to the film's focus on violence as embedded in the military as an institution. However central this national institution is, it is not an all-encompassing institution. In this sense, there is an outside, a border, a form of containment between what happens in the military and what happens in civilian life (though rapists in the military also figure high statistically as rapists when they return to civilian life). It is this form of containment that makes thinkable social outrage and a protest movement calling for legislative and cultural changes regarding military justice.

In *Operation Fine Girl*, however, there is no such containment, as it is *as* civilians that young girls, teenagers, and women were sexually abused. This lack of containment is embodied in the way in which tears spill over. As tears are always on tap, these young women let them dry on the face or habitually wipe them away without notice. There is no outside to suffering, no ordinary life which has been momentarily though repeatedly disrupted and to which one might return. Suffering is life, and there are few expectations for justice: the victims decry the fact that it is the perpetrators who seem to benefit, while there is little help for the victims. The only option for these women is to go on, as all eyes are watching them. However, as the film concludes with a scene of one of the young victims holding her child, looking over the landscape and into the future with a trace of a smile on her face,[18] the activist proscription of positive affect circumscribes the political reflexivity of the tears. It is rather through the spilling over of tears that the viewer confronts his or her own distance, confirming the failure of the transnational community as well.

Notes

1. I am grateful to Vibeke Pedersen, expert in media studies and gender studies, for useful conversations on these issues, and to Cristina Masters, for conversations during the workshop 'Sex Gender Violence Desire?' at the University of Gothenburg, June 7, 2014.
2. For a historical overview of sexual violence and war, see Schott (2011: 6–7).
3. These films are just two out of a great many documentaries that have now been produced on sexual violence committed during warfare. This list includes *Calling the Ghosts: A Story about Rape, War and Women* (1997), about the rapes at the Bosnian Serb-run Omarska Camp; *Rape of Nanking* (1999) made for the History Channel, one of many films relating the mass murder and mass rape committed by Japanese soldiers in Nanking over a six-week period beginning in December 1937 that left 300,000 persons dead; the five-part series *Women, War and Peace* (2011) produced for PBS; *Weapon of War: Confessions of Rape in Congo* (2009), about the systematic use of rape in Congo; and the newly released *Mission Rape: A Tool of War* (2014), about rape victims in Bosnia and the limitations of justice at the International Criminal Tribunal for the former Yugoslavia (ICTY).
4. *The Invisible War* has had a wide reception, winning the Audience Award for Best Documentary at the Sundance Film Festival in 2012 and being nominated for Best Documentary at the Academy Awards in 2013. Two days after viewing the film, then US Secretary of Defense Leon Panetta issued a directive ordering all sexual assault cases to be handled at the rank of colonel or higher, thereby ending the practice of commanders adjudicating cases within their own units. However, in March 2014, the US Senate rejected a bill that would remove military commanders from decisions over the prosecution of sexual assault cases in the armed forces. The military sexual assault trial of Brig. General Jeffrey A. Sinclair suggests both recent political pressures to address these issues and the difficulties in producing results.
5. The occasion was the Rodney King, Jr. incident, in which a bystander captured evidence of police brutality on his handheld video camera (see also Andersen's chapter for a discussion of Rodney King and video activism). See www.witness.org/about-us (accessed June 17, 2014).
6. Angela B. Ginorio, Associate Professor in Gender, Women and Sexuality Studies at the University of Washington, suggested this phrase while I was in residence at the University of Washington in February–March 2014.
7. See also Errol Morris' 2008 documentary on Abu Ghraib, *Standard Operating Procedure*. Judith Butler argues that the Abu Ghraib photographs reveal the nexus of violence and sexuality at the heart of the myth of a progressive, civilizing sexuality paraded by the US Army (Butler 2009: 128, 132).
8. See www.oxforddictionaries.com/definition/english/pathetic (accessed June 17, 2014).

9 The Foca case was the first in which sexual assault and sexual enslavement were judged to be crimes against humanity.
10 At the Nuremburg trial, twenty top Nazis were tried for crimes at the end of World War II.
11 This relates to a complex theme of class, gender, and nationalism in the representation of tears. For a good discussion, see Rabinowitz (1999: 44–47).
12 In the closing credits, there are approximately 180 names listed as 'courageous survivors' who helped make the film.
13 Tim Hetherington, collaborator with Sebastian Junger on the documentary *Restrepo* (2010), observed the positive aspects of military masculinity. In Junger's 2013 documentary *Which Way is the Front Line from Here? The Life and Time of Tim Hetherington*, Hetherington says, 'Afghanistan was a great place to be a man', and he entitled his photograph of soldiers digging a ditch 'Man Eden'. Both Hetherington and Junger view conflict as a form of bonding, and they see war as the only opportunity for men to love each other unconditionally, to be part of a group that is not reproducible in wider society (see also van Munster's chapter, this volume).
14 Butler (2009: 26, 31). Butler argues for a social ontology of the body, which acknowledges that one is always 'given over to others, to norms, to social and political organizations'. She calls this condition of exposure 'precariousness', 'the condition of being conditioned' (Butler 2009: 23). Precariousness points to the way in which life is injurable and finite, and provides the basis of obligations toward others. She introduces the notion of 'precarity' as a political notion, which refers to the differential allocation of this generalized condition of precariousness (Butler 2009: 25).
15 One doctor notes that 90 percent of the girls over twelve years old who come to the hospital have been raped, all have sexually transmitted diseases, and some have had their breasts and buttocks cut. Another doctor notes that all of these women and their children have HIV, and he is concerned about their easy disappearance in the population as a health problem. Here, the social contamination of being associated with rebels becomes a medical and psychic contamination of society.
16 One Revolutionary United Front (RUF) Colonel claimed: 'we are not 100 percent perfect' and 'we expect these things to happen'. He also claimed that if any woman identified a soldier, he will never go free, though this comment has little credibility, following his previous remarks.
17 Mabel describes herself at eighteen years old as having 'gone downhill in my life' – at an age when we imagine life as beginning for a young woman.
18 This positive tone at the end of the film is reinforced by Christiana Thorpe, director of the school and rehabilitation center, who observes that women are now mobilizing and one can be 'hopeful for the future of women in Sierra Leone'.

Films

Calling the Ghosts: A Story about Rape, War and Women (1997) Directed by Mandy Jacobson and Karmen Jelincic. USA, Bowery Productions.
Mission Rape: A Tool of War (2014) Directed by Annette Mari Olsen and Katia Forbert Petersen. Denmark, Sfinx Film.
Operation Fine Girl: Rape Used as a Weapon of War in Sierra Leone (2001) Directed by Lilibet Foster. USA, WITNESS.
Restrepo (2010) Directed by Tim Hetherington and Sebastian Junger. USA, Outpost Films and Virgil Films and Entertainment.
Standard Operating Procedure (2008) Directed by Errol Morris. USA, Participant Media.
The Invisible War (2012) Directed by Kirby Dick. USA, Chain Camera Pictures.

The Rape of Nanking (1999) Directed by Sammy Jackson. USA, Lou Reda Productions.
The Reckoning: The Battle for the International Criminal Court (2009) Directed by Pamela Yates. USA, Skylight Pictures.
Weapon of War: Confessions of Rape in Congo (2009) Directed by Ilse van Velzen and Femke van Velzen. The Netherlands, IFproductions.
Which Way is the Front Line from Here? The Life and Time of Tim Hetherington (2013) Directed by Sebastian Junger. USA, Goldcrest Films International.
Women, War and Peace (2011, TV series) Created by Abigail E. Disney, Pamela Hogan and Gini Reticker. USA, PBS.

References

Alcoff, Linda Martín (2012) 'Then and Now', *Journal of Speculative Philosophy*, 26, 268–278.
Brownmiller, Susan (1981 [1975]) *Against our Will; Men, Women, and Rape*. New York, NY: Bantam.
Butler, Judith (2009) *Frames of War: When is Life Grievable?* London: Verso.
Dunham, Will (2011) 'Obama Hails End of US Military Restrictions on Gays', Reuters.com. Available at: www.reuters.com/article/2011/09/20/us-usa-gays-military-idUSTRE78J3WP20110920 (accessed May 28, 2014).
Halonen, Irma Kaarina (1996) 'Mama, Mama. My Hand is Gone! Images of Women in War News Reporting', translated by Charly Hultén, originally published in Finnish in Marianna Laiho and Iiris Ruoho (eds) *Naisen naamio, miehen maski*. Helsinki: Kansan Sivistystyön Liitto. Available at: www.nordicom.gu.se/sites/default/files/kapitel-pdf/37_halonen.pdf (accessed July 14, 2014).
Jefferson, Andrew (2014) 'Performances of Victimhood, Allegation, and Disavowal in Sierra Leone', in Steffen Jensen and Henrik Ronsbo (eds) *Histories of Victimhood*. Philadelphia, PN: University of Pennsylvania Press, 218–238.
Johnston, Claire (1973) 'Women's Cinema as Counter-Cinema', in Claire Johnston (ed.) *Notes on Women's Cinema*. London: Society for Education in Film and Television, reprinted in Bill Nichols (1976) *Movies and Methods: An Anthology*. Berkeley and Los Angeles, CA: University of California Press, 208–217.
Lesage, Julia (1978) 'The Political Aesthetics of the Feminist Documentary Film', *Quarterly Review of Film Studies*, 3–4, 507–523.
Marcus, Sharon (1992) 'Fighting Bodies, Fighting Words: A Theory and Politics of Rape Prevention', in Judith Butler and Joan W. Scott (eds) *Feminists Theorize the Political*. New York, NY: Routledge, 385–403.
Mayne, Judith (1985) 'Feminist Film Theory and Criticism', *Signs; Journal of Women in Culture and Society*, 11, 81–100.
Meyers, Diana Tietjens (2011) 'Two Victim Paradigms and the Problem of "Impure" Victims' Humanity', *An International Journal of Human Rights, Humanitarianism and Development*, 2, 255–275.
Nichols, Bill (1991) *Representing Reality*. Bloomington, IN: Indiana University Press.
Nichols, Bill (2001) 'Documentary Film and the Modernist Avant-Garde', *Critical Inquiry*, 27, 580–610.
Peterson, Susan Rae (1977) 'Coercion and Rape: The State as a Male Protection Racket', in Mary Vetterling Braggin, Frederick A. Elliston and Jane English (eds) *Feminism and Philosophy*. Totawa, NJ: Rowman and Allenheld, 360–371.

Rabinowitz, Paula (1999) 'Sentimental Contracts: Dreams and Documents of American Labor', in Diane Waldman and Janet Walker (eds) *Feminism and Documentary*. Minneapolis, MN: University of Minnesota Press, 43–63.

Schott, Robin May (2011) 'War Rape, Natality and Genocide', *Journal of Genocide Research*, 13, 1–21.

Sivakumaran, Sandesh (2005) 'Male/Male Rape and the "Taint" of Homosexuality', *Human Rights Quarterly*, 27, 1274–1306.

Sontag, Susan (2003) *Regarding the Pain of Others*. London: Hamish Hamilton/Penguin.

Spelman, Elizabeth V. (1997) *Fruits of Sorrow: Framing Our Attention to Suffering*. Boston, MA: Beacon Press.

Waldman, Diane and Janet Walker (eds) (1999) 'Introduction', in Diane Waldman and Janet Walker (eds) *Feminism and Documentary*. Minneapolis, MN: University of Minnesota Press, 1–36.

Weil, Simone (1965) 'The Iliad, or the Poem of Force', translated by Mary McCarthy, *Chicago Review*, 18, 5–30.

Young, Iris Marion (2007) 'Feminist Reactions to the Contemporary Security Regime', in Robin May Schott (ed.) *Feminist Philosophy and the Problem of Evil*. Bloomington, IN: Indiana University Press, 299–307.

9 Meta-mediation, visual agency and documentarist reflexivity in conflict film

Burma VJ meets *Burke + Norfolk*

Rune Saugmann Andersen

Introduction

With the globalization of video recording and distribution technology in the first decade of the twenty-first century and the related globalization of the imagined recording and viewing communities, visual agency has emerged as an important part of the processes that make up international politics. Soldiers' video recordings of atrocities such as those in Abu Ghraib, protesters' visual denunciations of the repression of dissent in the Arab Spring and visual artists' questioning of security practices attest to the power of visual agency, as do increasingly ubiquitous bans on filming. On the other hand, meta-coverage of political events has been criticized for shifting the focus from the events themselves to mediation or the media aspects of events. While the increasing prominence given to visual agency and the mediation of conflict makes these interesting themes for documentary filmmaking, they raise tricky questions about how to negotiate attention to the visual agency of documenting within a genre that, for the most part, has seen itself as neutrally observing the world.

The present chapter considers questions of visual agency and meta-coverage in the documentary films *Burma VJ: Reporting from a Closed Country* (dir. Anders Østergaard 2008) and *Burke + Norfolk* (dir. Luke Tchalenko 2011), while paying particular attention to how these films understand their own roles vis-à-vis the visual agency they depict. The analysis of these themes is closely related to recent technological and political developments. The first decade of the twenty-first century witnessed a globalization of image-based communication that was hardly conceivable during the 1990s. The Internet and the digitization of the technologies for recording, distributing and showing video and photographic images redefined the ways in which images spread and meet the spectator. In a parallel development, imagined visual communities also underwent transformations, as largely private and local forms of visual agency became redefined as important public acts on the world scene (Andersen, forthcoming). As the documentary films discussed in this chapter illustrate, this double globalization has influenced international politics. Repression of dissent is not only a problem of achieving superiority of force; such force is now a potential (visual) liability that reconfigures the economy of force used (Andersen 2013). This type of visual liability is excellently portrayed in *Burma VJ*, a commercially produced award-winning film about the mediation of the 2007 Burmese protests. The second film considered here, *Burke + Norfolk*, is a short documentary about photographer Simon Norfolk's work in Afghanistan, produced for the Tate Museum. *Burke + Norfolk* attests to the power of visual agency by considering how Norfolk visually questions the occupation of Afghanistan by Western coalition forces.

Despite important differences, both films depict the role of visual (or pictorial) agency in violent political conflict. They also explore the practices of meta-mediation or meta-picturing, in which journalists, scholars, artists, citizens and the documentarists themselves engage. This chapter looks at the space of reflection provided by documentary film in meta-mediating pictorial agency in contemporary conflict. It does so by contrasting *Burma VJ* and *Burke + Norfolk* as films that picture the role of picturing in relation to violent conflict and by exploring the relationship between the meta-picturing of the documentary film and the pictorial agency they depict. I argue that both films stick closely to a tradition of documentary filming in which the choices made by documentary filmmakers remain hidden. This contrasts with the emphasis on picturing as an act that the subjects of the films articulate.

The chapter first introduces the concepts of meta-mediation and meta-pictures, discussing how, apart from a focus on mediation as a crucial part of reality, they are defined by reflexivity as a core discursive feature. Subsequently, it moves to an analysis of *Burma VJ*, and thereafter contrasts the depiction and enactment of visual agency in *Burma VJ* with the views expressed in *Burke + Norfolk*. Finally, the discussion centres on how the films enact and depict visual agency in world politics.

Meta-mediation

The increasing attention being given to visual agency in international affairs is paralleled by a growing attention to different forms of meta-communicative practices (see, for example, Esser 2009; Mitchell 1994). For the purposes of this analysis, the concepts of meta-coverage and meta-picturing are most relevant. First, the concept of meta-coverage has been employed to describe the recent trend in news coverage of war to privilege the media-related aspects of war and conflict. To Esser, meta-coverage is 'defined as news stories that report on war topics in their connection to the role of news journalism or political public relations' (Esser 2009: 709) – a central theme of *Burma VJ* – but it also encompasses stories that treat the broader mediation of war and conflict (Andersen 2012; Mortensen 2012). Meta-coverage can be seen to potentially displace the political aspects of conflict by focusing on its media coverage (Mortensen 2012). The phenomenon has also, however, been credited with fostering a reflexive attitude to mediation. Breaking with the 'strategic ritual' of invoking objectivism in news journalism (Tuchman 1972), meta-coverage calls for journalists to constantly examine their own efforts and those of other journalists (Tumber and Palmer 2004: 7, cited in Esser 2009).[1]

Second, the visual culture theorist W. J. T. Mitchell has pointed to meta-mediation as a powerful visual discourse running through the history of picturing, from cave paintings to cell-phone videos. In an essay on meta-pictures, Mitchell (1994: 35) defines these as 'pictures that refer to themselves or to other pictures, pictures that are used to show what a picture is'. This practice of referencing is central to *Burke + Norfolk*, in which Simon Norfolk contrasts his work with that of his nineteenth-century predecessor John Burke, as well as with contemporary war photojournalism. Key to Mitchell's thinking about meta-pictures is the view that these constitute a kind of pictorial *theorizing* in and of themselves, since such 'pictures might be capable of reflection on themselves, capable of providing a second-order discourse that tells us – or at least shows us – something about pictures' (Mitchell 1994: 35). When most powerful, the meta-picture 'offers [...] an *episteme*, an entire system of knowledge/power relations' (Mitchell 1994: 58). In depicting depicting, images of images not only enquire into the nature and production of images, but also point beyond the frame to the ways in which we look at things (including images): 'they show us what vision is, and picture theory' (Mitchell 1994: 57). In so doing, meta-pictures question the subject positions that are related to visual representation. They ask the spectator to question whether (s)he is a spectator or an image producer, depicting or depicted. To Foucault's analysis of *Las Meninas*, this means that 'we do not know who we are, or what we are doing. Seen or seeing?' (as cited in Mitchell 1994: 63).

In contemporary culture, in which the image of cameras depicting almost any thinkable event has become commonplace, the gesture of the raised camera (often in front of screens used at concerts, conferences and other events) has become an important marker of shared experience (Becker 2013). Perhaps it would be more accurate, then, to shift our analytical focus from meta-pictures to meta-*picturing* – that is, to the *activity* of depicting depiction – and to examine how this activity tackles the questions of reflexivity and agency originally posed by meta-pictures.

Watching *Burma VJ*

The 2008 documentary film *Burma VJ: Reporting from a Closed Country* presents both a nuanced and a troubling account of the 2007 Rangoon protests and their mediation. This immensely successful film concentrates on a group of illegal reporters who film the Burmese protests, smuggle the footage out of the country and broadcast it back into Burma from the TV station Democratic Voice of Burma (DVB) located in Oslo, Norway.[2] *Burma VJ* is mainly a meta-mediation of the conflict; its central focus is on mediation, even though it also relates this to the course of events that unfolded in Burma. The spectatorship of protest footage is central throughout the film, both driving the narrative about the mediation of the conflict and serving to explain what happens in the protests. The viewing is mainly framed by the voice of the protagonist, 'Joshua', whose viewing of protest footage and its international re-broadcasting carries the story of the film. 'Joshua's' comments and his phone calls to clandestine reporters in Burma from a safe house in Thailand function as voice-over for the majority of the film and situate the footage shot by VJs.[3] *Burma VJ*'s meta-mediation of the work of the VJs establishes its view of pictorial agency as crucial to world politics. Three interrelated narratives or arguments, all drawing on and contributing to theorizations or trajectories of pictorial agency in world politics, are crucial to this aspiration: (1) the idea of the camera as a weapon; (2) the idea of political action as a (news-)network effect; and (3) the idea of amateuristic aesthetics as a marker of authenticity. Together, these arguments shape and elaborate the overall argument of the film: that remediated protest video constitutes a 'weapon of the weak' against state repression.

'The police shoot us, and we shoot them': the camera as weapon

Burma VJ opens with a tableau where a sole protester is seen standing outside a gate, holding up a placard containing English text. A jump cut takes us inside a bag, in which we see a video camera being turned on and prepared for shooting. The actions are quick, precise and routine – not unlike the loading of a firearm. The scene underlines the film's main message that video documentation of protest is an extremely powerful form of pictorial agency that can function as a weapon against the regime. The first encounter with the journalist protagonist 'Joshua' is in his role as a spectator reviewing the footage of the protesting man on his Handycam. He tells us of the nervousness that always plagues the first moments of 'shooting'. As we witness the protester being taken into a car by plainclothes police, 'Joshua' observes that 'when I pick up the camera, maybe my hands are shaking', but 'after shooting for a while it's OK. I have only the subject in my mind. I just shoot.'

The idea of video as a weapon of mass exposure that can turn state repression into a problem for the state has a history, as video has previously proved able to transform otherwise mundane events of state-sanctioned repression into topics of world politics. Arguably, the most important precedent is the video filming of the beating of Rodney King in 1991.[4] If this video was instrumental in establishing the politically transformative capacity of visual mediation, the idea that private video can produce a global audience was already apparent from Abraham Zapruder's legendary footage of US President Kennedy's assassination. The Zapruder film was the first time that a privately held video camera brought an event of world politics to the screens of TV spectators around the world (Gunthert 2008). In this sense, it foreshadowed the contemporary situation, where the permeation of private video technology in society means that it is more likely that a 'citizen journalist', rather than a traditional media professional, first captures a scene of historical significance.

In *Burma VJ*, the idea that video recording is a source of powerful protest is underlined by the ways in which the regime targets the undercover journalists. In one scene, police yell 'He's got a camera', after which they proceed to arrest 'Joshua' and confiscate his camera and footage. Another scene shows the police shooting a Japanese photojournalist and, so it seems, collecting his camera (Japan News Review 2007). In a third scene, Buddhist monks are initially sceptical of the intentions of a camera-carrying journalist, advising him: 'Don't film; you will only create problems.' As civilian police agents try to arrest the journalist, however, the monks intervene to protect him. Thus, *Burma VJ* is saturated with references to the camera as a weapon.

Action as a (CNN) network effect

Burma VJ also stresses the importance of the remediation of protester footage by (international) news networks. While introducing his ambition that 'I want to fight for democracy', 'Joshua' reviews footage from the 1988 student protests in Burma, the hitherto largest protests in the history of the military regime. At times, he fast-forwards the analogue tape and comments on the episode as his prime motivation for becoming a video reporter. However, he also expresses his doubts about the achievements of these protests: 'Sometimes I feel they died for nothing. There's nothing left from '88, it's like everything's been forgotten.' The film underplays the fact that the 1988 protests did, in fact, lead to an international movement, widespread isolation of the military junta and the establishment of Aung San Suu Kyi as an internationally recognized, Nobel laureate leader of the democratic alternative to the military regime. This leaves Joshua vesting his hopes for change not so much in the protests as such, as in the democratizing potential of networked images. In *Burma VJ*, the answer to this stipulated futility of the 1988 protests is a highly optimistic media-effect narrative that stresses (and makes use of) international meta-coverage of the protests.[5]

The clearest enactment of this occurs when Joshua is reviewing footage, while a voice-over from CNN sets out the importance of network mediation: 'The information and the pictures and the photos that we're getting from iReporters is crucial.' The notion of iReporter refers to the corporate, branded name for CNN's initiative to harvest footage from citizens (in this case, Burmese citizens).[6] Upon receiving such footage, CNN remediates, curates and vets it by cross-referencing it with other images from the same location or event. This is all done to substantiate the claim to authenticity that drives the news value of citizen journalism.[7] According to the voice-over: 'It's telling the world what's going on. They [iReporters] are the world's eyes and ears in this sort of situation.' By including news network remediation of the protest footage shown on BBC, CNN and German-language TV, *Burma VJ* implies that a global community is being constituted through listening and watching. A CNN clip shows former US President George W. Bush commenting on the crisis as a sign that 'the people's desire for freedom is unmistakable'.[8] Besides highlighting the political economy of global media corporations receiving free footage while staying out of harm's way, this sequence bolsters the film's narrative that visual exposure is an agent of political change. It locates the political effect of protest not in the act of protesting itself, but in the ability of protestors to generate global media coverage that can lead to international pressure on the regime.[9]

Thus, while sanctions had already been imposed by the EU and US, and aid cut by Japan (BBC 2007), the film's exclusive focus on the pictorial agency of undercover journalists gives the impression that decisive change will only result from remediation.

The idea that international media exposure promotes pro-democratic change – repeated and elaborated throughout the film – draws on a rich tradition of thinking about photography, one that connects visibility closely to representation and participation.[10] For instance, Hannah Arendt (2003: 199) argued, in connection with the civil rights movement in the United States, that in 'the public realm, where nothing counts that cannot make itself seen and heard, visibility and audibility are of prime importance'. A similar belief in exposure underlies Susan Sontag's call to

> let the atrocious images haunt us. Even if they are only tokens and cannot possibly encompass most of the reality to which they refer, they still perform a vital function. The images say: this is what human beings are capable of doing.
>
> (Sontag 2004: 89)

Burma VJ's belief in the power of exposure is thus not without foundation.[11] Moreover, the idea of a CNN effect that runs through the film is a less sophisticated rendering of these ideas, although, as Sontag (2004: 81) remarks, it is one that is 'fast approaching the stature of platitudes'.

Burma VJ leaves out demands for political action (such as intervention) and simply equates news network exposure with 'pressure' and something good; as when a text superimposed on images at the beginning of the film states that: '[i]n the autumn of 2007, the secret reporters would set the world agenda in a way they had never imagined'. To Bignell's (2002: 128) Barthes-inspired analysis, the popularized effect theories are based on the mythic power of global media: 'If a news story is broadcast by CNN news, it carries the mythic meaning of global significance simply because CNN broadcast the story.' The idea that the private camera or the act of filming can decisively change a situation from one of everyday repression to a global event draws on this discourse. A similar idea underpins the Al-Jazeera effect, which holds that citizens' access to viewing and producing journalistic products erodes previous government monopolies of the media (Seib 2008). This effect is invoked explicitly in *Burma VJ*, both in the overlaid text claiming that the VJs 'counter the regime's propaganda and misinformation' and in the assertion by a CNN news anchor that VJs 'are the world's eyes and ears in this sort of situation, *because* we as journalists can't fulfill our role properly because we are *banned by the authorities from going in*' (emphasis added). In sum, *Burma VJ* convincingly combines the idea of the camera as a weapon with that of the network effect. It uses the Myanmar state TV's propaganda to drive the argument that new forms of journalism can dismantle government monopolies. Particularly, one tableau features international remediation of the protest footage, including the story of how it was smuggled out and its importance for international media; juxtaposing the authenticity of VJ footage to that of government propaganda. Thus, we are presented with claims by the Governmental Television National News[12] that international media is airing a 'skyful of lies' and that they are 'killers in the air waves'. This is followed by a street footage clip with Joshua's voice-over saying that '[m]ilitary people are hunting any person with a camera', together with footage from a government press conference denouncing the DVB.

The aesthetic strategy of amateurism

In 2005, the launch of YouTube accelerated a shift that was already underway in the publication of user-made digital video. Its catch-phrase slogan, 'broadcast yourself', invokes the publishing model, gestures to the private origins of the authority of video and points to the visibly 'homemade' and 'non-professional' (yet sometimes carefully choreographed) traits of authenticity in videos (cf. Burgess and Green 2009). Throughout *Burma VJ*, handheld camera aesthetics plays a major role in conveying the immediacy of protests and the authenticity, danger and urgency of the situations depicted. Here, the film draws on the aesthetics of citizen-made video and the visual display of non-professionalism (Andersen 2012; Weber 2008). In this sense, the footage from Burma shares some of the features that made the Rodney King video effective, including the 'authentic feel' produced by the low-resolution, handheld-type of footage. This kind of amateuristic aesthetics brands the original as well as reenacted footage in *Burma VJ* with a 'this is how it was' stamp (Barthes 1977: 44), visually testifying to its authenticity. Because it is visually and audibly distinct from professional genres of TV journalism and documentary film, the footage enables practices of meta-coverage and remediation in more professional genres (Bolter and Grusin 2000).

However, the insight that visible non-professionalism is an asset rather than a liability is not new either. The phenomenon had already been explored in the feature film *Wag the Dog* (dir. Barry Levinson 1997) about the production of a made-for-TV mock war in a Hollywood studio. Still, the trend has accelerated with the spread of digital video and online video-hosting platforms through which protesters can disseminate their stories. Visually slick, carefully choreographed and professionally edited visual media representations have long been described as being at 'the heart of society's real unreality' (Debord 1994: para. 6). By contrast, the lack of professional elaboration in *Burma VJ* powerfully reinforces the 'unreal reality' of the images and bolsters its claim to authentically 'capture' something that was really there.[13]

The 'low resolution' aesthetics in *Burma VJ* is not simply attributable to the equipment used. It also permeates – and this is perhaps where *Burma VJ* starts to resemble *Wag the Dog* – the reenactments that are part of the film. Bignell (2002: 192) has warned that 'mythic meanings may appear to take precedence over the "content" which the news medium communicates', because of strong myths of authenticity attached to various media formats. When *Burma VJ* creates protest images that look authentic – e.g., by mimicking chaotic recording conditions or through non-professional camera use – it leaves the spectator with no way of distinguishing between reenactment and actual street footage. Playing to the mythic meaning of the amateur format, it uses the look and feel of protest images as an aesthetic strategy to convey the immediacy of its message. Indeed, the reenactments weave together the story and provide some of the most emotionally charged moments in the film.

The seamless recreation of protest images is, however, troubling, given the strong agency that *Burma VJ* attributes to pictorial action. While the inclusion of reenactments might be relatively unproblematic in a different type of documentary, they threaten to undermine the narrative of *Burma VJ*. While the latter considers visual resistance crucial to politics and resistance, the use of reenactments simultaneously banalizes the work undertaken by undercover journalists. It undermines the notion that the camera is an effective weapon or the myth that low resolution is a sign of the perilous recording conditions under which the VJs operate. The power attributed to remediated images implicates the spectator as one of the agents through which the chain of networked agency works. By viewing and caring about what happens on the screen, spectators (are supposed to) create political momentum against the repression of dissent. This connection is beautifully enacted in the film: we see Joshua in his new workspace after he has been forced into exile in Thailand. He is depicted in silhouette, hanging a framed image of Aung San Suu Kyi on the wall. The framed image reflects the light entering from outside, but Joshua's dark silhouette blocks the ray of light. As the dark silhouette turns the TV screen into a mirror, the spectator's own image appears inside Joshua's silhouette. The message is clear: the spectator enables the actions of undercover journalists, who, in turn, enable dissidents and protesters.

The scene also, however, enacts the pictorial agency of the filmmaking crew, actively framing the story of how audiences and Suu Kyi connect (by putting both them and Joshua inside her picture frame). On the one hand, it firmly situates the spectator in a web of pictorial agency; on the other hand, it simultaneously contradicts this claim of agency by the failure to distinguish between protest film and reenactment. This not only confuses the spectator, but also creates a highly ambiguous subject position, in which the spectator is both asked to identify with her role in pictorial agency and to disavow this role as the passive spectator of an (entertaining) docudrama. As Andrew Marshall, a journalist who covered the Burmese uprising, writes in his review of the film:

> I felt moved by a sequence showing protesters gathering on a Rangoon backstreet in defiance of the junta. But when I learned that it had been shot from scratch in the northern Thai city of Chiang Mai, I felt something else: manipulated.
>
> (Marshall 2009)

The embedding of the use of video in a weaponized discourse of opposing forces draws attention to the agency of both underground journalism *and* documentary film about this phenomenon. Agency is at the core of the film's narrative, but it is also central to its motive. According to director Østergaard: 'Somehow the film manages to portray, I hope, the people there not just as victims in a burned village, but as people with the power to do something about their lives' (2008). Yet *Burma VJ* arguably fails to attend to the interpretative effects of its meta-mediation and reenactments – a troubling paradox, given that it is a film about visual agency in world politics. During the film, the narrative carried by Joshua's storytelling is set to shots of him using video-editing equipment, subtly suggesting that he is editing material into a narrative. The 'recording as resistance' narrative takes precedence, however, and the film is conspicuously devoid of any more explicit reflections on its own involvement in the struggle that is reenacted, and how it squares with the desire to portray VJs as powerful.

To get a sense of why this is problematic for the film, it is useful to contrast it with another documentary that also revolves around meta-mediation.

Burke + Norfolk: beauty as photographic agency

Burke + Norfolk, a Tate documentary about photographer Simon Norfolk's work in Afghanistan, displays a strikingly different approach to how images depict political conflict. As a documentary produced for an institution, *Burke + Norfolk* does not face the same pressure to generate revenues as commercial productions – it mainly has to satisfy the commissioning institution. Such differences notwithstanding, *Burma VJ* and *Burke + Norfolk* are remarkably similar in their documentarist indifference to the choices involved in their own production.

Burke + Norfolk also centres on meta-picturing pictorial agency. The film shows how contemporary art photographer Simon Norfolk encounters the work of the nineteenth-century British photographer John Burke. Norfolk's 'romantic gesture of following in his [Burke's] footsteps' and his visual meta-mediation on Burke's photography is the central theme of the film. Norfolk is shown meditating on the differences and commonalities between his and Burke's role and status and how this is reflected in their work. We follow Norfolk to Afghanistan – a country marked by occupation and war – as he re-photographs some of the scenes Burke captured when the Second Anglo-Afghan war marked the country. Apart from some interviews with other characters, the major part of the story is carried by Norfolk's voice-over as he explains his work. Perfect imitation of Burke's photography is not Norfolk's ambition; rather, 'as Burke moves through Afghanistan, I am shadowing him in some ways.'

This shadowing enacts an interesting, reflective kind of collaboration far removed from the frustration and regret Joshua felt towards his predecessors. Norfolk highlights the collaboration and points out how it produces his own images and enacts them as part of a history. Finding himself in another British war in Afghanistan, Norfolk does not chastise the futility of earlier war documentation, but calls the result 'a collaboration ... a kind of archeological act, ... or even like a piece of forensic evidence of a crime. It is an evidence of a crime.' In effect, Norfolk's images transform Burke's work from that of a commercial photographer struggling to make a living in the British Empire to that of a central witness in the investigation of war as crime.

While the basic narrative is thus relatively similar in the two films – following the production and producers of images – the engagement with contemporary conflict is remarkably different. While Joshua's undercover point-shoot-and-run video journalism results in grainy, blurry images, Norfolk's elaborate attention to light, detail and composition places him in the genre of slow photography (cf. Lisle 2011; Shapiro 2008). Still, the political aims are compatible: 'The beauty of these things', says Norfolk against the background of a series of pastel-colored shots of Afghan scenery, 'is only ever tactical':

> The reason why I am here is not to make beautiful pictures. The reason why I am here is to articulate the anger of my politics about what is happening in this war and the brutality that is being visited on Afghanistan. Beauty is just a vehicle.

The visual aesthetic strategy thus differs in the two films, but their use of such strategies for political agency is similar.

Norfolk's slow, forensic approach to photography emphasizes how the social position of the photographer inevitably influences the images produced. He criticizes the photojournalistic images coming from Afghanistan as 'like from some kind of sewer pipe with a crack in the side of it'. Norfolk's photography is not the product of pointing and 'just shooting'. Rather, it is intensely attentive to how the photographic process and the choices made by the person filming conditions the viewing and meaning of images. In contrast to the blurry aesthetic of undercover journalism that produces a sense of immediacy and urgency, slow photography does the opposite by encouraging pause and reflection. Yet, as Barthes remarked in his later works: 'Photography is subversive not when it frightens, repels, or even stigmatizes, but when it is *pensive*, when it thinks' (Barthes 1981: 38 [emphasis in original]). Barthes' renowned point seems to be at the heart of Norfolk's aesthetic strategy, informing his reimagining of Burke's work on British warfare in Afghanistan. 'By making the pictures very beautiful', Norfolk states, 'you're almost tricked into coming inside that photograph's space for a while, and engaging with it and *being in conversation with* the photograph. And then, by surprise, you might find that you've listened to a whole lot of my arguments' (emphasis added).

The strategy employed by Norfolk points to the role of the audience in pictorial agency. The determined, slow approach enacts the audience as a critical and reflective public, corresponding to the space in which it is circulated. As Shapiro remarks: '[m]useum exhibitions have sufficient exposure over time to "frame" and often "reframe" a society's conversations. Like some other artistic genres, they make available for extended public witnessing and discussion what daily media has forgotten' (Shapiro 2008: 182). Highly unusually, however, Norfolk's work won a 2012 World Press Photo award, suggesting that his production transcends a single genre and that genre borders are permeable and movable, rather than fixed.[14]

Not unlike the filming done by undercover journalists in Burma, Norfolk's work in Afghanistan exposes him to dangers that news networks and others would seek to avoid. At one point in *Burke + Norfolk*, we learn that the British Embassy is shocked to discover that Norfolk spent seven weeks in Kabul with no security apart from his local guide. While setting up equipment in a crowded street overlooking a river in Kabul, his voice-over (like that of 'Joshua') also ponders questions of personal safety:

> It was hairy, and on a few occasions it was downright dangerous, but it's possible to do it, and I would say that if you call yourself a journalist you're obliged to do it, rather than come to Afghanistan, live inside some armoured compound in a five-star hotel, and then tell me that you're reporting from Afghanistan. You're not, you're reporting from an armoured compound and a five-star hotel.

Regardless of the Barthesian strategy of slow, pensive photography, personal danger is an acute issue in picturing conflict. While directly targeting reporters in Afghanistan, Norfolk's condescending remark could just as well be directed at the reenactors in *Burma VJ*. Norfolk himself avoids the reenactment trap by shooting the same scenes that Burke captured, but under markedly different conditions. For example, while Burke's images are black and white, Norfolk's are photographed in 'a pre-dawn and post-sunset light, a much bluer, more melancholy, more disappointed light'. The documentary follows the same color aesthetics, but is distinguished from Norfolk's photography by its video (i.e., moving pictures), and the occasional inserts of Norfolk's photographs are well marked and unmistakable (perhaps marking a sort of reverence of the artist photographer who is the subject of the documentary and whose consent is its condition of possibility).

Reflections: documenting visual resistance and the politics of aesthetics

Both documentaries considered in this chapter employ visual aesthetic strategies that anticipate as well as enact the audiences they target, as do the image producers whose work they document. Indeed, both films strike a powerful rapport with their audiences by having a major show at Tate and in being remediated by CNN, BBC and others, and their respective aesthetic strategies are tailored to this end. Norfolk's pensive or slow photography emphasizing beauty and subtlety speaks to and enacts the viewer as a reflective visitor of a museum. Beauty is deployed as a vehicle for fostering a dialogue that escapes the narrow confines of the verbal day-to-day political distributions of the sensible (Rancière 2006; van Veeren 2010). Similarly, the aesthetic feel of *Burma VJ* marked by the authenticity and chaos of clandestine protest footage speaks to the selection criteria, discourse and (imagined, cosmopolitan) audiences of international news. This is most evident when Joshua tells a nun in a monastery raided by security forces: 'Don't worry, the whole world will know about it.' Here, the film relies on an imagination of audiences that neatly follows the 'mythical meaning' of CNN.

The filmic and aesthetic strategies are not, however, without challenges for the films as films (rather than for Joshua and Norfolk as characters). First, the dialogue between image producer and audience is not a one-way street. Audiences have agency and are potentially able to bring new, unanticipated meanings, distribution and agency to images.[15] This points to the possibility, pointed out most famously by Rancière, that spectatorship is not a passive consumption of visual spectacles, but a situation in which 'those in attendance learn from as opposed to being seduced by images; where they become active participants as opposed to passive voyeurs' (Rancière 2009: 4). Second, the strategy chosen may well have an impact on the coherence of the film as a filmic intervention in political debate.

Although *Burke + Norfolk* remains committed to a traditional documentary aesthetic that is silent on its editorial choices, it distinguishes well between the layers of mediation in the film, leaving Norfolk's opinions to dominate, but without them being visually reinforced by the filmmaker. *Burma VJ*, on the other hand, is more vulnerable in this respect. The combination of handheld aesthetics with slick and narrativized drama won *Burma VJ* the International Documentary Film Festival Amsterdam's (IDFA) most prestigious award and a number of other awards, including the editing prize at Sundance. The film gained well-deserved attention among a Western documentary-interested audience and was nominated for an Academy Award for Best Documentary Feature. Yet the price of this success is arguably high, especially when one bears in mind the director's ambition to use the film to showcase people's power. In essence, the story is dramatized to such a degree that the film hides its own intervention, while intervening rather forcefully. The strong narrative and footage that is 'edgy, visceral and raw, as you would expect from VJs who must shoot from the hip and run like hell to evade the junta's thugs' (Marshall 2009) does, at first sight, portray visually driven people power. Yet the concealed reenactments threaten to render it a remake of *Wag the Dog* in the age of citizen journalism: a slick imitation of amateur authenticity. The concealment of reenactments is an aesthetic strategy that can be criticized or embraced in various documentary productions, but in a film whose *raison d'être* is the importance, power and authenticity of visual resistance, it marks a deep ambivalence and raises (timely) questions about the ethics of documentary filmmaking. These are *problematiques* that are common to most documentarists, but the road taken by *Burma VJ* – that is, not admitting its own intervention – is clearly controversial.[16]

Apart from the problems that *Burma VJ*'s simultaneous commitment to and masking of a second-order truth creates, it also makes the film hard to classify. Thus, it sits ambiguously in the typology of van Munster and Sylvest (2013: 6), as they show how the commitment to a higher or second-order truth usually comes with a privileging of telling over showing, in which 'a deeper reality of truth [...] requires narrative excavation', rather than with a visual aesthetic of extreme reality. The aesthetic strategy of *Burma VJ* is one of extreme reality: it claims to put the spectator on the street in Rangoon, rather than telling a story of a historical event. Usually when such a strategy is employed, the narrative is less pronounced and leaves the emancipated spectator with more room for interpretation (see, for example, van Munster's reading of *Armadillo* and *Restrepo*, this volume). Indeed, in its careful manipulation of a visual aesthetic of extreme reality, *Burma VJ* replaces the detached war correspondent with a new mediascape of remediation and underground or citizen journalists. Doing so, however, has two problematic effects. First, it risks trivializing the actual footage included in the film by rendering it indistinguishable from reenactments. Second, it disempowers the viewer and risks reversing Rancière's thesis on spectatorship. The viewer is not enacted as a reflexive world citizen who can be trusted to make her own interpretative efforts, but as a consumer to be entertained.

In sum, there is a striking tendency in both films to render themselves transparent, even if they deal with how images are used for political purposes. This stands out in relation to both the visual actors they depict and discussions of meta-pictures and journalistic meta-coverage, where reflexivity is accorded much attention. While both Norfolk and 'Joshua' are acutely aware that they are engaged in pictorial agency, the documentarists portraying them seem uncomfortable with reflecting upon whether and how such agency extends to the documentary films' meta-mediation of visual resistance. The aesthetic practice of the documentaries thus partly undermines their arguments about pictorial agency. Moreover, it seems that the self-understanding and conventions of the genre – for example, in understanding the documentary as external to the documented – themselves play a role here. Paradoxically, the strongest argument for the agency of documentarism comes from 'Joshua' when he remarks on how documenting world politics is also doing world politics. When commenting on the footage of the brutal repression of a one-person protest, he states: '[i]t was a big moment for us, and a big mistake for them. Because they did so many brutal things in front of people and we could document that. We are shooting this, and the police are shooting us.' Whether this is a statement written by director Østergaard or an expression of the undercover journalist's opinion is, symptomatically, impossible to discern. At any rate, it leaves the spectator wondering: 'We do not know who we are, or what we are doing. Active participants or passive voyeurs?'[17]

Notes

1 Despite meta-coverage being a powerful discourse through which recent conflicts have been understood – think, for example, of the role phenomena such as embedded journalism or social media mobilization were attributed in the Iraq and Afghanistan wars or the Arab Spring – the increasing prevalence of meta-coverage as a frame for understanding world politics has not made its way into International Relations (IR) scholarship.
2 *Burma VJ* won the International Documentary Film Festival Amsterdam's (IDFA) most prestigious award, the Joris Ivens Award (IDFA 2008), as well as the 2009 World Cinema Documentary Film Editing Award at the Sundance Film Festival, and was nominated for an Academy Award the following year.

3 The film uses the acronym VJ to designate Video Journalists or undercover reporters filming the protests.
4 The Rodney King video turned a routine event of police violence and racial prejudice into a crisis that stirred debate and drew condemnation from all over the world. Even though the footage failed to convince the (all-white) jury that eventually acquitted the police of wrongdoing, it nonetheless demonstrated that a private, citizen-recorded video could turn the case into an event 'the whole world was watching' (Deibert 1997: 157).
5 Indeed, this media-effect narrative is so optimistic that it could fit a parody version of John Law's theorization of action as a network effect. Law's theory sees 'everything in the social and natural worlds as a continuously generated effect of the webs of relations within which they are located' (Law 2009: 141). The parody involves the substitution of the heterogeneous actor networks in Law's theory with those of news networks.
6 The term and its derivatives have been copyrighted by the CNN corporation. Citizens whose material appears in the program are not paid for their images.
7 Tellingly, the Burma footage is treated like this, even though it was made by undercover journalists of an illegal news network, rather than by citizen journalists.
8 Bush also refers to a '19-year reign of fear' that either implies that the military rule was benign until 1988, or mistakes its origin in 1962 for the 1988 protests.
9 As *Burma VJ*'s clever subtitle, 'reporting from a closed country', states, the film attempts to further the political goal of the VJs by reporting on what took place in Burma. But the subtitle can also be read as referring to what the VJs do.
10 I am indebted to Frank Möller for raising this point in our enlightening conversations about art and invisibility (Andersen and Möller 2013).
11 This liberal tradition also underpins Robert Hariman and John Lewis Lucaites' (2007) investigation of celebrated photojournalistic icons and liberal-democratic citizenship.
12 The name of the TV segment as it appeared in *Burma VJ*. Why this station would broadcast in English, which most Burmese do not understand, is not explained.
13 Sontag (2004: 46) has remarked on how the notions used for filming, such as 'capture', suggest a passive engagement with reality.
14 I shall return to the correspondence between aesthetic strategy, circulation and the enactment of the role and qualities of the spectator in the concluding section.
15 There is a parallel here with the Zapruder and Rodney King videos that were active in constituting a global public for private video by being appropriated by major news networks.
16 Partly sparked by the controversial strategies of documentarists like Michael Moore, the debate about the ethics of documentary filmmaking intensified at the time of the Toronto International Film Festival in 2009. One outcome of the debate was a survey among filmmakers on the ethical challenges they encounter and the ways in which they handle such challenges. A report based on the survey of thirty well-known documentary filmmakers showed that many films are committed to an ethics of telling the 'honest truth', even at the expense of factual or literal deceptions of the viewer. Filmmakers 'see themselves as executors of a "higher truth", framed within a narrative' (Aufderheide et al. 2009: 20) and, '[i]n relation to viewers, they often justified the manipulation of individual facts, sequences, and meanings of images, if it meant telling a story more effectively and helped viewers grasp the main, and overall truthful, themes of a story' (Aufderheide et al. 2009: 1). With specific reference to the question of reenactments, one documentarist pointed out that '[p]eople have to know and feel it's a recreation. You have to be 99.9 percent sure that people will know' (Aufderheide et al. 2009: 18).
17 This point alludes to Ranciere's concept of spectatorship, as well as to Foucault's reaction to *Las Meninas*: '[W]e do not know who we are, or what we are doing. Seen or seeing?' (cited in Mitchell 1994: 63)

Films

Armadillo (2010) Directed by Janus Metz Pedersen. Denmark, Fridthjof Film.

Burke + Norfolk: Photographs From the War in Afghanistan (2011) Directed by Simon Norfolk. UK, available at: www.tate.org.uk/context-comment/video/burke-norfolk-photographs-war-afghanistan (accessed 28 May 2014).

Burma VJ (2008) Directed by Anders Østergaard. Denmark, Kamoli Films and Magic Hour Films.

Restrepo (2010) Directed by Tim Hetherington and Sebastian Junger. USA, Outpost Films and Virgil Films and Entertainment.

Wag the Dog (1997) Directed by Barry Levinson. USA, Baltimore Pictures, New Line Cinema, Punch Productions and Tribeca Productions.

References

Andersen, Rune S. (2012) 'Remediating #IranElection: Journalistic Strategies for Positioning Citizen-Made Snapshots and Text Bites from the 2009 Iranian Post-Election Conflict', *Journalism Practice*, 6(3), 317–336.

Andersen, Rune S. (2013) 'Epistemic Authority, Lies, and Video: The Constitution of Knowledge and (in)Security in the Video/Security Nexus', *JOMEC Journal*, 4. Available at: www.cardiff.ac.uk/jomec/jomecjournal/4-november2013/Andersen_VideoSecurity.pdf (accessed 13 February 2014).

Andersen, Rune S. (forthcoming) 'Video: A Ma(r)ker of the International', in Mark B. Salter (ed.) *Making Things International*. Minneapolis, MN: University of Minnesota Press.

Andersen, Rune S. and Frank Möller (2013) 'Engaging the Limits of Visibility', *Security Dialogue*, 44(3), 203–221.

Arendt, Hannah (2003) *Responsibility and Judgment*, intro. by Jerome Kohn (ed.). New York, NY: Schocken Books.

Aufderheide, Patricia, Peter Jaszi and Mridu Chandra (2009) *Honest Truths: Documentary Filmmakers on Ethical Challenges in Their Work*. New York, NY: Center for Media & Social Impact. Available at: www.cmsimpact.org/making-your-media-matter/documents/best-practices/honest-truths-documentary-filmmakers-ethical-chall (accessed 24 December 2012).

Barthes, Roland (1977) 'Rhetoric of the Image', in Roland Barthes, *Image Music Text*. London: Fontana Press, 32–52.

Barthes, Roland (1981) *Camera Lucida: Reflections on Photography*. New York, NY: Hill & Wang.

Becker, Karin (2013) 'Performing the News', *Photographies*, 6(1), 17–28.

Bignell, Jonathan (2002) *Media Semiotics (second edn)*. Manchester: Manchester University Press.

Bolter, Jay and Richard A. Grusin (2000) *Remediation: Understanding New Media*. Cambridge, MA: MIT Press.

Burgess, Jean and Joshua Green (2009) *YouTube: Online Video and Participatory Culture*. Cambridge: Polity.

British Broadcasting Corporation (BBC) (2007) 'Bush Ramps Up Sanctions on Burma', *BBC News*, 19 October 2007. Available at: http://news.bbc.co.uk/2/hi/asia-pacific/7053000.stm (accessed 1 May 2012).

Debord, Guy (1994) *The Society of the Spectacle*. New York, NY: Zone Books.

Deibert, Ronald (1997) *Parchment, Printing, and Hypermedia: Communication in World Order Transformation*. New York, NY: Columbia University Press.

Esser, Frank (2009) 'Metacoverage of Mediated Wars: How the Press Framed the Role of the News Media and of Military News Management in the Iraq Wars of 1991 and 2003', *American Behavioral Scientist*, 52(5), 709–734.

Gunthert, André (2008) 'Digital Imaging Goes to War', *Photographies*, 1(1), 103–112.

Hariman, Robert and John L. Lucaites (2007) *No Caption Needed: Iconic Photographs, Public Culture, and Liberal Democracy*. Chicago, IL: University of Chicago Press.

International Documentary Film Festival Amsterdam (IDFA) (2008) 'Burma VJ: Reporting from a Closed Country', *IDFA.nl*. Available at: www.idfa.nl/nl/tags/project.aspx?id=3d2422cc-bdaf-4905-b62b-c2177bc3c2b3 (accessed 19 August 2012).

Japan News Review (2007) 'New Footage of Journalist Shot in Burma Shows Soldier Leaving Scene with Camera', *Japan News Review*. Available at: www.japannewsreview.com/society/international/20071009page_id=2350 (accessed 24 December 2012).

Law, John (2009) 'Actor Network Theory and Material Semiotics', in B. S. Turner (ed.) *The New Blackwell Companion to Social Theory*. Oxford: Blackwell, 141–158.

Lisle, Debbie (2011) 'The Surprising Detritus of Leisure: Encountering the Late Photography of War', *Environment and Planning D: Society and Space*, 29(5), 873–890.

Marshall, Andrew (29 January 2009) 'Burma VJ: Truth as Casualty', *Time*. Available at: http://content.time.com/time/magazine/article/0,9171,1874773,00.html (accessed 19 August 2012).

Mitchell, William J. (1994) *Picture Theory: Essays on Verbal and Visual Representation*. Chicago, IL: University of Chicago Press.

Mortensen, Mette (2012) 'Metacoverage Taking the Place of Coverage: WikiLeaks as a Source for Production of News in the Digital Age', *Northern Lights*, 10, 91–106.

van Munster, Rens and Casper Sylvest (2013) 'Documenting International Relations: Documentary Film and the Creative Arrangement of Perceptibility', *International Studies Perspectives*, DOI: 10.1111/insp. 12062.

Østergaard, Anders (2008) 'Full Feature: Anders Østergaard'. Available at: http://ifa-amsterdam.com/features/ANDERS-OSTERGAARD/11327437 (accessed 24 December 2012).

Rancière, Jacques (2006) *The Politics of Aesthetics*. London: Continuum.

Rancière, Jacques (2009) *The Emancipated Spectator*. London: Verso.

Seib, Philip (2008) *The Al Jazeera Effect: How the New Global Media are Reshaping World Politics*. Washington, DC: Potomac Books.

Shapiro, Michael J. (2008) 'Slow Looking: The Ethics and Politics of Aesthetics', *Millennium – Journal of International Studies*, 37(1), 181–197.

Sontag, Susan (2004) *Regarding the Pain of Others*. New York, NY: Picador.

Tchalenko, Luke (2011) *Burke + Norfolk*, Tate. Available at: http://channel.tate.org.uk (accessed 24 December 2012).

Tuchman, Gaye (1972) 'Objectivity as Strategic Ritual: An Examination of Newsmen's Notions of Objectivity', *The American Journal of Sociology*, 77(4), 660–679.

Tumber, Howard and Jerry Palmer (2004) *Media at War: The Iraq Crisis*. Thousand Oaks, CA: Sage.

van Veeren, Elspeth (2010) 'Captured by the Camera's Eye: Guantánamo and the Shifting Frame of the Global War on Terror', *Review of International Studies*, 37(4), 1721–1749.

Weber, Cynthia (2008) 'Popular Visual Language as Global Communication: The Remediation of United Airlines Flight 93', *Review of International Studies*, Supplement S, 137–153.

10 *The Reckoning*

Advocating international criminal justice and the flattening of humanity

Wouter G. Werner

Introduction

In March 2013, the latest documentary film on the International Criminal Court (ICC; hereafter, the Court) was launched at the annual human rights documentary film festival, Movies that Matter, in The Hague. Movies that Matter emerged out of the Amnesty International Film Festival and has now developed into one of the leading organizations dedicated to the promotion of human rights documentary films in the world.[1] Over the past few years, Movies that Matter has shown and promoted several documentaries on the ICC, almost as if a human rights film festival in the 'legal capital of the world' would be incomplete without a documentary on international criminal law. The documentary, called *The Court* (dir. Marcus Vetter and Michele Gentile 2013), was widely publicized on the Internet, as well as via the promotional material of the festival itself. The most distinctive aspect of the promotion of the documentary was a picture combining the images of five people: Judge Fulford, presiding judge of the Trial Chamber in the *Lubanga* case; Luis Moreno Ocampo and Fatou Bensouda, the former and current Chief Prosecutors of the ICC; Ben Ferencz, Chief US Prosecutor in the *Einsatzgruppen* case at Nuremberg and currently part of the ICC Prosecutor team; and finally Angelina Jolie, Hollywood celebrity and human rights activist. At some point, the pictures of Jolie and Ferencz were removed from the poster, thus leaving only the judge and the two prosecutors to promote the film. The nature of the poster, however, remained basically the same: a tongue in cheek representation of the ICC modeled after a US courtroom drama (see Figure 10.1).

The appearance of members of the Court in a flashy picture ironically mimicking an advertisement for a Hollywood movie is the most recent example of the ICC 'going pop'.[2] Members of the Court – in particular, members of the ICC Prosecution (hereafter, the Prosecution) – have appeared in virtually all advocacy documentaries on the ICC, often deliberately blurring the line between their formal role as Court professionals and their role as the main characters in a pro-ICC documentary film reaching out to a broad audience. Besides *The Court*, some recent examples include *The Prosecutor* (dir. Barry Stevens 2010), *The Reckoning* (dir. Pamela Yates 2009), and *Kony2012* (dir. Jason Russell 2012). In particular, documentaries have helped to present edited presentations of the 'humanity' in whose

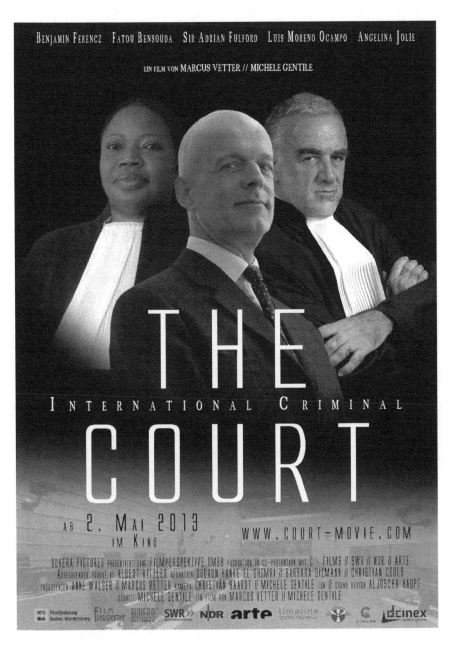

Figure 10.1 Theatre poster of *The Court* (without Jolie and Ferencz). Reprinted with permission from Marcus Vetter.

name the Office of the Prosecution and the ICC in general claims to operate. Documentary films have added images, perspective, sounds, pace, plot and narrative to the more usual expressions of 'humanity' in texts of international law; they attempt to portray 'humanity' at work and to show how an intangible international community takes the form of investigators and judges bringing justice to the world.[3]

In this chapter, I analyze in more detail how 'humanity' is crafted in one of the best known documentaries on the ICC, *The Reckoning*. I have selected *The Reckoning* for three main reasons. First, it is a widely used documentary associated with two influential non-governmental organizations (NGOs): the Coalition for the ICC (CICC)[4] and the International Center for Transitional Justice.[5] Before the documentary was actually produced, the documentary makers included influential NGOs on the advisory board, thus securing a link with organizations such as Human Rights Watch, the International Center for Transitional Justice and Amnesty International – organizations that later helped promote and disseminate the film. In addition, the documentary makers managed, in their own words, to establish 'common ground' with the Prosecutor and his team, which helped them obtain cooperation and support for the film from the ICC.[6] The documentary won an award from the American Bar Association – which also publicly endorsed the documentary as a useful teaching tool – and it was highly recommended in journals of visual anthropology, sociology and social justice.[7] Moreover, it was broadcast at human rights documentary festivals, ICC celebrations, for educational purposes.[8] *The Reckoning*, in other words, is important to study, as it has the potential to affect (or solidify) the opinions and attitudes of a broad audience. Second, *The Reckoning* is not about a specific trial, but reflects on the project of international criminal law in general, albeit with a specific focus on the ICC. As a consequence, the documentary makes an attempt to spell out the *rationale* of international prosecutions for crimes that affect the international community. Many of the arguments made in *The Reckoning* are echoed in broader discourses on international criminal law; what the documentary adds, however, is sounds, images and a specific plot revolving around its main character, the then Chief Prosecutor of the ICC, Luis Moreno-Ocampo. Third, many of the perspectives, images, sounds and arguments that appear in *The Reckoning* can also be found in other pro-ICC advocacy documentaries, such as *The Court*, *The Prosecutor* and even to a certain extent in the more activist film *Kony2012*. All these documentaries, while claiming to educate the viewer about the ICC as such, mainly focus on the role of the Prosecutor as the central agent charged with responding to inhumane acts that shock the conscience of mankind. They all use similar tropes of historical progress, portray the Prosecutor as fighting for global justice in the face of stern opposition in a troubled world and overlap in their presentation of victims crying out for the intervention of the ICC.[9]

At the same time, the exclusive focus on just one documentary naturally comes with some methodological constraints. This chapter cannot do justice to the different types of documentary that have been produced in recent decades, and thus no conclusions can be drawn regarding the nature and role of documentaries in international criminal law in general. More specifically, this chapter does not go into documentaries that present a more distanced perspective on international criminal justice, critically exploring how fighting crimes through criminal law may marginalize alternative methods of dealing with past atrocities.[10] Instead, the main aim of this chapter is to provide an in-depth, explorative study of how an influential pro-ICC documentary has added word-images to the verbal narratives that seek to justify international criminal law. In particular, I focus on the ways in which the documentary uses the 'inhumanity/humanity' dichotomy to convince its audience about the ICC's role in human progress. The mere fact that the 'humanity/inhumanity' distinction is invoked in the documentary is hardly surprising; after all, the whole fabric of international criminal law is built on the idea that some crimes are the business of the international community, as they 'shock the conscience of mankind'.[11] However, it matters a great deal *how* the concepts of humanity and inhumanity are invoked. Those working within the tradition of Hannah Arendt, for example, would understand 'humanity' as an inherently political concept, one that comes with questions of power, exclusion and responsibility (see, for example, Luban 2004). One of the striking aspects of *The Reckoning*, however, is that 'humanity' is used in an attempt to portray the Court as standing outside politics, as a non-political force that civilizes those in power. In this way, the documentary seeks to immunize the Court from the world of power, as if the Court is an untainted bringer of light to the dark world of politics. As I will argue below, the denial of the political nature of the ICC itself comes at a high price: it not only creates unrealistic expectations of what the ICC can achieve, it also fails to do justice to the victims of international crimes and to the very idea of humanity as a pluralistic political community.

The Reckoning as educational

The Reckoning opens with two people walking in a field with high grass in total silence, apart from the soft sounds of crickets and birds. One person, who looks like a local who has survived mass atrocities and knows the way through what, to the audience, appears to be an endless field, shows the exact location of a skull and the remains of a skeleton in the field. He shows the skull and skeleton to a man holding papers, whose appearance is that of an observer, a professional, an outsider. Whereas the local survivor's face is filled with grief, the spectator's appearance is committed yet distanced, almost analytical. He holds and studies the skull in a pose reminiscent of the classic *Hamlet* scene: at a distance, as if he is about to start talking to the remains of the human head. Then tragic, slow music sets in, followed by images of a line of men walking through the field. The men all appear to be survivors or first-hand witnesses to mass atrocities. The first spoken words in the documentary are from one of the men in the field, giving an implicit endorsement of the project of international criminal law: 'In this place killers go unpunished. Without justice people have no respect for each other. If this goes unpunished, it will happen again. Communities will go on killing each other' (1:30). The tragic music grows louder, and we see the tormented face of the survivor from the opening scene. Then we hear a chairman's hammer, and the survivor looks up as if he is hearing the same sounds. Coming from afar, we hear a woman's voice, '[t]he International Criminal Court is now in session', followed by images of a member of the Prosecution team, who puts the local suffering in global and historical perspective: 'During the previous century millions of people were the victims of unimaginable atrocities' (1:52). It was the realization that such crimes concern the international community and should not go unpunished, the Prosecutor continues, that led to the creation of an independent, permanent criminal court.

The Reckoning was produced by Skylight Pictures, a company specialized in the production of independent documentary films that seek to educate a broad audience on issues of human rights and global justice.[12] The nature of the productions of Skylight Pictures is thus nicely captured in one of the older terms used to designate documentaries: 'educationals' (Aufderheide 2007: 3). The director of *The Reckoning*, Pamela Yates, has been a rather well-known maker of human rights documentaries since the 1980s, when she made films about the Ku Klux Clan (*Resurgence* 1981) and international crimes committed in Guatemala (*When the Mountains Tremble* 1983). Since then, her work has primarily focused on international crimes, (transitional) justice and counterterrorism – all films that seek to educate a broader audience through artistic and journalistic means.[13] This also applies to *The Reckoning*, a film, in the words of Yates herself, made 'for general audiences both here and abroad who had never heard of the ICC', and whose hearts and minds are to be won

> with all the filmic tools – carefully thought out cinematography that is beautiful, sad, epic; unifying music throughout the film that captures the emotional highs and lows, well written narration spoken by a soulful narrator, and always an emphasis on the victims and survivors at the center of this justice initiative.[14]

In line with the educational ambitions of *The Reckoning*, the images in the opening scene are primarily meant to teach the audience about international crimes and international criminal law. Take, for example, the skull and skeleton in the initially unspecified African field,[15] without any accompanying music or voice-over. In semiotic terms, the skull and skeleton simultaneously function as icons, indexes and symbols.[16] As may be recalled, an *icon* represents an object through resemblance. This is how the first images in *The Reckoning* work: they represent, in two-dimensional form, the real skull and skeleton lying in the African field, just as the sound of birds and crickets mimics the sound of the animals present at the time of filming. The audience should learn the actual, the real situation. An *index* represents an object through relations of causality or proximity. The classic example is 'smoke', indicating that there will be 'fire' nearby. The skull and skeleton work as index for what has happened earlier: atrocities, crimes and the resulting human suffering. Here, the documentary seeks to convince its audience that basic norms have been transgressed and that fellow human beings suffer as a result – a message underlined by the bodily expression of the man in the field. Finally, a *symbol* stands in a cultural or conventional relationship to what it represents. The classic example is language, which consists of signs that, through conventional rules, are related to objects. However, symbolic representation can also take a non-verbal form, including sounds and images. In the case of *The Reckoning*, this takes the form of what an audience can anticipate in a documentary on the ICC: the silence accompanying the skull and skeleton in the field cannot remain unanswered; someone is about to give voice to those who suffered, calling to account those who are ultimately responsible for what happened.

Reading *The Reckoning* through the lens of Piercian semiotics reveals the different messages that are sent out simultaneously. Another way of carving out the different lessons communicated in the documentary is to study the different levels of truth, taking into account Richard Sherwin's distinction between factual truth, symbolic truth and higher truth (Sherwin 2000). Documentaries generally make a claim to factual truth, in that they seek to convince the audience that what is shown and argued accurately represents reality. *The Reckoning*, for example, claims that the numerous examples of atrocities shown and narrated in the documentary actually took place (and there is no reason to doubt this assertion). The factual truth is subsequently linked to what Sherwin calls 'symbolic truth', the common tropes, 'the conventional stories that we use to make sense of the world' (Spence and Navarro 2011: 22). In case of *The Reckoning*, this takes the form of the Second World War and the crimes committed by the Nazis, as an archetype for the organized evil of modern times. Moreover, it takes the form of the Nuremberg trials, which are archetypical for a civilized, rule-of-law informed response to organized evil. *The Reckoning* moves back and forth between these archetypes and the ICC, most directly in the form of its presentation of Ben Ferencz, the then 27-year-old prosecutor at Nuremberg. The documentary shows footage of Ferencz' impressive opening speech at the trial, a slim, young figure standing behind a big rostrum, symbolizing the grandiose task he was facing. The speech is then continued by Ben Ferencz in 2009, an old man looking back on his great moment. The personality/character of Ben Ferencz symbolizes the link the documentary seeks to make between Nuremberg as a response to the Second World War and the ICC's response to crimes committed in the twenty-first century. In similar fashion, the person of Luis Moreno-Ocampo, then head of the Office of the Prosecution,[17] is embedded in a narrative of progress. *The Reckoning* shows Ocampo as a young man, responsible for prosecuting the *junta* in his homeland of Argentina, prosecutions that were 'the first trials after Nuremberg in which generals were prosecuted for massive crimes' (7:11).[18] All his work in Argentina, an older, more reflexive Ocampo states in *The Reckoning*, was just the prelude to his current job as prosecutor for the ICC. In this way, the ICC is situated in a progressive unfolding of history, from an ad hoc tribunal based on victors' justice in 1945, via learning experiences at the domestic level and ad hoc tribunals in the 1990s, towards a permanent, independent court in our times.

Finally, the term 'higher truth' refers to basic norms and principles that often work as institutional facts within a given community. A telling example is the well-known phrase from the US Declaration of Independence: 'We hold these truths to be self-evident, that all men are created equal ...'. In similar fashion, *The Reckoning* relates the sound-images of factual truths to basic principles, such as the principle that international crimes should not go unpunished. The need to 'end impunity' is the plot that brings most of the images of atrocities, human suffering and international institutional practice together in a coherent narrative. In addition, it seeks to demonstrate that the ICC not only serves, but is also *constrained* by higher truths – in particular, the basic principles of a fair trial – and that this is what sets a court of law apart from mere revenge.[19] For the purposes of this chapter, however, I am mostly interested in the 'highest' truth that *The Reckoning* seeks to communicate: the 'truth' that the ICC is an agent and enactor of 'humanity'. The articulation of this truth claim will be analyzed in more detail below.

The International Criminal Court and humanity

The opening scene of *The Reckoning* relates to three interrelated truth claims about 'humanity': (1) humanity has a counterpart in the inhumane; (2) the ICC gives voice to the victims of inhumanity, thus enacting what 'humanity' is about; and (3) for 'humanity' to be enacted, cosmopolitan lawyers should have the courage to speak 'law to power' – humanity is as much a professional vocation as a normative ideal.

The Reckoning starts out by showing what inhumanity looks like: the skull and skeleton, together with what is apparently a group of survivors of mass atrocities, represent the appalling effects of international crimes. The pictures bring together direct victims, survivors and shocked outsiders, all underpinned by silence or tragic music. What is shown here is the working of *inhumane* acts, of crimes that are inhuman in nature and that violate the humanity of their direct victims and survivors. What characterizes this form of (in)humanity, among other things, is its localized and bodily character. The documentary starts off by pointing at an actual place where actual people were killed and actual survivors still suffer. The documentary does this without even explaining what happened, who did what to whom. The crimes, the perpetrators, the victims, they all remain silent (or silenced) about what happened. Yet, the shots used in the opening scene fit archetypical imageries of mass atrocities well enough to make us understand what this is about: a specific place where specific crimes happened against specific individuals. Moreover, the direct victims of mass atrocities are shown most of all as *bodily* manifestations. In the opening scene, this takes the form of skulls and skeletons; later in the documentary, it takes the form of mutilated faces, corpses, split-open skulls, hollow-eyed survivors of concentration camps and images of people in pain. In this way, the documentary tries to picture 'unimaginable atrocities' (thereby, of course, paradoxically making an attempt to imagine the unimaginable). By showing actual bodily suffering, the documentary appeals to a very thin understanding of (in)humanity. Victims are not shown as individuals whose individuality and political agency is frustrated,[20] but primarily as suffering bodies, with hardly any voice of their own. If victims speak in the documentary, it is mainly to underscore the need to end impunity, because otherwise crimes will be repeated; or to show how organizations such as the Lord's Resistance Army (LRA) trick local communities into believing that arrest warrants ought to be withdrawn (see further below). This fits in with later accounts by the executive editor of the film, Peter Kenoy. Reflecting on *The Reckoning*, Kenoy explains that the documentary revolves around two main characters: on the one hand, victims as seekers of international justice and, on the other hand, the ICC. As a result, *The Reckoning* primarily shows victims as either voiceless pictures underscoring the need for an ICC or as those more actively searching for ICC intervention.[21] Victims of inhumane international crimes thus enter the picture only in a very abstract capacity, as 'human beings'[22] or as supporters of the ICC. On the other hand, this implies that the international community that is claiming to be hurt by the atrocities is also understood in a rather abstract (and quite thin) sense. As one commentator has put it, if the inhumane nature of international crimes justified international interventions, such interventions would rest on 'pre-institutional responsibilities that we have to all human beings as such' (Renzo 2012: 470). In this formulation, the use of the unspecified term 'we' deserves attention. The rights of abstract individuals can apparently be claimed against an equally abstract 'we', an apolitical multitude of individuals who share a very basic characteristic with the direct victims – their 'being human'. As the documentary purports to show, this multitude now has found a more concrete form to articulate its thirst for justice in the form of the newly established ICC.

Humanity as a vocation

As was indicated above, one of the main ambitions of international criminal law is to reconnect the localized and bodily experience of atrocity and inhumanity to a world of voice and meaning. This is also what *The Reckoning* seeks to establish. In the opening scene, this takes place through the future-oriented reflection by one of the local survivors, who argues that the culture of impunity that apparently reigns in his region should be ended and that a next round of violence can be expected if criminal courts do not perform their function. Most of all, however, this happens through the distant voice coming from The Hague declaring the first session of the ICC opened. These words initially come across almost as a Genesis 1 experience: the ICC speaks, and a new reality appears from the troubled fields of East Congo, with future crimes looming large in the ordered reality of a courtroom in the legal capital of the world.

The documentary is quick to point out, however, that the ICC can only be understood as the provisional endpoint of a long, progressive history that started off in Nuremberg. It was blocked during the Cold War and gained new momentum with the establishment of the ad hoc tribunals and the proliferation of mixed tribunals all over the world. In a similar fashion, the destroyed world of the portrayed victims is linked to a larger story of crime and suffering, with millions of people being killed since the bloody twentieth century started, and almost invariably with impunity for the perpetrators. The question animating the Court, according to a spokeswoman for the Prosecution, is whether 'humanity can do better than this?'– a question followed by what looks like the official beginning of the documentary, with the title *The Reckoning* prominently projected on to the screen. It is as if the opening scene functions as a sort of prologue, with a clear message: the Court is there to give voice to the intensely localized and bodily experiences of inhumanity by linking them to a larger narrative of a progressive world community. While the physical killing cannot be undone, the symbolic meaning of what happened can be transformed from the destruction of the world of the victims by international criminals into a story of humanity confronting inhumanity; humanity critically investigating itself and coming to the conclusion that ending impunity is the answer to mass atrocities. This is reinforced by the sequence of images presented to the viewer: from the field in East Congo (again) to Second World War bombers/fighters in flight (with a low, solemn voice-over informing the viewer that during the war humanity came face to face with its own depravity) to the Nuremberg trials and the speech of then 27-year-old prosecutor Ben Ferencz, labeling the trial 'a plea of humanity to law'. This plea, the documentary contends, gains even more relevance in light of the atrocities of the twentieth century and the early twenty-first century that followed it (some of which are shown in quick succession in the documentary), all leading up to an 'accelerated demand for a system of global justice', which is then symbolized by an image of Rome, pictured as a city upon the hill, as the home of the newly established International Criminal Court.[23]

This last image links up with another way in which humanity is used in the documentary: as an institutional reality and a professional vocation. The most important message that *The Reckoning* tries to get across is that giving voice to victims of inhumanities requires a commitment from the professionals who speak 'the law of humanity to power' and who are willing to fight egoistical and ideological politics in the name of the dehumanized victims. The term 'humanity' here takes on a double meaning. On the one hand, it is used to refer to the international or world community, a community of all the peoples in the world asking for justice. This meaning of the term is symbolized by images of the adoption of the Rome Statute: a room filled with delegates from all over the world, literally applauding the coming into existence of the Court, their faces filled with excitement and joy about the historic event they have just brought about. This image is followed by a text on the screen listing the state parties to the ICC,[24] underscored by sober, yet promising music. At the same time, however, the voice-over warns the audience that the newly established court will not achieve its goals lightly, as 'it had to fight for its very survival' (6:32) – a sentence that once more signifies that the abstract idea of humanity is now being translated into a concrete institutional reality. This becomes even clearer when the Prosecutor of the ICC, Moreno Ocampo, makes his first appearance in the documentary. 'The drivers of this Court', Ocampo argues, 'are the dreamers, those who dream of a world with justice.... But then my task is to put the dreams into reality' (6:45). Humanity here thus appears as the world community, represented by the states adopting the Rome Statute, who dream up a world of justice and entrust it to the professionals of the ICC to realize humanity's dream of a better world where justice reigns.

This links up to a further meaning of the term 'humanity' invoked in the documentary: the ICC is portrayed as fighting for *humane* ideals, against those who seek to corrupt these ideals in the name of power, self-interest or ideology. Take, for example, the way in which Skylight Pictures markets *The Reckoning*:

> A David & Goliath battle of titanic proportions unfolds as ICC prosecutor Luis Moreno Ocampo faces down warlords, genocidal dictators and world superpowers in his struggle to tame the Wild West of global conflict zones and bring perpetrators of crimes against humanity to justice.[25]

The metaphor of David and Goliath nicely captures the way in which *The Reckoning* portrays the ICC Prosecutor. Ocampo is pictured as standing *against* those in power, speaking humanity and law *to* those in power and as the hero eventually *overcoming* those in powerful positions. In this context, it is interesting to compare *The Reckoning* to *Why We Figh*t (1942–1945) – a classic propaganda[26] educational used by the US Government to convince the American public about the necessity of entering the Second World War. Of course, the institutional and historical context of *Why We Fight* is completely different. Whereas *The Reckoning* is the work of a human rights NGO advocating international criminal law solutions to atrocities, *Why We Fight* was a government production aimed at soliciting support for sending military forces abroad. What makes it nevertheless interesting to compare the two documentaries is that both rely heavily on conceptions of humanity to convince their audiences. In order to convince those advocating isolationism, *Why We Fight* argues that not participating in the war is a naïve and dangerous strategy, as the enemies of the US seek nothing less than world domination. Germany, Japan and Italy are portrayed as a 'slave world', run by manipulative and ruthless dictators and masses who have given up their human dignity.[27] The 'slave world' is confronting the 'free world', most prominently symbolized by the US, whose democratic constitution is pictured as the culminating point of a history of human progress through figures such as Moses, Mohammed, Confucius, Jesus, up to the freedom fighters of modern history. For the US, therefore, entering the war is both an act of enlightened self-interest and a service to humanity. This is probably best symbolized by the statement of Secretary of War Henry Stimson, shown at the beginning of *Why We Fight* (1:21): 'We are determined that before the sun sets on this terrible struggle our flag will be recognized throughout the world as a *symbol of freedom* on the one hand ... and of *overwhelming* power on the other'. To underscore the latter point, the documentary not only shows the US flag waving proudly, but also numerous US soldiers marching and busy factories producing war materials.

Now compare this to the way in which humanity is invoked in *The Reckoning*. Here, humanity is enacted by legal professionals who take pride in *not* having power and principally in *fighting* those in power. This juxtaposition of ICC professionals to those in power structures the way in which the documentary discusses the US opposition to the Court. Showing an apparently concerned Ocampo, pacing up and down in his office overlooking The Hague, the voice-over announces that 'lack of international support was a growing problem for the Court' (17:20), with major powers refusing to join and the US even openly fighting the ICC. Yet, notwithstanding the severe opposition of the world's most powerful state, as symbolized in the determined face and voice of John Bolton, the Prosecution's Office proudly concludes that the US failed to stop the ICC, because '[w]e represent interests that are much broader than the United States' (19:00). The imagery of the Court invoked in *The Reckoning* is that of legal professionals embodying an idea of humanity that, at the end of the day, proves stronger than the opposition of those holding power.

The lack of power other than that of 'humanity' also informs the way in which *The Reckoning* portrays the Court's activities in Colombia, Uganda and Darfur. As the one responsible for realizing the dreams of humanity, Ocampo is portrayed as operating in the difficult space between high cosmopolitan hopes and the bitter realities of (world) politics and local conflicts. The heroic aspect of his job is illustrated by shots of Ocampo in a taxi in Bogotà, reflecting on his attempts to use his position as the representative of an international community to push the powers that be towards ending impunity. Or by shots of him standing alone in the rain, looking slightly tormented but still determined, walking towards the taxi after intense arguments in the Security Council with those who apparently sought to protect Sudanese President Omar Al-Bashir from ICC prosecution. It is further underlined by Ocampo recalling the difficult decisions he has taken in the face of severe political opposition and advice from 'everyone' to focus on easier cases. The opposition to the Court seems to be everywhere: in the US, in the Security Council, at the level of national governments or at the level of rebel groups such as the LRA, who, according to *The Reckoning*, only seek to 'push their anti-ICC case' when they manage to convince a local community that the arrest warrant against the LRA top brass is detrimental to the peace process (43:00). However, all this opposition only strengthens the Prosecution and the Court. Not unlike the main character in a *Bildung* novel, the Prosecutor grows because he learns to deal with these difficult situations, all in order to 'establish the law to people in power' (57:07).

One of the final shots of *The Reckoning* is one of Ocampo alone on the beach in Scheveningen, the Netherlands, looking small and vulnerable against the background of a seemingly endless North Sea with big ships passing by on the horizon. Ocampo once more reflects on one of the main problems of international criminal justice: the fact that the people against whom arrest warrants are issued have so much power. However, invoking the example of Augusto Pinochet, the documentary ends with the hope that 'one day there will be justice' (58:28); a hope underscored by Ferencz' closing words: 'If we try hard enough and long enough to make it a more humane world ... I am confident it will come about'. The final message of *The Reckoning* is thus almost eschatological: in the end, the voice of humanity will transform the world, even though it now only speaks against those in power.

Concluding thoughts

It is now time to return to the main questions that have informed my analysis of *The Reckoning*: (1) how is humanity and its negative counterpart construed; (2) to what extent does the protagonist claim a right to represent or speak on behalf of humanity?; (3) how are texts, sounds and images construed to deliver the message of the documentary, and what are the purported affective effects of this construction?; and (4) what is outside the frame of the documentary? As is (hopefully) clear from the previous sections, the answers to the four questions hang closely together.

The Reckoning uses iconic, indexical and symbolic representations of human suffering in an attempt to show 'inhumanity at work'. Victimhood is shown through images of bodily mutilations, death, grief and sorrow – often portraying the direct victims of mass atrocities as voiceless or as longing for an end to impunity – and, in any case, in need of representation. The International Criminal Court then enters the stage as the voice of humanity, representing a world community as well as the notion of humaneness. *The Reckoning* literally brings the voice of the Court into the dark corners of Africa, where survivors of international crimes mourn and despair. The Court is also presented as the culmination of a progressive humanity in search of the institutional structures that can end impunity. Through linkages between images of the trials in Nuremberg, a young Ocampo prosecuting the military junta and the current ICC, *The Reckoning* seeks to establish historical continuity and progress. The Court, and especially the Prosecutor, is portrayed as the institutional embodiment of humanity, as the one that is fighting to put the dreams of humanity by the world community into reality. A large part of *The Reckoning* shows the Prosecutor as a lonely hero, struggling against those in power in order achieve a world of peace and justice. He is the one 'speaking humanity to power', keeping alive the hope that one day justice will reign.

The affective effects of *The Reckoning* are hardly subtle: the audience cannot but feel sympathy for the suffering of the victims and nod affirmatively when confronted with the call to respond to the atrocities that are shown throughout the documentary. The documentary zooms in on one particular way of responding: through prosecution by the ICC. The grand narrative of progress in which the Court is embedded entices feelings of hope and empowerment: however horrible the world is, we *can* do something about it. What is more, the documentary shows the Prosecutor as the one who actually *is doing* something about it. Although constantly faced with the opposition of the powerful, he keeps on struggling to put the dreams of humanity into reality. Not coincidentally, the narrative is presented as a fight between David and Goliath, with the figure of David symbolizing the good cause: the absence of power and the triumph of seemingly powerless universal ideals over power politics and ideology.

By framing the Court as speaking law to power, the documentary fits within a broader self-image of international criminal law as standing outside power politics. The different ways in which the Court is implicated in power struggles, the ways in which the Prosecutor has aligned himself with governments that are seeking to delegitimize their enemies, are thus left outside the frame (Nouwen and Werner 2010). In this way, the documentary is vulnerable to the critique that has been voiced by critical legal scholars for decades now: the attempt to define international legal institutions as somehow beyond politics is not just naïve, but politically problematic. It obscures the choices and biases that come with attempts to pursue political aims through legal institutions, thus making it more difficult to subject them to critical debate (see also Kennedy 1987; Koskenniemi 2002a, 2002b). To mention just one example: the documentary does not confront the question of how the pursuit of justice through the institutional structure of international criminal law may push aside and marginalize alternative conceptions of justice that may mean more to local communities than the expert vocabulary of international criminal law (Nouwen and Werner 2013). When showing shots of Ugandan village communities opting for alternative mechanisms of conflict resolution and justice, *The Reckoning* frames these as successful attempts by international criminals to mislead and intimidate the local population. The lack of attention to alternative conceptions and mechanisms of justice hangs closely together with the dominant framing of victims as voiceless or as longing for intervention by the ICC. The 'humanity' at work in *The Reckoning* is therefore not a pluralistic humanity composed of political agents with different views of justice and reconciliation.[28] Instead, 'humanity' appears as a more abstract category. It operates as the antithesis of the 'inhumanity' done to victims, victims who are portrayed as seeking rescue through international criminal trials and whose interests are presented as coinciding with a 'world community' in search of an end to impunity.

In similar fashion, the documentary directly connects notions of 'victimhood' and 'humanity' to intervention by the ICC. As a result, processes of mediation and translation that unavoidably come with legal processes are left unaddressed. Through the use of images of suffering, tragic music and narratives of progress, the ICC is presented as the unfiltered voice of victims and humanity. It is exactly this lack of attention to the mediating role of law in the articulation of concepts such as 'humanity' that has driven earlier critiques of humanitarianism in international law (*inter alia* Koskenimmi 2002; Orford 2003). The lack of attention to law's mediating role may be explained by the fact that *The Reckoning* seeks to educate a public that is largely unaware of the workings of the ICC. Complicated messages about the politics of the Court and the problems that come with translating sociopolitical issues into the formal language of law will make it more difficult to convince an uninformed and maybe skeptical audience. Yet, the price paid for leaving out the realities of legal interventions is likely to be quite high. The documentary evokes unrealistic expectations about the ICC's ability to do justice to victims as well as to 'humanity' and is thus bound to create disappointment about the actual achievements of the Court. This is not just because the ICC is frustrated by external factors (as the documentary wants us to believe), it is also the result of the deep structure of international criminal law, which requires a very specific construction of sociopolitical reality, in terms of its own vocabulary, tropes of argumentation and biases. A good example of the difficulties and downsides that come with ICC interventions can be found in *Carte Blanche* (dir. Heidi Specogna 2011), a documentary about the trial of Jean Pierre Bemba. The film works without voice-over or underpinning music, thus opening up more space for the people involved in the documentary to appear as people with their own lives and stories. Rather than portraying the ICC as the embodiment of humanity, the documentary shows the problems that come with building a legal case after villages have been subjected to mass violence, including the mismatch that can exist between the experiences of victims and the language that experts of different kinds need to speak (see also Werner 2013). None of these complexities enter *The Reckoning*, which first and foremost presents the ICC as the voice of humanity, as well as the answer to the search for justice by victims. The fact that international criminal law is itself part and parcel of power politics, that it may marginalize alternative concepts of justice, that it unavoidably distorts the experiences of victims – all that is suppressed in an attempt to educate a broad audience about the beneficial effects of interventions by the ICC. And, indeed, *The Reckoning* has been very successful in reaching a broad audience. The message communicated to this audience, however, is quite problematic, with humanity flattened, victims stereotyped and the Court portrayed as a messianic institution.

Notes

1 For more information, see: www.moviesthatmatter.nl/over_ons (accessed 21 October 2014). Some 34 human rights film festivals have since developed their own organization, the Human Rights Film Network, which supports and coordinates the showing and promotion of human rights documentaries around the world (see www.humanrightsfilmnetwork.org, accessed 21 October 2014).
2 The phrase 'going pop' is borrowed from Richard Sherwin (2000).
3 Or as Amann (2003: 170) has phrased the promise of the human rights movement: 'when individuals or states commit certain offenses, even against their own people, the international community will take action'.
4 Available at: www.iccnow.org (accessed 21 October 2014).
5 Available at: www.ictj.org (accessed 21 October 2014).
6 Robyn Hillman-Harrigan, 'Interview with Director Pamela Yates', *Huffington Post*. Available at: www.huffingtonpost.com/robyn-hillmanharrigan/emthe-reckoning-em--int_b_230516.html (accessed 21 October 2014).
7 The following quotes regarding the reception of *The Reckoning* have been kindly suggested to me by Isadora Teixeira Caporali, student in the Law and Politics of International Security at VU University, Amsterdam. Rothenberg (2010) says that: '*The Reckoning* provides an excellent, compelling and dramatic introduction to the ICC. The film is ideally suited for the classroom use.' Kardaras (2010: 71) says that:

> Instructors will find *The Reckoning* to be an eye-opener for students who may have limited knowledge of global events, human rights issues, international law

and the UN.... In short, *The Reckoning* provides ample opportunities for students to engage in deep sociological thinking, reflection and analysis.

The Reckoning is listed among its 'Recommended Films' by *Peace Review: A Journal of Social Justice* (2010). Available at: www.tandfonline.com/doi/pdf/10.1080/10402651003751594 (accessed 21 October 2014). For the American Bar Association (ABA) award, see: www.Americanbar.org/content/dam/aba/migrated/publiced/gavel/2010ABASilverGavelAwardsProgramFinalDoc.authcheckdam.pdf (accessed 21 October 2014), with public endorsement at: www.Americanbar.org/content/dam/aba/images/public_education/learninggateways.pdf (accessed 21 October 2014).

8 For a list of nominations and shows, see: http://skylightpictures.com/article/the-reckoning-nominee-for-major-award (accessed 21 October 2014).
9 For a comparative analysis of some pro-ICC documentary films, see Werner (2013).
10 For an example, see *War Don Don* (dir. Rebecca Richman 2010) or *Peace v. Justice* (dir. Klaartje Quirijns 2012).
11 See, for example, the preamble to the ICC Statute, where the state parties indicate that they are '[m]indful that during this century millions of children, women and men have been victims of unimaginable atrocities that deeply shock the conscience of humanity'.
12 Skylight Pictures presents itself as follows on its website:

> For 25 years Skylight Pictures has been committed to producing artistic, challenging and socially relevant independent documentary films on issues of human rights and the quest for justice. Through the use of film and digital technologies, we seek to engage, educate and increase understanding of human rights amongst the public at large and policy-makers, contributing to informed decisions on issues of social change and the public good.

Available at: http://skylightpictures.com/about/ (accessed 28 January 2013)
13 For an overview of Yates' work, see: http://skylight.is/?s=pamela+yates (accessed 21 October 2014).
14 Robyn Hillman-Harrigan, 'Interview with Director Pamela Yates', *Huffington Post*. Available at: www.huffingtonpost.com/robyn-hillmanharrigan/emthe-reckoning-em--int_b_230516.html (accessed 21 October 2014).
15 A field which later in the documentary appears to be located somewhere in East Congo.
16 The triad of icon, index and symbol were introduced by the founding father of semiotic theory, Charles Sanders Pierce, for whom the three corresponded to his phenomenological categories of firstness, secondness and thirdness. In documentary theory, Pierce's work has been taken up *inter alia* by Louise Spence and Vinicius Navarro (2011: 14–15, 23). A related structure is presented by Nichols (1991: 26, 27), who argues that images in documentaries can be taken realistically (they show what actually is the case), functionally (how they contribute to the main argument of the documentary film) or intertextually (what kind of images we expect in a documentary on a specific topic).
17 Luis Moreno-Ocampo was the first Prosecutor of the ICC from 16 June 2003 until 15 June 2012, at which point he was succeeded by Fatou Bensouda.
18 Note that the claim to novelty can be questioned, given the earlier examples of criminal prosecutions in, for example, Greece and Portugal. For a discussion, see Kathryn Sikkink (2011).
19 Most directly, this is symbolized through the short narrative on the mistakes made by the Prosecutor in the first trial – that of Lubanga. In this case, the Prosecutor had failed to disclose relevant information to the defense, which almost led to the trial being aborted early. The documentary shows this episode, mainly as evidence for the ICC's respect for the principles of a fair trial.

20 For an account of international crimes as attacks on the possibilities for political agency, see Arendt (1964: 268–269), Vernon (2002), May (2005) and Luban (2004).
21 For an analysis of torture in terms of 'body' v. 'voice', see Elaine Scarry (1985). The expression 'destruction of the world' is taken from Scarry.
22 Paradoxically, however, all that makes these victims *human* – their sociopolitical identities, their capacity, etc. – would be stripped out if such an approach to international crimes were adopted.
23 The last element should be taken literally, as Rome was, indeed, the city where the Statute of the ICC was signed.
24 This list of countries is taken up again at the very end of the documentary, where it shows how the Court has gradually expanded since its inception.
25 Available at: http://vimeo.com/9160246 (accessed 21 October 2014).
26 Note that the term 'propaganda educational' is used here in the technical sense, not in any pejorative sense. In documentary theory, 'propaganda' refers to documentaries produced or adopted governments, in order to solicit support for a specific cause or program – in this case, US participation in the war.
27 The terms 'slave' and 'free' world are taken from Vice-President Henry Wallace's speech in New York, 1942, which framed the Second World War as 'a fight between a free world and a slave world' (4:37).
28 For a critical analysis along similar lines (using Mutua's savage-victim-savior metaphor), see Jeff Handemaker (2011).

Films

Carte Blanche (2011) Directed by Heidi Specogna. Switzerland and Germany, PS Film Zürich and Specogna Filmproduktion.
Kony2012 (2012) Directed by Jason Russell. USA, Invisible Children.
Peace v. Justice (2012) Directed by Klaartje Quirijns. Netherlands, Submarine Productions.
Resurgence (1981) Directed by Pamela Yates and Tom Sigel. USA, Skylight Pictures and Emancipation Arts.
The Court (2013) Directed by Marcus Vetter and Michele Gentile. Germany, Filmperspektive GmbH.
The Prosecutor (2010) Directed by Barry Stevens. Canada, White Pine Pictures.
The Reckoning: The Battle for the International Criminal Court (2009) Directed by Pamela Yates. USA, Skylight Pictures.
War Don Don (2010) Directed by Rebecca Richman Cohen. USA, Naked Edge Films and Racing Horse Productions.
When the Mountains Tremble (1983) Directed by Pamela Yates and Tom Sigel. USA, Skylight Pictures.
Why We Fight (series) (1942–1945) Directed by Frank Capra, Anatole Litvak and Anthony Veiller. USA, Signal Services (US Army) and Signal Corps Army Pictorial Service.

References

Amann, Diane Marie (2003) 'Assessing International Criminal Adjudication of Human Rights Atrocities', *Third World Legal Studies*, 16(9), 169–181.
Arendt, Hannah (1964) *Eichmann in Jerusalem: A Report on the Banality of Evil*. New York, NY: Penguin.

Aufderheide, Patricia (2007) *Documentary Film: A Very Short Introduction.* Oxford: Oxford University Press.

Handemaker, Jeff (2011) 'Facing Up to the ICC's Crisis of Legitimacy: A Critique of *The Reckoning* and its Representation of International Criminal Justice', *Recht der Werkelijkheid.* Available at: www.bjutijdschriften.nl/tijdschrift/rechtderwerkelijkheid/2011/3/RdW_1380-6424_2011_032_003_008 (accessed 21 October 2014).

Kardaras, Basil (2010) 'Film Review: The Reckoning: The Battle for the International Criminal Court', *Teaching Sociology*, 38(January), 70–72. Available at: http://tso.sagepub.com/content/38/1/70.full (accessed 21 October 2014).

Kennedy, David (1987) *International Legal Structures.* Berlin: Nomos.

Koskenniemi, Martti (2002a) *From Apology to Utopia: The Structure of International Legal Argument.* Cambridge: Cambridge University Press.

Koskenniemi, Martti (2002b) '"The Lady Doth Protest Too Much": Kosovo, and the Turn to Ethics in International Law', *The Modern Law Review*, 65(2), 159–175.

Luban, David (2004) 'A Theory of Crimes Against Humanity', *The Yale Journal of International Law*, 29, 85–167.

May, Larry (2005) *Crimes Against Humanity: A Normative Account.* Cambridge: Cambridge University Press.

Nichols, Bill (1991) *Representing Reality, Issues and Concepts in Documentary.* Bloomington, IN: Indiana University Press.

Nouwen, Sarah and Wouter Werner (2010) 'Doing Justice to the Political: The International Criminal Court in Uganda and Sudan', *European Journal of International Law*, 21(4), 941–965.

Nouwen, Sarah and Wouter Werner (2013) 'Monopolizing Justice: Ending Impunity as Hegemonic Politics'. Paper presented at the COST conference *Globalization and the Boundaries of Law*, Weimar, 10–12 December 2013 (on file with author).

Orford, Anne (2003) *Reading Humanitarian Intervention: Human Rights and the Use of Force in International Law.* Cambridge: Cambridge University Press.

Peace Review (2010) 'Recommended Films', *Journal of Social Justice*, 22(2). Available at: www.tandfonline.com/doi/pdf/10.1080/10402651003751594 (accessed 21 October 2014).

Renzo, Massimo (2012) 'Crimes Against Humanity and the Limits of International Criminal Law', *Law and Philosophy*, 31, 443–476.

Rothenberg, Daniel (2010) 'The Reckoning: The Battle for the International Criminal Court (review)', *Visual Anthropology Review*, 26(1). Available at: http://onlinelibrary.wiley.com/doi/10.1111/j.1548-7458.2010.01060.x/pdf (accessed 18 May 2010).

Scarry, Elaine (1985) *The Body in Pain: The Making and Unmaking of the World.* New York, NY: Oxford University Press.

Sherwin, Richard (2000) *When Law Goes Pop: The Vanishing Line between Law and Popular Culture.* Chicago, IL: The University of Chicago Press.

Sikkink, Kathryn (2011) *The Justice Cascade: How Human Rights Prosecutions are Changing World Politics.* New York, NY, and London: W. W. Norton & Company.

Spence, Louise and Vinicius Navarro (2011) *Crafting Truth, Documentary Form and Meaning.* New Brunswick, NJ: Rutgers University Press.

Vernon, Richard (2002) 'What is a Crime against Humanity?' *The Journal of Political Philosophy*, 10(3), 231–249.

Werner, Wouter G. (2013) '"We Cannot Allow Ourselves to Imagine what it All Means": Documentary Practices and the International Criminal Court', *Law and Social Problems*, 76, 3–4.

11 Strange encounters

Past, present, and future conceivable life

Juha A. Vuori

Viewpoint

In the present chapter, I examine three documentaries that consist of encounters with 'strange' Others: North Korea in *The Red Chapel* (dir. Mads Brügger 2009),[1] the Central African Republic in *The Ambassador* (dir. Mads Brügger 2011),[2] and future beings in *Into Eternity: A Film for the Future* (dir. Michael Madsen 2010).[3] Of interest to me here is how these fairly recent Danish documentaries present the possibility of communication across 'difference' and how they produce social imaginaries of diplomacy. The focus is on the apprehension or conceivability of strange life: how do documentaries of distant communities – whether in terms of geographical, political, or temporal distance – apprehend or fail to apprehend life. To achieve this, I utilize two notions of Judith Butler's (2006, 2010) in reading the films. First, how do the documentaries present 'life' when the subject matter is outside the sphere of the contemporary liberal-democratic order? Second, how does 'temporality' play into this? Can communication and recognition take place outside 'our time'? Furthermore, how do documentaries merge into more general semiotic flows of signs and social imaginaries on the (im)possibility of communication with life beyond the documentarian's norm? How are encounters with the strange imagined in terms of representation, representativeness, and mediation? These three films suggest that communication across strangeness and temporalities is difficult.

The Red Chapel: the assertion of identity politics fails to recognize life outside its norm

Diplomacy can be taken to work as a mediation of the 'strange', or 'something actual that seems unreal or out of place', 'something familiar but foreign' (van Wyck 2005: xi). Mediation functions as a connecting link between the familiar (the home) and the strange (foreign). One way to cross the divide between the familiar and the strange is cultural exchange. In this form of public diplomacy, mediation does not take place between professional diplomats and envoys, but through artists, entertainers, and athletes instead. The first film addresses the theme of mediation precisely through this kind of diplomacy.

In the documentary film *The Red Chapel*, director Mads Brügger goes to North Korea with two Danish-Korean comedians on the pretence of conducting a cultural exchange in the form of a comedy show in honor of the Dear Leader Kim Jong-Il. The director wants to achieve what no one has been able to do before – that is, to 'expose the very core of the evilness of North Korea'. This would happen via the 'X-factor' of Jacob Nossel, a Danish-Korean comic who is, in his own words, 'spastic'. The troupe of comics receives the usual treatment given to foreign dignitaries and is taken to see the statue of Kim Il-Sung, a school, museums, the demilitarized zone, and finally a 'peace demonstration'. Beyond these cultural experiences, the film follows how they rehearse their deliberately bad and illogical comedy show and how the troupe uses various opportunities to insert absurdity into venerated situations unbeknownst to their hosts. In accordance with his plan, the director allows the Koreans to mould the absurd comedy show into an even more 'grotesque' form that attempts to hide Nossel's handicap and insert North Korean ideology into it.

In terms of van Munster and Sylvest's (2013; Introduction, this volume) typology of the politics and visual modalities of the documentary, the political aim of *The Red Chapel* is to disclose the truth about the North Korean regime. The goal of the director is to force the operatives of the system to reveal their true nature through deception in the form of 'playing along' by putting them in apparently uncomfortable situations with a handicapped person and by performing postmodern irony in hallowed situations in order to reveal how ridiculous dictatorship is. This kind of disclosure does not happen through showing, but through saying: the voice-over of the director is perhaps even more potent than is usual in documentary films.

The use of voice-over is already strongly present in the opening scene of the film, which gives us a clue to what it is about; the opening address by the documentarian constitutes a location and position of the filmmaker from which the plan of the film is articulated (Butchart 2006: 436). In the opening scene of *The Red Chapel*, the director, who is also the main character and protagonist, lays on a hotel bed and reads something that his voice-over tells us is a manual of revolutionary filmmaking written by the Dear Leader, Kim Jong-Il.[4] He also tells the viewer to bear in mind that the footage has been shot under North Korean censorship and with the secret police's 'sentiment' in mind. He goes on to make it clear that only one member of his troupe was able to say what he really thought, while the others 'had to' continually lie to the Koreans.

This opening scene sets the film up as one about faking and deception from two sides: the North Korean censorship and the director's deception, and unnecessarily continuous lies. Indeed, the whole exercise is based on a lie: the stated purpose of the director is to strike at the comedic soft spot of all dictatorships by presenting them with a deliberately illogical and qualitatively poor comical performance, thereby forcing them to reveal their 'evil' nature. The director's assumption is that everything and everyone they will encounter is fake, acting, and 'evil', and that everything he does is therefore deceptive and false, too. In this way, Brügger is following Louis XI's instructions to his ambassadors: 'If they lie to you, see to it you lie more to them' (Der Derian 1987: 1).

The film's position makes the role of the narrating 'voice of God' even more powerful than usual. In general, narration in documentary films has political repercussions: the narrative voice is assumed to represent the decision between truth and falsehood. When the footage is shot under major constraints, the role of narration becomes even more crucial, as the director does not have the freedom of expression that is usually assumed to exist in choosing where and what the frame of the camera can capture. This also means that the ethics of the director should have stronger foundations than usual: as the images are biased by the political order of North Korea, the narration should be reflective of its own biases, too.

Indeed, Garnet Butchart (2006: 428) notes that, although documentarians have the right to artistic expression, the rights of participants should be protected by the disclosure of the intentions of the 'image maker' so as to avoid victimization through informed understanding and consent. The job of the documentarian is typically assumed to be delivery on the truth claims that the 'voice of God' produces in the documentary (cf. Butchart 2006: 429). From this point of view, documentarians should present their footage in a manner that is as unbiased, unfiltered, and truthful as possible. In political orders such as North Korea, the strict systems of censorship may require that not everything can be disclosed. At the same time, the documentarian should not cause severe harm to the participants through unethical practices. However, Brügger fails to be unbiased, even though he does consider whether his bias is the right way to approach North Korea. He repeats generally held beliefs about the mistreatment of the handicapped and the existence of concentration camps for political prisoners in his voice-overs, but he fails to provide any evidence to back up these claims. Indeed, the only 'gigantic lie' he is able to evidence with his footage is that in North Korea the Korean War is claimed to have been begun by the US – hardly a very significant or new finding for anyone who is familiar with Korea's contemporary history.

Furthermore, the deception used in the film produces a strong potential for harm to be caused to participants, particularly in the case of the 'caretaker of the virtual reality which the North Koreans had arranged', Mrs Pak. Brügger states that all the people they meet along their way are 'sycophants and informers', that their displayed emotions are false, and that everything they say is considered to be a lie of the deadly dictatorship. Consequently, even as his comedians push the issue of morality and ethics on the director, he replies that he has no moral scruples whatsoever in dealing with the North Koreans. Theodor W. Adorno (Horkheimer and Adorno 2002) warned against the use of violence in the name of civilization: even though such use is justified by referring to the barbarity or sub-humanity of the enemy, it also reveals the barbarity of the civilization that justifies it. Brügger does not heed this lesson, as he justifies his deception and break with ethics by referring to the uncivilized practices prevalent in North Korea. He does not recognize the life of Mrs Pak or any of the other participants as requiring protection from harm, as he does not recognize them as life to begin with. When a life is not recognized, it does not matter if it is hurt by your actions. Indeed, to harm a certain life is acceptable in order to reproduce the frame of recognized life. The assertion of identity politics overrides the harm produced for a life that is not recognized.

Butler notes how liberal freedoms are assumed to stem from a hegemonic culture of 'modernity' that relies on a certain account of increasing freedoms. Perhaps paradoxically, the uncritical assumption of such a culture as a prerequisite for liberal freedom easily becomes a source for the justification of cultural hatred and abjection. In temporal terms, then, North Korea is not 'of this time or our time, but of another time' (Butler 2010: 109). The existence of North Korea is thus an anachronistic aberration in the time of liberal-democratic modernity and the life that is recognizable for it. North Korea belongs to a past time, a remnant of twentieth-century totalitarian dictatorship, and thus cannot be conceived of as life in ours. It is a past that should no longer exist.

Indeed, North Korea seems ridiculous in the light of contemporary European values and thus appears as an open-air museum of totalitarianism. The assumption is that with time culture progresses towards more freedom. In this sense, North Korea is portrayed as frozen in time, having been, in Brügger's words, in 'hermetically sealed cultural isolation for more than 50 years'. The taken-for-granted building blocks of liberal freedoms are explicit with regard to tolerance of 'minorities' being an indicator of progressive modernity or pre-modern backwardness: the 'spastic' in the director's troupe works to show how tolerant and open his culture is, whereas North Korea remains pre-modern in its intolerance of handicaps. This is the director's admitted 'working theory', with Nossel as the X-factor. In terms of identity politics, this means that Brügger and the viewer are placed culturally in an advanced position, while North Koreans remain barbarians.[5]

Furthermore, Brügger's troupe produces and consumes a certain type of comedy, which it aims to provide to the North Koreans, albeit in a deliberately illogical, inconsistent, and tasteless manner. The director characterizes the skit they intend to play as 'the most innocent and classic Danish comedy sketch' of a senior citizen transvestite who has a strange relationship with a shopkeeper who speaks like a spastic. Yet, the troupe fails to play their original sketch: the North Koreans 'suggest' alterations to the skits, and Brügger deliberately plays along to pose the question of why the Koreans allow such a bad spectacle to take place, which he answers with reference to propaganda. This puts the troupe in a superior position, as they can grasp the type of humor by deciding what is funny and what is not, which the Korean authorities, bent on propaganda functions, cannot. The show's audiences similarly do not seem very amused by the hybrid production presented to them. This exercise produces the frame and conceptions of the troupe as contemporary, 'postmodern', 'ironic', and thus superior, and the actions and reactions of the Koreans as quaint if not exotic. As ironic postmodernists, the troupe can wear the North Korean uniforms, badges of trust, and partake in demonstrations, while the Koreans are assumed to be oblivious to how false they are. The lack of humor and inability to recognize irony reinforces the trajectory of North Korea in the film as outside contemporary civilization, working to justify the uncivilized actions of the director.

Such temporal disparities have an effect on the assumed possibility for communication across strangeness, too. The presumption of cultural exchange would provide an opportunity not only to examine the practices of North Korea, but also to destabilize the received frame of North Korea. This would be particularly opportune, as the country is perhaps the furthest away from the liberal-democratic norm in terms of political orders in the contemporary world. The documentary provides a potential to bridge this gap. For Jacques Rancière, translation is at the heart of learning and thus of emancipatory endeavors; for him, distance is not an evil to be bridged, but a part of any communication. In this sense, the strange, the alien, is not much further away than any other interlocutor. It is a matter of translating and counter-translating intellectual adventures (Rancière 2011: 10, 11). As Slavoj Žižek (2002: 66) also emphasizes, universal ideologies or values should not be assumed or imposed; instead, universality should be taken as a shared space of understanding among cultures that requires an infinite task of translation and reworking of one's particular position.

Rather than a shared space, what is seeable and sayable, and what remains invisible and unsayable in *The Red Chapel* is conditioned by two social structures, those of censorship and prejudice. The censorship affects what can be filmed and where the frame of the camera can be directed, yet perhaps a stronger constraint for the frame of the film is the prejudice of the director. *The Red Chapel* does not provide a voice for the Other of North Korea. Even though we hear the Koreans speak and express emotions, the director tells us that it is all acting or a lie. He presents us with certain images and sounds, while telling us what they mean with his 'voice of God'. But the bodies he presents are incapable of returning the director's gaze, nor can they respond to his spoken words. They become 'an object of speech without themselves having a chance to speak' (Rancière 2011: 96). The director deciphers for the viewer the meaning of the images he has created. He portrays the view that his subjects are merely cogs in the totalitarian machine of North Korea, 'the most heartless and brutal totalitarian state ever created'. Despite the opportunity to translate intellectual experiences, as Nossel does, Brügger remains within the frame he has chosen from the outset, thereby reproducing and reifying the frame of North Korea without a true voice.

But despite such frames, people actually live their lives in North Korea; North Korea is not just an aberration outside the liberal-democratic norm and temporality – it is life for millions of individual people who have to negotiate their existence within the system. Brügger works to colonize this, with no regard for the consequences of his actions. In the words of Nossel, Brügger 'makes things more [sic] worse' by 'playing along' to a much greater degree than the others would. Indeed, he is thought to have 'the weakest nerve' of the group. This hubris also appears in his concern that an appearance on national television would make them 'too visible'. Yet nothing happens.

The Red Chapel appears as a colonizing myth. The documentary reproduces the dominant social imaginaries and myth about North Korea as bad or mad. For Brügger, 'North Korea is a sanctuary for crazy people'. It seems that the director is unable to imagine or conceive of liveable life in North Korea. According to

Barthes (2000: 151), when someone incapable of imagining the Other 'comes face to face with him, he blinds himself, ignores and denies him, or else transforms him into himself'. Such a blinding effect is even suggested by the director, as for most of the film he wears sunglasses, thereby insulating himself from eye contact with the Koreans, and self-admittedly waits behind his shades for the moment when his trap will be sprung by the Koreans (which fails to happen). Even his troupe of comics finds this disturbing, and somehow wrong.

Barthes (2000: 151) notes that 'all the experiences of confrontation are reverberating, any otherness is reduced to sameness[;] This is because the Other is a scandal which threatens his essence'. The way out of such reverberations is to make the Other exotic: 'a pure object, a spectacle, a clown. Relegated to the confines of humanity, he no longer threatens the security of the home.' *The Red Chapel* produces this effect by creating a farce – namely, to show how ridiculous the regime of North Korea is. In this sense, the politics of the film could be viewed as destabilization (van Munster and Sylvest 2013; Introduction, this volume). Yet, there is no actual destabilization: the film fails to destabilize the general impression of North Korea. Furthermore, there is no destabilization or questioning of orientalizing assumptions about North Korea. Instead, the film reproduces and reifies them, becoming an assertion of Brügger's hubristic identity politics and circulating the hegemonic frame of liberal-democratic life.

However, there is one possible caveat to the above reading. As the director himself brings up the issue of postmodern irony, and as the film represents absurdist farces, could it be that the film aims at a *Borat*-like (dir. Larry Charles 2006) effect of unease in the spectator, that the prejudices of the director are being faked in order to tease out the prejudices of the viewer? This was my preferred assumption before viewing the film, yet such a reading does not seem plausible and would be far too generous, as the effect of prejudice is not produced in the interaction with the Koreans, but in the director's voice-over. Furthermore, although Nossel reflects on what he has learned through the experience and states that there are always two sides to a story, Brügger still tries to entrap Mrs Pak with his deceptions and lies. Indeed, Brügger seems unflinching in his denial of the life of 'sycophants and informants', those whom the 'regime trusts'. Indeed, one searches in vain for indications that his presentation of North Korea is ironic and will work to destabilize the commonly held imaginaries of it. The film may depart from postmodern irony in taking the mickey out of the Koreans, with silly poetry and fart jokes in classic fables, but the irony does not seem to reach the director himself. Instead, Brügger seems closer to the views that produced the 'cartoon crisis' in Denmark, and he displays the failure to produce shared streams of life-worlds in his assertion of identity politics.

The Ambassador: a colonial farce of corrupt diplomacy

Identity frames produce accounts of who we are, as well as how we would like others to see us. Yet, for these frames to be felicitous, others must recognize us for whom we frame ourselves to be: identities are social facts, which come about through social interaction (Ringmar 2012: 5). Recognition legitimizes the narratives and frames that we produce of ourselves. Legitimizing recognition needs to come from someone or something, which is, in turn, recognized. This kind of reciprocal recognition produces imagined communities and eventually turns into a system of diplomacy, which is based on reciprocal orientations of recognition between entities (Der Derian 1987: 110). Of import here is that the value of recognition derives from the reciprocal partner. What or who grants recognition has to be viewed as deserving of recognition in itself. Thus, alienation and bridging the communicative gap between societies is a vital question for diplomacy, which evolved into a formalized practice precisely as the result of alienation and estrangement. Indeed, diplomacy can itself be viewed as a system of communication and communication flows. Diplomacy tends to be understood as the exchange of accredited envoys who have certain privileges and serve the interests of the accreditor (Der Derian 1987: 2). Perhaps the most persistent social imaginary of diplomacy is envoys enjoying drinks at diplomatic receptions. This is also the image that the second film builds on.

In the film *The Ambassador*, Mads Brügger poses as a Danish businessman, Mr Cortzen, who tries to buy diplomatic papers to become a consul of Liberia in the Central African Republic (CAR), in order to smuggle out conflict diamonds under the cover of diplomatic immunity. In his opening statement and plan of the film, Brügger tells us how he exchanges his life as a Danish journalist for one where he 'can operate freely beyond all moral boundaries known to man while still being a respectable member of society' and 'travel the world with a suitcase full of diamonds'. Not only that, the stated plan was to get his hands on as many diamonds as possible. *The Ambassador* is about 'life as an African diplomat', about the corrupt combination of business and diplomatic privilege, suggesting how such outside actors keep the CAR in perpetual insecurity. Through secretly filmed footage and recorded phone calls, the film exposes corrupt and racist behavior and shows how money can buy diplomatic status from Liberia. Mr Cortzen interacts with locals, expats, and state officials in Bangui under the pretence of establishing a match factory, but actually makes a contract for acquiring illicit diamonds for export. Despite his vast use of bribes, or 'envelopes of happiness', the character of Cortzen fails to obtain the proper accreditation for most of the film. In the end, though, he manages to get his hands on illegal diamonds, at which point the film is brought to a puzzling end regarding whether he is actually going to smuggle the diamonds out. It is also made to appear that Mr Cortzen is finally granted the status of a Liberian consul in the CAR.

In terms of van Munster and Sylvest's (2013; Introduction, this volume) typology of the politics and visual modalities of the documentary, the political aim of *The Ambassador* is to expose the corrupt practices involved in buying diplomatic accreditation and of the diamond business in the CAR, stating how the colonial past is still being played out in African diplomacy. Yet, the aesthetic and other choices made direct the film towards problematization and destabilization. The question is whether these choices destabilize the topical phenomenon of the film, or whether they merely pull the rug out from underneath the edifying purposes of the film itself.

The documentary combines two styles: the exposure of hidden and nefarious activities, mixed in with a postmodern farce that includes hints of and references to fiction. The use of hidden cameras to show criminal activities is a classic means of *exposé* documentaries, and such techniques represent *vérité* in this genre of documentary. Brügger's team manages to obtain revealing footage of the corrupt practices that are prevalent in the brokerage of diplomatic credentials in both Liberia and the CAR. In addition, they show politically incorrect views of race and nationalities, as well as candid comments on political situations like the connection between the illicit diamond trade, militant organizations in Sudan, and France's great power politics. In this way, Brügger infiltrates corrupt practices and shows how they are still in operation, despite the Liberian Government's declarations that it has cleaned up its act. Money can buy diplomatic credentials, even for criminal purposes. By playing a caricature of the corrupt white colonial diplomat, Brügger gets closer to what *Borat* or *The Yes Men* (dir. Dan Ollman, Sarah Price, and Chris Smith 2003) achieve than he did in *The Red Chapel*: by performing overtly racist and colonial speeches, he gets some of his interlocutors to present their own similar views and to partake in corrupt practices like bribery. Like *The Yes Men*, he presents the logic of prevalent practices in politically incorrect ways without his audiences paying it any attention.

But Brügger's absurd and racist performance art at the expense of people not involved in either the diplomatic community or the diamond trade also undermines the apparent exposures of corruption and prejudice: ridicule of working people is not necessary for the political purpose of exposure. Stepping on the downtrodden does not make for good satire: Brügger ends up victimizing already exploited groups of pygmies and potential match-factory workers. He even admits to doing this in his voice-over: 'All along I knew perfectly well that this match factory never would come into existence. Thus, I was giving these people a false sense of hope.' How he justifies his unethical behavior is more revealing, though: 'Let me assure you, diplomats do this every day on a daily basis and on a much larger scale all over Africa. It's part of the game.' In this way, he fails to recognize the lives of these individuals, but exploits them like he claims others do, too. Brügger describes the CAR not as the heart of darkness, but as its appendix, as 'a Jurassic Park for people who long for Africa of the 1970s'. In such a 'park' outside our time, the character of Mr Cortzen operates without concern for the lives he touches, and the director Brügger performs exploitation in order to criticize exploitation.

Granted, the absurd elements of the film could be viewed as an entertainment vehicle to make the revelation of the hard political realities more digestible, as a critique of developmental NGOs and exploitative businesses ('Because I believe in sustainable development and support tribal people, I want to employ pygmies'), or even as a play on prejudices and racist stereotypes (pygmies are 'small and black'; 'I have a problem with Asian people'; they are sneaky and greedy). In such a reading, farcical performances work to destabilize these kinds of efforts and practices. Yet, how this satire is accomplished merely risks the reification of preconceptions and victimization of the documented. Accordingly, we see the iconic images of an African dictator in exuberant regalia, child soldiers, and people dancing in traditional clothing. Brügger's *exposé* does document corruption in Liberia and the CAR, but he generalizes this as applying to all of Africa. This works to reify the prevalent European frame of Africa as a corrupt and dangerous place, stuck in its past.

This persistent imaginary freezes Africa in temporal terms. Indeed, the aesthetic choices and voice-overs present the CAR as not only dislodged from international norms as 'a lawless territory' without ever having had a working state structure – whereby you can operate there without moral boundaries – but also as dislodged from time: 'Time moves backward in Bangui'. Against the modern imaginary, progress does not happen in the CAR. In secretly filmed footage, the head of state security explains how this is the deliberate policy of France, but this is also emphasized by Brügger's choice of music and attire. The soundtrack is from the 1930s to the 1950s,[6] he wears colonial safari clothing and a large 'the good mark' ring of the Phantom – a comic-book series established in the 1930s, the protagonist of which has pygmies as aides.

The Ambassador reifies the image of diplomacy as the exchange of accredited representatives who wear certain types of attire and enjoy special privileges which can be used for their own corrupt purposes. Concomitantly, it reproduces the dominant European imaginary of Africa as an underdeveloped, dangerous, and corrupt playground for nasty adventurists exploiting diplomatic practices. The CAR remains an aberration of the European colonial past. The pygmies are made to look strange, with stony-faced expressions that do not seem to appreciate Mr Cortzen's antics, like playing whale songs to them. Throughout the performance of corruption and racism, Brügger turns these practices into farces, whereby they can no longer threaten the expected norm. The film shows corruption, but makes the CAR and its exploiters exotic, caricatures in a playground of France's colonial past that still reverberates today. Instead of limiting itself to presenting criticism of corruption and France's policies and working to destabilize the dominant frame of Africa as exploitable, the film ends up reifying this very frame. When you are outside the liberal norm everything is permissible, but with the risk of ending up 'dead in a ditch in Africa'.

Into Eternity: a wistful fable for the future

Recognizability characterizes the general conditions that affect a subject's recognition as a living being. Categories, norms, and conventions – political imaginaries – are what constitute the conditions for recognition. Such conditions allocate recognition unevenly; different frames of intelligibility establish varying domains of the knowable. For Butler (2006, 2010), a life has to be intelligible as a life: a recognized life conforms to certain conceptions of what life is. The concept of time is also an important aspect here. Butler asks (2010: 102): 'What time are we in? Are all of us in the same time? Who has arrived in modernity and who has not?' Such questions are relevant, as notions of progress tend to be defined against pre-modernity and the transition to modern technologies and values. Such social imaginaries are part of the background of our assumptions about life, being essential for what we conceive life to be: these form a 'picture of ourselves as speaking to others to whom we are related in some way' (Taylor 2004: 26). Estranged relations among individuals, groups, or entities require mediation, which can take on many forms (Der Derian 1987: 6). As we have seen from the two previous films and the social imaginaries they partake in, cultural practitioners, ambassadors, and consuls have been important diplomatic representatives. Yet, representations as such can also be representatives. For example, the Voyager spacecraft was equipped with representations of humans and humanity for possible extraterrestrial encounters. To convey messages across vast distances or temporalities requires non-human representatives.

The issue of non-human communication is pertinent for the documentary *Into Eternity: A Film for the Future*, about the safety and difficulties of storing nuclear waste. It depicts the construction of a permanent underground storage site for Finnish nuclear waste. This repository of spent nuclear fuel should last for 100,000 years, which corresponds to the time it takes for nuclear waste to stop being harmful to biological organisms. Such a lengthy period of time creates difficulties in how to construct the site, and how or even whether to communicate the purpose and dangers of the repository for future generations of humans or other intelligent beings that might develop over such a lengthy period. The film is structured around the themes of Waste, Interim Storage, Permanent Solution, Human Intrusion, Warning the Future, and The Law.

In van Munster and Sylvest's typology (2013; Introduction, this volume), the film works to produce a destabilizing effect by using the visual to make strange what the people being interviewed say. At the same time, the film grants the viewer access to processes that would usually be off-limits. While it is possible to visit nuclear power plants, the removal of fuel rods and the digging of a vast underground facility are not everyday images for most people. In this way, the politics of the film could be viewed as exposition, yet the melancholic message of the voice-over, the visual style, and the auditory messages work to destabilize the efforts of the documented.

The film begins with a slow motion descent into an underground installation along a road, while a disembodied voice (which later turns out not to be that of the director) says:

> I would say that you are now on [sic] a place where we have buried something from you to protect you. And we have taken great pain [sic] to be sure that you are protected. We also need you to know that this place should not be disturbed. And we want you to know that this is not a place for you to live in. You should stay away from this place, and then you will be safe.

As this initial scene and the title of the film suggest, *Into Eternity* is a documentary for the future about the folly of 'our civilization', about what and how to communicate to the future the mistakes of our time. The film is a wistful message in a bottle (cf. Horkheimer and Adorno 2002),[7] or perhaps in a time capsule, as one of the participants describes the feeling of being in the 'Onkalo' – the Finnish word for a cavernous hiding place that the repository is called. But unlike the time capsules that were in vogue in the 1950s and stored representations of forms of life for interpretation by future archaeologists, this repository is built like the tombs of the Pharaohs, never to be opened again.

The film poses questions for future humans or other intelligent beings, which is achieved in the form of a fable told in darkness for the length of time a match takes to burn out. In Rancière's (2006: 5–6) view, films are fables that depend on other fables by extracting fragments from previous fables to construct new ones. Such new fables reappropriate and silence the fragments in order to make them speak in a new manner. As an art, cinema is the making of fables with other fables. In the field of the documentary, Ilona Hongisto (2011: 90) calls this process 'fabulation'. Fabulation takes place when a character starts to 'make fiction' and thereby contributes to the invention of a 'people'. Such a 'people' is to envision a collectivity beyond that which exists in actuality.

In the fabulation of a future past, the director produces a present community, his 'civilization, totally dependent on energy', which tried to harness the 'power of the Universe', yet had to bury its fire underground, where it would burn 'into' eternity. The fables told in the light of a match are reminiscent of campfire stories and combine the elements of past fables of fire-bringers to the future fable of the past: 'Once upon a time man learned to master fire.' In his match, the director is the creator and the bringer of light, as well as the one who creates the fiction of his civilization.

The aesthetic choices in both the visual and the auditory also work to emphasize the passage of time and the fable-like quality of the film. The participants of the documentary are presented as somehow strange and isolated. Subjects in a half-body shot are presented in isolation from the linguistics and spatiotemporality of the interview. They are pulled out of the flow of the film and presented for the examination of the spectator in a still form. We see silent, slightly amused people, either still or in slow motion, with the detached voices of others. In *Into Eternity*, this effect is emphasized with the stark lighting of such shots and with sterile surroundings and empty desks. This makes the subjects seem cold and detached, perhaps even uncaring. They become archetypes in the fable presented by the director; they represent man's [sic] folly in attempting to harness the power of the Universe with his engineered science. In parallel, the use of slow motion and transparency effects make the people seem like appearing and disappearing ghosts, or lost souls. The cold, artificial environment of the engineers is juxtaposed with desolate images of nature.

Into Eternity explicitly takes on the question of time and cultural, economic, political, technological, and even evolutionary change. The inter-visuals deployed in the film also seem to work towards this function: the topics of the film are introduced one at a time as circles within circles. This visual is reminiscent of the television show *Time Tunnel*. The motif of engineered artefacts doing a waltz has been used in the science fiction classic *2001: A Space Odyssey*, dirty mechanical devices in gritty darkness were used for great effect in *Alien*, while the promotional video of Onkalo is like the underground installation in *Resident Evil*. The musical choices of the score also chime with the sense of hopelessness, the passage of time, future encounters with the strange unknown, science gone bad, and death.[7]

Indeed, for the director, '100,000 years is beyond our imagination'. As this is the case, can we learn from an incomprehensible past to communicate with an unknown future? What will come after our time? Will humans or some other creatures be as modern life was in its infancy, or will it be completely outside our time, and life? Can we recognize life outside our time, be that in our past or the distant future? There is a veil between our time and future time, and thus our life and future life.[8] The question then becomes how to communicate to future humans, or even other creatures, that the site should not be disturbed?

One suggestion has been to mark the site with a marker that would last through the millennia, conveying the instruction to keep away from this enduring danger. In this way, the marker touches upon 'cultural conceptions of time and history, and the very idea of communicativity' (van Wyck 2005: xvii), producing a confrontation with cultural Otherness and unimaginable estrangement. This is troubling for the engineers of Onkalo, as well as the director of *Into Eternity*: we 'cannot assume people or creatures in the future will understand very much'. Messages of long-lost civilizations have been found and disregarded by our time; faced with the most extreme estrangement, the warnings of unrecognized life will be disregarded by future beings, too. This is why some suggest not leaving any marker or message on or of the site.

The length of time it takes for radioactive waste to become harmless requires that diplomatic messages be approached from the viewpoint of mythology: millennia are too long a time to present direct messages. Instead, systems of sacred symbols that order and communicate human experiences, a form of 'mytho-diplomacy' (Der Derian 1987: 49–50), are needed. The director, too, asks the future whether they have learned of the burial ground of the last glow of his civilization through legends. Mytho-diplomacy is 'a largely atemporal and symbolic mediation of estranged relations between groups and entities' (Der Derian 1987: 68). Madsen tells the future that ancient legends have reached us and that perhaps future legends will reach them. Such mediation will be achieved through ritual, sacrifice, and ceremony, which have all been vital aspects of mythologies. They have also been previously suggested as one means of communicating the danger of such sites to future beings. Folkloristic means should be combined with a kind of priesthood of the marker (Sebeok 1984). Rituals of obedience turn into customs and become the common heritage of communities that allow them to live as communities (Der Derian 1987: 55). The keepers of the marker could become one such community; the priests of the marker would be those in the know, the inner circle, but for the whole congregation the marker would be about ritual and custom, a mediating link between the estranged past and future.

Past, present, and future conceivable life 195

The marker would not be a monument, but a mediator of estrangement, a representation as a representative, a diplomat bearing a message. Although particular, the marker would not be unique in this regard. The difficulty with conveying intentions and achieving appropriate perlocutionary effects is that contemporary life has not recognized previous life: robbers and archaeologists have not heeded the warnings and commands not to disturb sites of import. Why would future beings be any different? How to communicate danger in a way that would be perceived as sincere, and be taken up, too? These questions may seem difficult through the time-span of millennia, yet the problems of communication and speech acts are present in any situation of interlocution. The issue is about conventions and social imaginaries. To make a marker work, the conventions of the language systems would need to be provided so they could be decoded. Yet, this would not resolve the problem of social imaginaries: can life with nuclear waste be imagined, or can we recognize life that cannot comprehend life with nuclear waste? What is life outside our time?

We can similarly ask what the message of the director is. His fable is a wistful apology of someone who has lost hope. Although the film appears as socially progressive, it does not provide alternative courses of action. The fire that burns without smell, taste, or visibility will burn into eternity, and cannot be stopped. In this sense, the melancholic pessimism of the director makes the film as hollow as Onkalo. The film produces an aesthetically pleasing experience, but remains politically unsatisfactory.[9] It places the documentarian as a Cassandra-like figure; the engineers in their trust of human engineering are wrong to think the problem has been solved. Onkalo can host only the waste of the five nuclear reactors in Finland; the vastly larger number of reactors and their waste are without even this kind of a 'solution' for the problem. Does the director want to wake people up to the problem? Or is he merely resolute in the melancholy of death? Does viewing the film produce a sense of accomplishing something towards the resolution of the nuclear waste problem? The director is worried for the future and his civilization. But is there a need to worry? Serious and capable people are working on the most tenable solution available at the moment. What would be the alternative? The film does not provide one; it merely underlines the folly of man (*sic*) who wanted to harness the powers of the Universe, which ultimately proved too unwieldy.

Vanishing point

At first glance, the three films on strange encounters appear to deal with different issues and topics: totalitarian dictatorship, corrupt diplomacy, and nuclear waste. Yet, they all partake in social imaginaries of the possibility of communication and mediation across strangeness. Social imaginaries can be affected by both factual knowledge and works of fiction. They are about how 'ordinary people' imagine their social surroundings that are 'carried in images, stories, and legends' and are 'shared by large groups of people' (Taylor 2004: 23). At issue are the ways in which people 'imagine' social existence, how they fit together with others, and what are normal expectations and their underlying normative notions (Taylor 2004: 23–24). Indeed, such imaginaries tell us something about how life in society should be conducted.

The modern social imaginary of liberal democracy has been colonized to cover the entirety of international relations and to produce a sense of homogeneous time (Taylor 2004: 157). It has become the prevalent view, to the degree that those political orders that go against its premises have to pretend not to be doing this. Such a strong imaginary brings a sense of security, as well as moral superiority, through its maintenance as something real (Taylor 2004: 182). Outside challenges to the dominance of the imaginary are considered threatening, as are our own actions that are taken to undermine or betray the imaginary, which challenges the sense of our own integrity and goodness.

Norms produce the idea of who is worthy of recognition and representation at all (Butler 2010: 138). The question is about the cultural and political frames of recognition: superficial difference can be subsumed into the frame of recognizable life as long as the strange is excluded. Recognition becomes part of social sorting in accordance with pre-existing norms. Indeed, when other societies rule and arrange themselves in a different manner than those of one's own norm, action against them is considered justified (Butchart 2006: 431). It is problematic if the features of life that are recognizable rely on a failure of recognition (Butler 2010: 141). Does the reproduction of the recognizable frame of liberal-democratic life in modernity rely on the failure to recognize life in strange forms?

All three documentary films examined here present the view that it is not possible to communicate across strangeness or across temporalities. Shared streams of life-worlds through signs cannot be produced, either because of assumed and actual deception or too much difference in social imaginaries. Such premises reflect the view that life outside the norm need not be recognized, as it cannot be communicated with. These assumptions reinforce the view that values and identities within frames of recognized life can be asserted without the need for any consideration of its effects outside it. But does this view really hold?

Notes

1 Presented at festivals in Canada, the US, Australia, Mexico, Croatia, Latvia, South Africa, Brazil, Spain, and Poland in 2010. Won the Best Nordic Documentary Award at the 2009 Nordic Panorama Festival, and World Cinema Grand Jury Prize: Documentary at the 2010 Sundance Film Festival. Broadcast in Australia, Norway, Denmark, and the UK. Available at: www.theredchapel.com/ (accessed 15 May 2014). Available on DVD and YouTube (without rights).
2 Presented at the 2011 International Documentary Film Festival Amsterdam (IDFA) in the Netherlands, an official selection at the 2012 Sundance Film Festival. Broadcast in Sweden and Finland. In the cinema in Norway and Denmark. Available at: www.theambassador.dk/ (accessed 15 May 2014). Available on DVD and Blu-ray, and YouTube (without rights).
3 Received 19 prizes at film festivals from 2009 to 2010. Streamed online twice in 2012. Available at: www.intoeternitythemovie.com/ (accessed 15 May 2014). Broadcast at least in the Nordic countries. Available on DVD and YouTube (without rights).

4 The clue and the synoptic place of the opening scene is given more gravity as the film's final act also begins with the same scene, but with a different voice-over that contemplates two different endings for the film, in accordance with the Dear Leader's instructions for the creation of lasting political effects.
5 The barbarian or exotic attitude of the director is evident, for example, in the assumption that '[i]f the North Koreans were ever able to learn the Danish language, they would never understand "spastic" Danish'; that 'I have been told that the important thing about Koreans is not what they say with their voices, but with their faces'; and that North Koreans have a 'group mind'.
6 Including the title track 'I don't want to set the world on fire' by The Ink Spots, a track which was given new life with its inclusion in the satirical Cold War nostalgic science fiction video game *Fallout 3*, and the ending track of 'Istanbul (not Constantinople)' by the Four Lads, which also plays with colonial nostalgia.
7 The sadness and wistfulness of the film is enforced by the musical choices on the soundtrack – for example, in how the director makes two stone drills 'dance' to Sibelius' *Valse triste*, a piece of occasional music from the play *Death*.
8 This is suggested by the end of Madsen's film, where two blasters enter the dusty darkness of Onkalo as they burrow deeper.
9 With the interviews edited out, the film could be enjoyed as an industrial ambient music video.

Films

2001: A Space Odyssey (1968) Directed by Stanley Kubrick. USA and UK, Metro-Goldwyn-Mayer and Stanley Kubrick Productions.

Alien (1979) Directed by Ridley Scott. USA and UK, Brandywine Productions and Twentieth Century Fox Productions.

Borat (2006) Directed by Larry Charles. USA, Four by Two, Everyman Pictures, and One America.

Into Eternity (2010) Directed by Michael Madsen. Denmark, Finland, Sweden, and Italy, Atmo Media Network, Film i Väst, Global HDTV, Magic Hour Films ApS, Mouka Filmi Oy, Sveriges Television, and Yleisradio.

Resident Evil (2002) Directed by Paul W. S. Anderson. UK, Germany, France, and USA, Constantin Film Produktion, Davis-Films, Impact Pictures, and New Legacy.

The Ambassador (2011) Directed by Mads Brügger. Denmark, Zentropa Real.

The Red Chapel (2009) Directed by Mads Brügger. Denmark, Danmarks Radio and Zentropa Productions.

The Yes Men (2003) Directed by Dan Ollman, Sarah Price, and Chris Smith. USA, Yes Men Films LLC.

Time Tunnel (1966–1967, TV series) Directed by Irwin Allen. USA, American Broadcasting Company, Twentieth Century Fox Television, Irwin Allen Productions, and Kent Productions.

References

Barthes, Roland (2000 [1957]) *Mythologies*, trans. Jonathan Cape. London: Vintage.
Butchart, Garnet C. (2006): 'On Ethics and Documentary: A Real and Actual Truth', *Communication Theory*, 16, 427–452.
Butler, Judith (2006 [2004]) *Precarious Life: The Powers of Mourning and Violence*. London: Verso.

Butler, Judith (2010 [2009]) *Frames of War: When is Life Grievable?* London and New York, NY: Verso.

Der Derian, James (1987) *On Diplomacy: A Genealogy of Western Estrangement*. Oxford and New York, NY: Basil Blackwell.

Hongisto, Ilona (2011) *Soul of the Documentary: Expression and the Capture of the Real*. Turku: University of Turku.

Horkheimer, Max and Theodor W. Adorno (2002 [1947]) *Dialectic of Enlightenment*, trans. Edmund Jephcott, ed. Gunzelin Schmid Noerr. Stanford, CA: Stanford University Press.

van Munster, Rens and Casper Sylvest (2013) 'Documenting International Relations: Documentary Film and the Creative Arrangement of Perceptibility', *International Studies Perspectives*, 1–17.

Rancière, Jacques (2006 [2001]) *Film Fables*, trans. Emiliano Battista. Oxford and New York, NY: Berg.

Rancière, Jacques (2011 [2008]) *The Emancipated Spectator*, trans. G. Elliott. London and New York, NY: Verso.

Ringmar, Erik (2012) 'Introduction: The International Politics of Recognition', in T. Lindemann and E. Ringmar (eds) *The International Politics of Recognition*. Boulder, CO, and London: Paradigm Publishers, 3–23.

Sebeok, Thomas A. (1984) *Communication Measures to Bridge Ten Millennia*. Columbus, OH: Office of Nuclear Waste Isolation.

Taylor, Charles (2004) *Modern Social Imaginaries*. Durham, NC, and London: Duke University Press.

van Wyck, Peter C. (2005) *Signs of Danger: Waste, Trauma, and Nuclear Threat*. Minneapolis, MN, and London: University of Minnesota Press.

Žižek, Slavoj (2002) *Welcome to the Desert of the Real! Five Essays on September 11 and Related Issues*. London: Verso.

Part III
Behind the scenes

12 Evil, art and politics in documentary film

Interview with Joshua Oppenheimer

Rens van Munster and Casper Sylvest

Introductory

Joshua Oppenheimer (b. 1974) is the director of several award-winning documentary films and Reader in Documentary Film and Artistic Director of the Centre for Documentary and Experimental Film at the University of Westminster. From 2007 to 2011, he was senior researcher on the UK Arts and Humanities Research Council (AHRC)'s Genocide and Genre project. For over a decade, he has worked with militias, death squads and their victims to explore the relationship between political violence and the public imagination. We sat down with him to talk about his Oscar-nominated film, *The Act of Killing* (2012), in which former Indonesian death-squad leaders reenact their real-life mass killings in their favorite cinematic genres, including film noir, westerns and musicals.

Documentary film

Q: Before we talk about the The Act of Killing, *we would like to start off with a more general question about how you conceive of documentary film. What is it that this genre allows you to do?*

JO: I came to documentary filmmaking from two angles. First, I came from a background in theoretical physics and an interest in the nature of being. Filmmaking is a way for me to explore aspects of the world that I otherwise would not see. It is a way of exploring and making visible aspects of our world that have previously been invisible. It offers the possibility of exploring what appears to be a simple factual reality, with certain objects as a given, like self, other, identity, place, nation and the like. But these objects are not given; they are made up of myriad and usually invisible stories, fantasies and projections that all interact in microscopic ways. Each time we posit these macroscopic objects – objects that make the world intelligible – we render invisible numerous relations and a rich interplay of social and political forces, stories, fantasies. For this reason, I do not conceive of non-fiction filmmaking as 'storytelling': the appearance of every object is inherently social, but when our primary focus, to the exclusion of all else, is the power of our storytelling, we render invisible the forces that make virtually everything what it is, including ourselves. For me, film has always been a way to unmask these social processes in the same way a physicist will try and find the microscopic, mutually entangled forms of energy that make the world what it is. That means accepting a crisis in objectivity – for observing these things inherently disturbs them. As in quantum mechanics, every observation is an intervention, even if it merely reinforces the *status quo* (which is decidedly *not* what I try to do).

Second, I came to film as an activist who saw in film the potential of documenting moments of confrontation, encounter and performance. Activism to me inherently involves performing social and political identities in public space, and from the outset I saw the camera as a way of documenting and staging such performances. I made my first film by infiltrating neo-Nazi and right-wing militia movements as a means of trying to understand paranoia, intolerance and fundamentalism in the US, particularly leading up to the turn of the millennium. As I could not enter those spaces safely as myself, I had to become the people I was documenting. This performance of identity was something I was using the camera to document in that early work.

Q: Your ideas of staging are very different from the conventional idea that in documentary a camera portrays the real or apparent. How do you think about this relationship between performance and truth?

JO: I have always been interested in the camera as something that could document and catalyze forms of performance. This is also why I have some

Figure 12.1 Behind the scenes of *The Act of Killing*. Reprinted with permission from Joshua Oppenheimer.

disaffection for the word 'documentary', because we tend to take with it a lot of baggage – namely, that the camera documents a pre-existing reality. Nothing could be further from the truth. The camera does *not* document a pre-existing reality.

For example, in filming, say, a single day in your life, together we would simulate a reality in which we simulate the camera's absence. That is, we pretend that the camera is not there, or at least that it's not having the overwhelming influence that it inevitably has. And to me, that is not the most interesting thing you could do with a camera. The moment I start filming you, you would be inherently self-conscious. You would start staging yourself. That, in turn, is actually an opportunity to make visible the ways in which you *want* to be seen and the ways in which you *want* the world to know you. The underbelly of that, also now visible, would be your insecurities, your fears, the vulnerabilities you are trying to hide. That is an opportunity that documentary normally misses, because documentarians try to get past the self-consciousness and pretend their camera is a transparent window on to the world, when nothing could be further from the truth. The myth that we are documenting a pre-existing reality obfuscates the real way in which documentaries are made and how they work.

Q: So how would you define documentary film?

JO: For me, it is useful to think of documentary as the staging of a series of occasions. In that sense, every documentary scene is inherently a collaboration between subject and filmmaker, and it is inherently performative, too. *The Act of Killing* is taking the performative *cinéma vérité* of Jean Rouch a step further. There should be no confusion between *cinéma vérité* in the context of Rouch and what has been wrongly called *cinéma vérité* in the UK, US and Denmark, which is fly-on-the-wall, observational cinema (properly called 'direct cinema'). You could say that I am taking Rouch's methods a step further, but in ways that would have been technologically impossible in his time. Instead of looking at filming as documenting reality, it is more apt to look at it as creating occasions with your subjects, occasions in which someone may do something they would not otherwise do, or only be half conscious of – for example, prolong an argument or make a confession. If you look at *The Act of Killing* from this perspective, every scene in the film is another occasion for Anwar Congo [a former commander of a death squad and the main character in the film, ed.] to explore and make visible a part of himself and often at the same time do paradoxical and contradictory things to approach his pain and run away from it.

Given that every time you film somebody they are self-conscious, self-consciousness is actually a resource that non-fiction film should make use of, because it is an opportunity to understand how people see themselves and want to be seen. The moment you film anybody they tend to stage themselves, and if you look at how people stage themselves and how they behave when they are self-conscious, you can, of course, see how they *want* to be seen, and in that you can see the stories they tell themselves – stories they tell in order to live with who they are or to project to the world (and to the camera) a person they wish they were. When you put that under a microscope, you can see that these are second-hand, half-remembered fragments of narratives taken from Hollywood, television, their parents, school and so on, and these stories interact in a kind of maelstrom we call identity and that we call a person. Human beings are made up of such fragments, and to ignore them is to speak in the macroscopic fictions I mentioned before.

Q: Elsewhere you have used the phrase 'documentary of the imagination' as what you aspire to create. What do you mean by that?

JO: I think *all* documentaries should strive to be documentaries of the imagination. When they are not, they are lying about the nature of what they are doing. Whenever we are not acknowledging that the moment you point a camera at a human subject one is documenting a form of performance, we are lying. The moment we stop telling that lie and start acknowledging that everybody is performing when we film them, then you are essentially subscribing to a manifesto for a documentary of the imagination.

The politics of evil in *The Act of Killing*

Q: One of the most striking and innovative aspects of The Act of Killing *is your decision to stage occasions with the perpetrators, rather than the victims, of the genocide in Indonesia in the mid-1960s. How did you come to make that decision?*

JO: Well, that decision was the outcome of a long process. I actually began the project in collaboration with the *survivors* of the genocide, but they were bullied into silence by the Indonesian army, who would not let them be filmed or even talk about what had happened to them. Meanwhile, the survivors would send myself and one of the film's two co-directors, Christine Cynn, on these very painful missions to film neighbors in a plantation workers' community, who were suspected perpetrators. We would go to these neighbors' houses, and we would ask circumspect questions about the past, thinking they would be unwilling to reveal their crimes. However, they would immediately respond with horrific stories of mass killings, told in a boastful register, often in front of their wives, children and grandchildren. This contrast between plantation workers – workers who were struggling to organize a union, afraid because their parents and grandparents had been killed for being in a union and who were forced by the army to remain silent forty years after the killings – and perpetrators, who were totally boastful and saying things far more incriminating than anything the survivors could possibly tell us, this contrast was horrific. It felt as though we had landed in Germany forty years after the Holocaust, but with the Nazis still in power.

When I showed the early material with the perpetrators to those survivors who wanted to see it and to the broader Indonesian human rights community, they urged me to continue: 'Keep filming the perpetrators', they said. 'You're on to something terribly important. Any Indonesian who sees this will be forced to acknowledge that we are all afraid, and forced to acknowledge the rotten heart of this regime. Keep going.' I felt I was entrusted by the survivors and human rights community to do a work of moral and political importance that they could not safely do themselves, so I filmed every perpetrator I could find, working my way up the chain of command from the countryside to the city. In the beginning, I thought it would be a much simpler political exposé of a regime of corruption built on mass graves, but I came to understand that here was an opportunity to show, above all, what happens to our *common humanity* when we build our normality on the basis of terror and lies. *The Act of Killing* addresses universal themes. It concerns, or should concern, us all – namely, about the nature of evil and the human condition – revealing that we are all much closer to perpetrators than we like to think.

Q: Could you explain to us how you think of this universal dimension of the film?

JO: In a very crude and simple way, my general view of the world is that evil is something produced systemically. As horrific as this situation is in Indonesia, I understood from the outset that this horrific situation of 'what if the Nazis had won' was actually not the exception to the rule, but the way our whole world works. For example, everything we as consumers buy is produced in places like Indonesia – places where there has been mass political violence, where perpetrators have won and have used their victory to build regimes of fear that are so intimidating that workers are too afraid or too suppressed to be able to get the human cost of what we buy incorporated in the price tag.

What *is* included in the price tag is a small premium for thugs like Anwar and his friends who keep people afraid. In that sense, we all depend on the suffering of others to feed ourselves, clothe ourselves, put petrol in our tanks. But I think that the human experience of living with that raises crucial questions: *how* do humans become agents of evil? How do we make sense of the consequences of that? And what difficulties does this pose for them? To do so, we must see human beings in all of their complexity. My task as a filmmaker is not to judge Anwar's evil. Any moron could do that from a transcript of the first meeting that I had with him. It would involve a long list of the things he did, and one could quickly find him guilty and condemn him. Much of our human rights documentary tradition is about cataloguing what we already know to be bad and pretending that it's a discovery. But what are the performative effects of condemning somebody? What are the performative effects of making the leap from 'this man has done something evil' to 'this man *is* evil?' The greatest function of condemning somebody in this way is to reassure ourselves that we are not like them. But in this process, we are not learning anything. We are actually un-learning something, which is that 'this man is human'. Such films just make us more stupid than we were to start with.

We may learn facts about a certain conflict or atrocity, but it really does not increase our *understanding*. So, yes, it is my position that evil is produced systematically, and I gradually came to live the consequences of that position when dealing with and filming Anwar – a human being who had committed evil. For me, that was a painful ethical dilemma: if I was close to Anwar, and if I thought of him secretly as a monster, I would betray him. I did not want to do that and actually had to overcome my fear of being like him and allow myself to like him. I would have to be open to him and not for a second allow myself to work with this man from a position of hatred or condemnation. Gradually, and maybe it already happened before I met Anwar – he was the forty-first perpetrator I filmed – I realized that the ethics of the relationship with this man would necessitate that I would not condemn him as a monster, even as I would never forget that what he *did* was monstrous.

Q: In doing so, The Act of Killing *addresses a real conundrum: how is it possible that everybody knows what is right and wrong – and yet we so easily do wrong?*

JO: Yes, especially since doing wrong harms you! In Anwar's case, I glimpsed this in the very first scene on the roof, where he used to kill his victims. On the roof, he dances the cha-cha-cha and says he's a good dancer. He explains: 'I would go out drinking, taking drugs, dancing in order to forget what I did.' He was the most stridently boastful of the perpetrators I filmed, and yet he actually gives voice to his conscience from the outset. In that, I saw the opportunity to understand and to answer a question about evil: he knows what he did is wrong, and yet he is all the more stridently celebrating it – how is that possible?

To try and understand that, I showed him the footage of himself dancing on the roof, wondering if he would recognize in the mirror of the film what he is doing. He looked very disturbed, but he does not dare say so, because he has never been forced to say it. Instead of confronting his deeds, he says: 'My clothes are wrong, my hair is wrong, my acting is wrong …' And so begins this process of embellishment, the engine of which from the very beginning was actually his conscience and his desperate fear of the tormenting effects of guilt. You see, Anwar and his friends got away with their acts and have been handed a justification by the army and the government in the form of propaganda that validates what they did. Anwar has clung to that excuse for his entire life. Adi Zulkadry, another perpetrator, says in the film that killing is the worst thing you can do, but if you can get away with it, and if you are paid well enough to do it, then go ahead and do it, but you must invent an excuse so that you can live with yourself afterwards and cling to it for dear life. And that is what Anwar has done.

Q: So, the reenactments force Anwar into a position where he needs to justify his deed to himself and others?

JO: Yes, each scene is almost a greater outrage than the previous scene, finally culminating in that waterfall scene, where the genocide victims thank Anwar for sending them to heaven. But this is not just about Anwar. The film reenacts a process which the *whole regime* has enacted since 1965: lying about evil to justify evil acts begets further evil.

The reenactments become the cinematic prism through which Anwar finally sees the meaning of what he has done and through which Indonesian society confronts its traumatic past – and the abuse of that traumatic past to uphold a corrupt and intolerable present. People lie about what they have done in order to justify it, *but also because they know it was wrong*. That triggers a downward spiral into further corruption and evil. Because, having gotten away with mass murder and justified it (in the form of propaganda), you must now blame the victims for what happened, because that is part of the excuse that sanctions your actions. You must dehumanize the victims, because it is easier to live with yourself if the people you killed are not fully human. And you must kill again, because if, for example, the army tells you to kill more people for the same reason as you killed the first, if you refuse the second time it's tantamount to admitting it was wrong the first time. This downward spiral can only end in a total moral vacuum.

Figure 12.2 The waterfall scene in *The Act of Killing*. Reprinted with permission from Joshua Oppenheimer.

The film witnesses this downward spiral of corruption and evil, and documents how it emerges not because the evil actors are immoral, but precisely because they *are* moral. They know that what they have done is wrong; they lie to themselves and build an ever more hollow and corrupt reality on the basis of that lie. From this, we glimpse one of the most startling findings of the film – namely, that so much of what we call human evil is intimately bound up with human morality. In Anwar, we see that this even applies to sadism, which turns out to be a furious and despairing defense against incipient remorse.

The reception of *The Act of Killing*

Q: *What were you trying to achieve in exposing the lie at the heart of the regime?*

JO: My hope with the film was to expose the nature of the corrupt downward spiral I mentioned. But there was also the hope that if I film the perpetrators boasting I could reveal the rotten heart of the regime, not so much for an international audience, but for Indonesians themselves. Indonesia needed a film that, like the child in the *Emperor's New Clothes*, points at the king and says: 'Look, the king is naked!' A film, essentially, that shows everybody what they already know, but have been too afraid to articulate. And shows it so powerfully that there is no going back, and no way of pretending that these things have not happened, and that on their basis, atop the mass graves, corruption, thuggery and terror have prevailed. That was my goal, but it was hard to maintain my faith over the seven years of making the film. In fact, I sometimes thought: 'No one will care about this film when it comes out.' I contented myself with the hope was that it would at least open up new directions for the medium of film and that it may be appreciated as such.

Q: *Obviously, the film has proved a success on both of these dimensions, but why did you think the film would not necessarily succeed in its political objective?*

JO: I was worried that Indonesians would think of the film as being made by a foreigner, conceived to make Indonesia look bad. To avoid that, I involved as much as possible the man who is now credited as an anonymous co-director of the film; he was my production manager, my assistant director, my second cameraman. He helped with the editing. But, above all, he was my main creative sounding board throughout the production. I think that our dialogue gave us the courage to go in a direction that I may not have had the confidence to go myself, because I was not sure it would be authentic. The dialogue with my anonymous Indonesian co-director was important in that respect, and because of it the film is seen as 100 percent authentic by

Indonesians and has been welcomed in Indonesia as a genuine work of Indonesian cinema. Take the waterfall scene at the end of the film: that is a scene where Indonesians weep, but they also laugh with the cathartic joy of seeing the regime unmasked by the perpetrators themselves. There is no going back after you have seen that, because the perpetrators say it themselves: this is a country where we have killed a million people, and the victims should thank us for it. That is the nature of this regime! There is this cathartic joyful laughter even as they cry, because the scene is an allegory of all of the rot that has come before it in the film – and it is a tragic moment for Anwar. I did not want the film to be seen as a grotesque cartoon-like image created by a foreigner. I wanted it to be a fully authentic image of Indonesia. Another key part of that was that Anwar was the author of all of those scenes. That gave it authenticity, but we did not want it to look like Anwar was insane. It had to be clear that all of his insane choices were manifestations of a social and political insanity that is utterly systemic – and in which we all participate, because we depend on it for our everyday living. (The insanity of *The Act of Killing* is the underbelly of our reality, after all.)

Q: The film has had a real impact in Indonesia. Can you tell us something about how the film was introduced into the country and how it was received?

JO: At the time, I worried if the film would speak to the leaders of Indonesian civil society. Would they care? But a new generation of educators, journalists, artists, filmmakers, writers, professionals are coming up, and they are not complicit in the same way as their parents' generation in the crimes of 1965. Nor are they traumatized by memories of the violence, like their parents' generation has been. And given that the perpetrators themselves so forcefully and undeniably identify the problems – corruption, impunity, thuggery, fear, etc. – it means that these can now be addressed more easily by this generation.

Still, it was difficult. Indonesia bans films dealing with Indonesian human rights violations. If we wanted to show the film in Indonesia, we would have to give it to the censorship board. But we knew they would ban it – and if they ban it, it is a crime to even show it in your house. If it is a crime to show the film, then it is an excuse for the Indonesian paramilitary groups to physically attack screenings. To get around that, we knew we had to build high-level Indonesian support for the film and then get the film out under the cover of that support.

In September 2012 we held a screening at the National Human Rights Commission in Jakarta for publishers, editors and producers of Indonesia's leading news outlets. All of them left the film devastated and deeply moved. What the film shows is undeniable, and showing it was the best strategy for building support.

What we did not know was just *how* powerful the media and the Indonesian audience would find the film. What happened with *Tempo* magazine,

Indonesia's most important news publication, is a good example. After watching the film at the National Human Rights Commission, the editor called me and said:

> There was a time before *The Act of Killing*, and now there is a time after *The Act of Killing*. I have been censoring articles on the 1965 killings for as long as I have been editing this magazine. I will not do this anymore, because your film shows me that I do not want to grow old as a perpetrator. We are going to break our decades-long silence on the killings, and to do so we are going to marshal fresh evidence about the atrocities and show that *The Act of Killing* could have been made anywhere in Indonesia, that the problems it underscores are systemic, that Anwar [the protagonist] is perhaps one of 10,000 perpetrators of his rank living around the country.

So they sent 60 journalists around the country and found boastful perpetrators everywhere they went – former death-squad leaders still in positions of power. They collected hundreds of pages of testimony, which they edited and published in a double edition of the magazine, alongside material about the film, interviews, reviews, historical surveys about other films about 1965 and an essay about how I came to make the film. *The Act of Killing* edition of *Tempo* was immediately sold out, they reprinted it, it sold out again, they reprinted it and it sold out a third time. Indonesians were astonished, after all, to see this holocaust upon which their whole society was based, but which is never discussed in the media, filling the most important news publication in the country. And after that, the rest of the media followed, producing their own investigating reports about the genocide. Then, of course, everyone was curious to see the film. So we held screenings for Indonesia's leading artists, filmmakers, celebrities, historians, writers, educators. All these people had read *Tempo* magazine, and they approached us to hold another screening at the National Human Rights Commission. After seeing it, they all said that everybody in Indonesia must see this film. Then, under the cover of that high-level support from across Indonesian civil society, they took the film back to their communities and screened it. Starting with International Human Rights Day in 2012, there were 50 screenings in 30 cities averaging in size about 200 people, but they range from 30 people up to 700 people. Most of them were 'invitation-only' screenings, which was a way of protecting people's security. By July 2013, there had been over 1,100 screenings in 118 cities, and many more organizations have since requested copies to hold screenings. On the anniversary of the start of the atrocities, 30 September 2013, the film became available for free download for anyone in Indonesia.

Q: It appears that that the film succeeds in combining universal questions about the nature of evil with a much more specific focus on the Indonesian atrocities. How did you achieve this balance?

JO: It is precisely because of the universal human significance that the film has not been rejected as the work of a foreigner saying: 'Look how evil Indonesia is'. In relating to Anwar as a human being, the story becomes universal. It implicitly says: 'Look, I am not necessarily any better than this'. This is why Indonesians have not rejected the film as the work of an outsider. The form of the documentary reinforces that. There is no looking down from a place of critical distance, and there is no authoritative voice-over or layer of text that explains either historical or contemporary political events. If we included that layer of expert commentary, it would be to look down from a higher analytical position and thereby patronize and treat the subjects with condescension. I think that would make the film unbearable for Indonesians – and for me. The film avoids being patronizing because it is not judgmental of human beings, while never suspending its judgment of specific acts that everybody knows are wrong.

Documentary, power, art

Q: As a form of mediation, The Act of Killing *seems to have more in common with art than with journalism. How do you think about the relationship between art and politics?*

JO: To me, the function of art is telling people what they already know in powerful and complex enough ways, so that the complexities that people normally do not want to look at – because they are frightening – are acknowledged and addressed. That, to some extent, is the function of art – not to show us something we did not know, but to show us something we already know, but have been too afraid or uncomfortable to say.

The relationship between art and activism is, in many ways, difficult and unpredictable. The first film I made in Indonesia with the plantation workers in West Sumatra – *The Globalization Tapes* – was meant to be an educational, activist tool. But after the film was done using my experimental performative documentary technique that I developed in London, it was cut into this horrible 60 minute corporate video. It was unrecognizable. It was used a lot in Indonesia to inspire Indonesian workers and maybe – I actually don't know – it had some effect. So when I began *The Act of Killing* I was very disillusioned about what art as activism could be, and I vowed never again to make a campaign film – and I still hold on to that vow. But as an artist, I never lost my sense that art is about showing us the nature of reality in its most painful and complicated form, in forms that are so mysterious, unfathomable, mystical and horrifying that we normally shudder to think of them. And that is inherently political.

After all, if art encourages, invites or forces people to articulate and address the most painful, frightening and mysterious aspects of who we are, it cannot but open up a space for activism of the most radical sort, but it is not activism in and of itself.

I later had this moment when I was with Werner Herzog, and he was looking at the special edition of *Tempo* magazine on *The Act of Killing*. After flipping through it, he looked me in the eye and said: 'Art does not make a difference'. Then Werner puts down the magazine, looks at me for a long time, smiles and says: 'Until it does'. He's right. You never know when that moment will come, and it's not always about art being great; it's about the moment being right.

Films

The Act of Killing (2012) Directed by Joshua Oppenheimer. Denmark, Final Cut for Real.
The Globalization Tapes (2003) Directed by Joshua Oppenheimer, Christine Cynn and Members of the Plantation Workers' Union of Sumatra. Indonesia, Independent Plantation Workers' Union of Sumatra, International Union of Food and Agricultural Workers and Vision Machine Film Project.

13 Bridging research and documentary film

Interview with Janus Metz and Sine Plambech

Rens van Munster and Casper Sylvest

Introductory

Janus Metz (b. 1974) is director of several documentary films, including *Armadillo* (2010), for which he received the Grand Prix de la Semaine de la Critique at the Cannes Film Festival.[1] Sine Plambech (b. 1975) is an anthropologist at the Danish Institute for International Studies specializing in human trafficking, international migration and gender. Together, Metz and Plambech made the films *Love on Delivery* (2008) and *Ticket to Paradise* (2008), both official selections at the 2008 International Documentary Film Festival in Amsterdam (IDFA). The outcome of a meeting between academic research and the art and craft of documentary filmmaking, the films explore migration and transnational ties and identities under conditions of globalization by focusing on marital arrangements among Thai women and men in provincial Denmark. *Love on Delivery* and *Ticket to Paradise* challenge conventional narratives of victimhood by focusing on the self-perceptions of Thai women as they make the life-determining choice to settle in an unknown country on the other side of the planet, leaving behind family and communities. We sat down with Metz and Plambech to talk about their collaboration and the opportunities and challenges of bringing together (anthropological) research and documentary filmmaking.

Research and film

Q: Before we discuss the relationship between research and film in more detail, could you explain to us how your collaboration began?

SP: I have worked with this group of Thai women for ten years now, and I have always been interested in communicating my research results to a wider audience. I wanted to show how a place like Denmark is connected to other places through these marital arrangements. It was not completely new to me to consider alternative ways of communicating my research, but until I met Janus I had not thought about film.

JM: At that time, I was already interested in making a film about migration. I had been researching young men in western Africa who travel to Europe through the Sahara Desert, but this turned out to be an almost impossible film to make because of the extreme conditions. Obviously, undocumented migrants want to live outside the spotlight, which made filming difficult. It was also dangerous, as these men would often experience robberies. I joined a trip on the back of a truck from the northern part of Mali up to the Algerian border and back again, but it was difficult to follow someone who would eventually cross the ocean on a raft. It was also very difficult to secure financing for that film. Within the Danish financing system for documentaries, you generally depend on a Danish broadcaster to secure funding from the Danish Film Institute. At the time, in 2006, African immigrants were perceived as something distanced and of little interest to Danish viewers.

When a mutual friend told me about Sine's research, it struck me that this was a similar story, but set in a community where you could actually film people's journeys and agency. It also had a 'Danish angle' that could appeal to the Danish broadcasting community.

SP: For the broadcaster, the focus on Danish men was crucial, even if for us and the producers of the film the women were always the more interesting characters – it is their relationship with men that drives the film.

Q: What role did Sine's research play in conceiving and shaping the film?

SP: My research provided access to the main characters. We did not have to apply for a lot of money for research or development, which you would normally do before filming. My theoretical background is in critical trafficking studies and post-colonial feminist transnational studies. Both fields focus very much on the agency of the subjects we study, and we tried to bring that focus to the screen: the agency of the women, how they were connected to specific areas in Thailand and so on.

JM: Once we decided to work together, everything happened very quickly. The first film premiered within a year from our first trip to northern Jutland [the region of Denmark where some of the Thai women portrayed in the film now live, ed.]. We were twenty steps ahead, because Sine knew the people, their way of operating, their everyday lives, their motivations and how they did things. Our ambition for the film was to make a double-sided portrait of a village in Thailand and a small-town community in Denmark and see how they affected each other through these marital arrangements.

SP: My research focuses on the political economy of migration, and I wanted this to be a story about global structures and labor migration. The marital arrangements should be understood in that light. Sometimes, anthropologists ask me why I did not stress the cultural practice of marriage more. They would say: 'Why is the cosmology muted?', or 'What about the Thai men, what is their opinion?' and 'Could you not have had a little bit of a voice-over explaining the context of marriage in Thailand?' For our story, however, it was important to me to portray these women as breadwinners,

Bridging research and documentary film 215

Figure 13.1 Niels Jørgen Molbæk and Sommai talk about their marriage. Film still from *Love on Delivery*, dir. Janus Metz. Photographer: Jacob Aue Sobol, Upfront Films.

whose decision to migrate was based on family relations and kin. In that way, my research came to bear upon the film's narrative. Of course, I do acknowledge that cosmology and the voices of Thai men are muted in the film, but not everything can be part of the film. Without wanting to sound too paternalistic, the film was a way to give these Thai women a voice and tell their stories. Had Janus collaborated with another anthropologist, he might have focused more on other, perhaps more cultural practices, such as temple visits or marriage ceremonies.

JM: Every film is also a practical operation, a piece of work, and some stories might just not fit the narrative. I remember we were filming a local marriage in the village where there was a lot of money being passed around in the presence of monks – that was interesting, but it did not involve the characters in our film. In such cases, representational or explanatory images of marriage and marital arrangements interfere with the narrative.

Q: So how, in the end, did you balance anthropological concerns with the filmic language?

JM: A film cannot directly incorporate an academic analysis. It would be completely disastrous if a voice-over explains what is actually going on. It would not only be offensive to audiences, but it would also be directly patronizing to the people whom you are filming. I have not seen a documentary that explains the actions of the characters in academic terms since the anthropological films made in the 1970s. They were not necessarily boring, but they were certainly a strange creature of filmmaking. An exhaustive analysis or explanation, which one probably would be asked to do in an academic paper, does not always work on film.

To me, a good film is always about drama. It has to reach an audience, and the worst thing is to consider film as simply conveying information. Film talks to the belly much more than the head. Rather than filming our characters seated in chairs talking to us about their experiences, we modeled the film around a set of active scenes based on the story of a woman coming to Denmark on a marital journey, to find a husband. This set into motion a story through which audiences can relate emotionally to the women and men in the film – their wants or needs, and their will to achieve a better life, to provide for their families or to get out of loneliness. From a dramatic point of view, the least successful scenes are the ones where the women merely *talk* about Thailand or about how Thai women are perceived in Denmark. Those are scenes that are only there because there is no better scene. It is a 'tell' and not a 'show'.

SP: How can you film transnationalism? That is one of the great questions you are confronted with as a researcher attached to a film project. As researchers, we *talk* about transnationalism, globalization and flows, but what do such phenomena *look* like? How do you visualize such theoretical concepts or human practices? I wanted to show the global connection between Thy and Thailand, but we were unable to go to Thailand for the first film. One way in which we brought this absence into view was by visualizing transnational political economy through everyday interactions, such as phone calls between a mother and her son or by a shot of women looking at photos of houses in Thai villages financed by remittances. By translating transnationalism from the written word to a moving image, film can actually help in making complex phenomena more tangible.

JM: Our strategy behind the film was this: let's tell the story about these women, but let's set it in northern Jutland and tell it from the narrative perspective of a 'stranger coming to town'. From a cinematic point of view that was extremely compelling and interesting, because it provided a fixed starting point, a stop date and a driving engine that pulled the plot forward. If the film had just been about Thai women, prostitution and sex bars in Pattaya, we would have made a different film – extremely interesting to go into, but that was not *our* film. The film was about the interlinked *flows* of people and money between a fishing community in northern Jutland and a rural area in Thailand.

That was also the main reason behind the making of the second film. If *Love on Delivery* was about the conditions for marriage between Danish men and Thai women, we conceived *Ticket to Paradise* almost as a prequel to that film. We wanted to explore what happened to women who could not go to Denmark, and we wanted to find out what impact the inflow of remittances had on their villages.

SP: I was extremely happy we were able to make a second film, because I did not want to tell a story about immigrants in Denmark without also including a more global perspective. A lot of films about immigrants have a national bias. Immigrants are presented as if their lives only begin when they arrive in their country of destination; prior to that they seem not to have had any existence, just as they are not seen to maintain their transnational lives with their families back home after arriving in a new country. I was really frustrated about this tendency, because my research showed that the lives of the Thai women were transnational, rather than national. This little village in Thy in northern Jutland was intimately connected to Thailand. It was very difficult to have this story included in a single, one-hour film, and the second film allowed us to expand on the transnational theme.

Documentary, fiction and reality

Q: If film needs drama, could you say something about your decision to make a documentary – a genre that is often seen as speaking to the mind more than the belly. In what ways does the genre of documentary allow you to unfold a drama?

JM: The power of documentary has a lot to do with its claims to reality and authenticity. It is about lived reality. The presence of real people and real people's lives creates a sense of intimacy that makes it hard to disregard what you see. Fiction films can do that as well, but they rely much more on a safe, confined space of art, where we can have an experience and then step out of it again. In contrast, documentaries have a presence of reality that has real, political implications for you and me and for the people in the film. It carries a greater urgency for action, identification and discussion. As a filmmaker, I would argue that fiction films can be just as or sometimes even more real than documentary films exactly because in the former you have a greater range of artistic freedom. You can orchestrate your film without the need to be sensitive about the fragile lives of the people in it. But for an audience, experiencing something that is not mediated by actors comes across as more real and pressing.

SP: We also focus more on the universal sentiments of a 'mother', 'daughter' or 'wife' that audiences can identify with. By conveying more universal aspects of these marital arrangements, we wanted to take out some of the cultural differences and the exoticism that is often at work in migration movies. By focusing on more 'universal' categories, we wanted to create an atmosphere of intimacy between the characters in the film and the audience.

JM: It is about finding a grain of sand that can become a larger image of how the world is stitched together and how human beings all struggle to navigate through the world. The most interesting part of the films is that globalized inequality is staged on the very intimate scene of two people – one from the Global North, the other from the Global South – that each have their own motivations and reasons for entering into this transnational relationship. In the West, we might have all kinds of prejudices about these women and their motivations, so the films were driven by an empathetic concern to find out what the globalized world looks like from the perspective and position of someone in the Global South.

SP: I like to think of my work as a study of the nitty-gritty of everyday life that conveys something about the world in a larger perspective. You look at small things and try to find the larger perspective in what happens in those everyday practices. Films are at their best when they show small practices, emotions and actions between people that succeed in addressing not necessarily a political, but an existential larger-than-life question.

JM: At a very early stage we defined the women as entrepreneurial heroines of globalization who were obviously entering into very fragile and vulnerable relationships. Sine's research provided a crucial understanding of the ways in which migration is a choice made by these women, if obviously not under circumstances of their own choosing. At the bottom of society, choices are constrained; you cannot pick and choose from every shelf. The use of this basic Marxian insight that human agency is constrained by larger structures helped to confront viewers with their own moral ideas about migration and the relationship between Thai women and Danish men. By showing the perspective of someone from the Global South, audiences in the West were able to bridge the gap between themselves and those who live far away.

Q: Currently, you are working together on a manuscript for a fiction feature on human trafficking based on Sine's research (with anthropologist Hans Lucht) on trafficked women from Nigeria. Given the power of documentaries to appeal to audiences, could you justify this choice to move to fiction?

JM: It is difficult to talk about a script that is not even finished yet, because we are still working on so many things.

SP: There are things you can do in a fiction film that you cannot do in a documentary. When I did my fieldwork in Nigeria, I encountered very strong narratives about migration. Yet I also realized that it is difficult to connect the different points in these narratives – that is, to connect Nigeria with Niger, the crisis in Libya, migrants' journeys to Italy and practices of deportation. That entire layout would be difficult enough to unfold in an anthropological analysis, let alone a short documentary film. Most of the migrants' lives are so complicated. For example, some women would experience multiple rapes during their journey or would witness others getting killed. They have a child or get deported. Their lives are so intense. Yet the translation of this intensity to the screen can be complicated. Emotionally, it is difficult to relate to someone who has been raped three times in a film. Perhaps you can, but then the film would be about *that* – a woman who has been raped three times – and only secondarily about something else.

JM: From an anthropological point of view, the story of a Nigerian migrant traveling to Europe is an important one to tell. But from a filmic perspective, you have to think of ways of mediating that experience that speak to the belly, rather than the mind. You would not be able to direct a person saying: 'Can you go on the roof and dream about Europe?' But you can say to an actor: 'Your dad just died, he is lying on the floor, bleeding.' Audiences can now picture her as a *daughter* in a situation where the breadwinner of the family is gone. What is she going to do? Now, that is strong drama, because it is a person we can relate to. We are no longer talking about a migrant, we are talking about a daughter. What we can then try to do is to authenticate the story in terms of anthropological sensitivity and understanding.

SP: For me it is a question not so much of objective truth but of authenticity, however that it is filtered. I do not feel that as an anthropologist I am fictionalizing my research, or that making a documentary would be more true to it. Not at all. In producing a film, we have to condense and cut out certain aspects, but as long as we create an authentic story, fiction film can be truthful. The challenge is to develop a character that is unique. If you want the main character to be representative, it might not be good drama, so you have to find that unique person around who you can build a story that is still authentic. We became increasingly interested in condensing the story of these women into one single narrative. The story we are trying to write is a story of one woman, but it is also a story that filters many other women's experiences into one strong narrative.

Ethics and responsibility

Q: Another consideration could be that in fiction film you do not need to expose real people in vulnerable positions to the public. To what extent have such concerns played a role in your work?

SP: There is a lot of hesitation in making documentaries about migration and migrating women, not just Thai women. We can never be sure how a documentary influences the lives of the participants. But because I had worked so much with these women, I knew they would be capable of making a decision on whether they felt it was appropriate for their lives to be filmed. It was very uncomplicated: I just asked them if I could come by with Janus, so they could meet him and we could all discuss what filming them would imply. Of course, we could not know how popular the film would become, so at the time we did not realize how well-known they would become throughout Denmark.

JM: Sine vouching for me was obviously hugely important, because it convinced them we were sincere in our efforts to try and understand who they were and where they were coming from. We also had a lot of fun! Still, everybody entered the process with some trepidation. I remember a husband that all of a sudden, the night before we would officially start filming, did not want to be in the film. He was worried I was going to take away his wife, and there were these jealousy issues. These little things are completely unforeseen. I think his wife was actually barking at him the entire night to get him to be in the film, because apparently it was important to her.

SP: Documentary filmmaking also allows the participants to make a political statement. Especially Sommai [one of the central characters in the films, ed.] developed a purpose of her own to be a part of the film. She wanted to convey the motives of Thai women and help deconstruct some of the stereotypes. She did not voice it that way, but it was obvious that she really wanted to explain to a Danish audience that Thai women primarily migrate to help their families. She always wanted us to go with her to Thailand as well, in order to film how women like her have helped develop their villages.

JM: As soon as you introduce the camera into a scene it affects that scene, because people relate to the camera. There is no recording like a fly on the wall. It has never existed, and it never will. In the best cases – and I think this was one of those cases – an almost therapeutic process begins when you press the 'play' button. The camera becomes a machine of confession, a process of creating meaning and truth that can be very therapeutic to people. That therapeutic process of filming became a trajectory of empowerment for some of these women, because their self-inquiry also brought to the forefront the price they had to pay and their past experiences as vulnerable subjects of prostitution. That is not something we could have known from the outset. In the second film, *Ticket to Paradise*, it was much harder for them to appropriate the scene, because it is closer to traditional social realism and more poverty-oriented; its ethics has more in common with traditional documentary films, where directors seek to tell audiences about the disadvantages of poverty in the hope that one day we can all hopefully live in a better world. *Ticket to Paradise* also delved more into issues of sex tourism and prostitution, which were only superficially dealt with in *Love on Delivery*. This also meant that the film did not go down well with some parts of the Thai community in Denmark. Some felt we were disclosing too many secrets and that the film was stigmatizing them. On the other hand, the film shows some of the more brutal social realities of these women's lives.

Q: Can you tell us more about your ethical deliberations behind specific scenes or filmic decisions and how they affected the final product?

JM: It is very difficult to pinpoint exactly how certain scenes found their way into the film and other scenes were left out. Rather, we had a constant dialogue about how to turn the scenes.

SP: For almost every scene, we discussed how we could display the agency of the women, their sexuality and the decisions they would make. In that way, their story became a part of the narrative structure. For example, for our second film, *Ticket to Paradise*, we discussed a childish, playful scene with Lom and Saeng, two young women who were sex workers. Since sex workers are often portrayed as children who do not have any opinion or are submissive, we decided to drop that scene, because it would just add to the stereotype we were trying to nuance. We also had a discussion about human trafficking. Sommai was quite pragmatic towards the notion that sometimes women have to make a decision to go into the sex industry for a period of time. In *Ticket to Paradise* she tells young women that to meet Western men they can go to work in the sex industry in Pattaya for a little while, but she also tells them that there are other ways for them to meet men. We discussed the possibility that in a Western context Sommai could easily be interpreted as a trafficker. We did not want to take the scene out, because older women or men sometimes do suggest these things to younger women in Thai communities. However, we did discuss how to balance that scene so that audiences would also understand her motives for making this kind of suggestion.

JM: One of the things we discussed and felt very clearly was that the sex industry in Pattaya is a surreal world where prostitution is open-ended. It is not a direct transaction as we know it from Denmark or many other parts of the Western world, where men go to brothels, pay at the door and go to a room for a limited time. It is different. You have all these girls and women like Saeng who come from rural areas and who are or become excited about the money. It almost becomes a drug to them. We tried to capture this in the film by shooting the lights of the nightclubs, the gazes and the little kisses. The way that montage is edited, cut and put into the film is intended to

Figure 13.2 Saeng and her friend at a bar in Pattaya, Thailand. Film still from *Ticket to Paradise*, dir. Janus Metz. Photographer: Lars Skree, Upfront Films.

capture Saeng's seduction by this environment. However, I do not *know* if that is exactly what Saeng felt and thought, but that was very much the sentiment we got from her and from dealing with other women in similar situations.

It is like watching someone take drugs for the first time. As audiences, we need to understand that mechanism, because otherwise we cannot understand where she is coming from, where she is going and why she is doing it. Showing the seductive power of this environment was important in telling Saeng's story, just as it was important to show that she had a little boy back in the village that she had to provide for. She could have provided for that boy in other ways. She did have other choices. We wanted to understand why some women do this when they could also work in a field, a factory in Bangkok or even pursue an education.

SP: Still, it is impossible to control how audiences react. After the films came out, we were contacted by a lot of Danish men, who had seen the film and wanted us to help them find a Thai wife. And some marriages actually came out of the films! You could say that documentaries create or sustain desires – like marrying a Thai – and in this way, the films unintentionally reproduce some of the phenomena they deal with.

Note

1 For an analysis of *Armadillo*, see van Munster's chapter in this volume.

Films

Armadillo (2010) Directed by Janus Metz Pedersen. Denmark, Fridthjof Film.
Love on Delivery (2008) Directed by Janus Metz. Denmark, Cosmo Doc.
Ticket to Paradise (2008) Directed by Janus Metz. Denmark, Cosmo Doc.

14 After-image

James Der Derian

> The fundamental event of the modern age is the conquest of the world as picture.
> (Heidegger 1977: 134)

As images multiply, screens proliferate, and the signal-to-noise ratios invert in an expanding infosphere, the arrival of *Documenting World Politics* is good news for viewers and readers alike.[1] Emerging from the fecund Copenhagen interpretation of international security studies, Rens van Munster and Casper Sylvest have assembled a cohort of critical thinkers intent on re-constituting the field and re-visioning the purview of world politics through documentary film. They do a splendiferous job of it, producing a book that is truly greater than the sum of the chapters (a rare thing in collected volumes). The result is a holistic view of a multifarious world politics through documentary film. Rather than rehearse the individual essays – and reduce the whole to less than the sum of its parts – I would like to push the vision of the volume further, into the not wholly unfamiliar territory of the *other* Copenhagen Interpretation, to explore how new and ubiquitous technologies of visual observation, documentation, and mediation are generating new uncertainties as well as new possibilities in world politics. The implications are quite radical, suggesting that the near-constant interventions of networked global media are producing a quantum interaction in world politics – in short, a multitude of worlds that only become real when mutually observed.[2]

The impact of images in world politics might just be the paradigm shifter. It is now cheaper, faster, easier to produce, transmit, and distribute images on a global scale. Technologies of reproduction have attained ever higher levels of verisimilitude as images progressed from still to moving, silent to sound, black and white to colour; from 16 to 35 to 70 millimeter frames and 16 to 24 to 48 frames per second; and from 2D to 3D to virtual immersion. Celluloid faltered in the reproducibility race after videotape – already becoming, like 'documentary film', an anachronistic misnomer – appeared on the scene. But with 4K video, 3D, and 7.1 surround sound the new (if sure to be short-lived) standard, the technology of representation has reached hyperreal levels. Drawing on software and hardware pioneered in video games, next-generation documentaries are unlikely to be shot by a camera; as with *Gravity*, the latest Hollywood excursion into cinematic virtuality, they will most likely be generated by computer – with some b-roll images thrown in from the archives for good measure. As the image of the world (*pace* Heidegger) becomes a multiverse of images, documentaries (*pace* U2) will become even better than the real thing (which is not, in the case of supermodels or superrealities, necessarily a good thing).

This is not to challenge the materiality of world politics; it is rather to acknowledge how world politics is increasingly produced and sustained through technologies of reproduction. Nor, at the other extreme, is it to endorse some kind of technological determinism which negates any critical inquiry; and is why Heidegger was adamant that the essence of technology is anything but technological. Technology is an artifice of the real as well as an art of the possible; or, to use the classical concepts of representation updated by Heidegger, technology copies (*mimesis*) and technology creates (*poiesis*). These concepts can help us understand the complementary imitative and creative practices operating in documentary film and world politics.[3]

Realpolitik and *cinéma vérité*

Film is a story told through technology. From its beginnings, the combination of technological form and narrative function introduced quantum properties of complementarity to film, including artifice and art, imitation and creation, effect and affect, fact and fiction. As we have learned in earlier chapters, because of the technological interaction between the mode and object of representation, no single picture can capture the reality of the moment. Even if apocryphal, the popular account of an audience fleeing in terror from the 1896 screening of the Lumière film, *Arrival of a Train at La Ciotat*, attests to the complementary properties of documentary film; but it is also evident in the famous fifty second, seven meter film that individual behavior in the train station crowd is altered by the presence of the Lumière's camera. In the 1920s, Dziga Vertov, an early and influential Soviet documentary filmmaker influenced by constructivists like Tatlin, Lissitzky, and Rodchenko, developed what he called 'kino-pravda' ('cinematic truth') to capture 'life as it is'. But he also introduced a menu of technical artifice uncommon to human optics and now quite commonplace in contemporary documentary film, like frame shifts through multiple lenses, slow-motion shots, and time-lapse editing. Perhaps most notoriously, Robert Flaherty, credited with making the first narrative documentary, *Nanook of the North* in 1922, introduced ethnographic practices to filmmaking, while restaging several scenes to conform to romantic notions he and a putative audience shared of indigenous subjects.

Observing world politics through documentary film reveals a mutual dependence upon the mimetic and aesthetic power of realism. The key tenet of realism, '*wie es eigentlich gewesen*', to 'show what actually happened', expresses in German what is epitomized in documentary film by the French concept of *cinéma vérité*. Moreover, documentary film and realist theory are backed by the same reality principle. Modern political documentary was born out of the First World War, came of age in the interwar, and reached its apex during the Second World War, when picture palaces presented the *world as picture* in the newsreel format of war, revolution, and international crises. This fitful dyad of the visual and the martial might be less strident today than in the interwar of the twentieth century, when futurists and constructivists as well as fascist and communist filmmakers first weaponized cinema (Virilio 1989). But the realist legacy still dominates the American way of film and war, most visibly in the *ex officio* motto of the military-industrial-media-entertainment network: 'All but war is simulation.'[4]

Documentary film, as opposed to, say, a novel, painting, or fictional film, might claim to show the world 'as it really is', rather than as one might imagine or wish it to be; but like realism, both upon closer viewing prove to be heavily dependent upon a host of mimetic proxies and aesthetic practices, including models and metaphors, techniques and tropes, framing and editing. Probably no thinker, including the philosophically astute but ideologically defective Heidegger, better understands the *faux vérité* of media than Walter Benjamin, who acutely captures the parallax view of interwar film and politics. Benjamin surely had the historian Ranke and his geopolitical apostles in mind when he wrote that 'the history that showed things "as they really were" was the strongest narcotic of the century' (Benjamin 1999: 463). But Benjamin also had early filmmakers in his viewfinder when he warned in his eventually influential essay, 'The Work of Art in the Age of its Technical Reproducibility' (1936), of the aestheticization of politics.

The power of the concept has not diminished with time and bears revisiting. As a mechanical copy of reality, film lost the authenticity as well as aura of the original. Also bypassed in modern forms of reproduction are the traditional rituals of artistic creation that mediate the differences and desires of mimesis. 'Every day the urge grows stronger', wrote Benjamin, 'to get hold of an object at close range in an image, or, better, in a facsimile, a reproduction' (Benjamin 2008: 23). Film seeks to accommodate this mimetic desire by, as Benjamin put it, aligning reality with the masses, and the masses with reality. In this manner, film becomes the 'most powerful agent of mass movements' (Benjamin 2008: 22–24).

This also helps explain film's over-familiarity with violence. Violence is immanent in the 'mimetic faculty', which Benjamin co-locates in the primordial 'shot' taken by hunter and artist of their prey: 'Perhaps the human from the stone-age sketches the elk so incomparably, only because the hand which leads the crayon still recalls the bow with which it shot the animal' (Benjamin 1974–1989: 127). René Girard takes this insight one step further, grounding the mimetic faculty in anthropology to identify mimesis as the desire for the desire of the Other, producing a rivalry dynamic that, if not displaced through ritual or mediated through art, leads to violence. This leads to the perennial question about art and violence: does a trip to the Cineplex, where mimetic violence is usually on full display, constitute a palliative ritual or a recycling of mimetic desire?

Film, lies, and videotape

Revisiting the controversy surrounding one of the earliest and most powerful political documentaries, *Triumph of the Will*, by Leni Riefenstahl – Hitler's favorite filmmaker – might shed some light on the question of film, violence, and the truth. Released in 1934, the film was highly popular and received several film festival awards, in spite and because of the criticism (depending on the ideology) that it bent the truth to accommodate political beliefs. Riefenstahl herself displayed no such doubts and went to her grave defending the realism of the film:

> If you see this film again today you ascertain that it doesn't contain a single reconstructed scene. Everything in it is true. And it contains no tendentious commentary at all. It is history. A pure historical film ... it is film-vérité. It reflects the truth that was then in 1934, history. It is therefore a documentary.
>
> (Thomson 2010: 822)

Riefenstahl has a point. More than one commentator has remarked on the cinematic nature of the Nazi regime. Eric Rentschler says it best: 'If the Nazis were movie mad, then the Third Reich was movie made'; he goes on to cite Hans Jürgen Syberberg's seven-hour opus, *Hitler: A Film from Germany*, lending some credence to Riefenstahl's claim that her documentary simply 'reflects the truth that was then' (Rentschler 1996: 1). This raises a more interesting question (than was it fact or fiction): were the Nazi's acting out, in a classic case of double mimesis, their own filmic reflection in the *Triumph of the Will*?

The debate over the realist pretense, aesthetic form, and political function of documentary film is understandably most intense during the interwar – a flux period of emergence, experimentation, and, yes, politicization of the documentary. But the issue of veracity in particular mushrooms with every international crisis and its representation. For instance, Riefenstahl's films, which were enjoying something of a revival as camp art rather than as diabolical agitprop, came under severe attack during the Vietnam War era. Leading the charge in a remarkable 1975 *New York Review of Books* essay, Susan Sontag decries Riefenstahl's celebration of violence dressed up in the aesthetics of purity and thinly veiled erotics. Calling *Triumph of the Will* 'the most successfully, most purely propagandistic film ever made', Sontag wrote: 'the document (the image) is no longer simply the record of reality; "reality" has been constructed to serve the image.'[5] Even with scare quotes around it, 'reality', especially wartime reality, rises to the top of the political litmus test for a documentary.

War and film clearly have more than a passing relationship (Virilio 1989). At the micro-level of technology, the chemistry between the two is more literal than romantic: the same nitrocellulose used in explosives were used to make the celluloid filmstrip. The same synchronizing gear of first film cameras were adapted for the 'interruptor' gear that made it possible to fire a machine gun through an airplane propeller. At the macro-level of economics, the war and film industries have obvious mutual interests, not least the seduction of the citizen consumer. Shrinking distances, increasing accuracy, and accelerating delivery, the technologies of war and film became entangled early in the century, and in the twenty-first have reached new levels of sophistication in their joint theatres of operations. At the meta-levels of international theory and film criticism, the transfiguration of realism from historical to political to structural to simulacral closely maps the journey of the documentary image, from photographic to cinematic to videographic to virtual. In short, modes of representation and destruction organized to represent, see, and kill the enemy while securing and seducing the citizen have converged in dual economies of sight and might.

From the herky-jerky footage of the First World War to the cult of pure war captured by Riefenstahl in the Second World War to the synchronization of gun and camera in the Iraq War, shooting film (or video) and shooting the enemy has undergone a technical, aesthetic, and political convergence, giving new meaning to the art of war. The dead body – on the battlefield, in the tomb of the unknown soldier, in the collective memory, and on the screen – continues to elevate the violence and sacrifice of war over other collective values.

The latest technological transformations in the preparation, execution, and representation of modern warfare as well as documentaries do raise new questions. Does the sanitization and virtualization of war (and the attempt to disappear the body) present a new challenge to realism and how it is represented?[6] Without the reality principle of war, will documentary film appear less truthful, authentic, or factual than other mimetic forms of representation, like the docudrama, reality show, or historical reenactment? With lower costs, easier distribution, and a burgeoning of documentarians, who will adjudicate truth claims and take responsibility for what might be called 'deceit effects'? Rather than wait for *Documenting World Politics 2*, I offer an early lesson I learned on the matter, presented as less of an answer and more of a cautionary tale.

Handle with care

If images do, indeed, represent a great new power in world politics, then it is also true that they present a great responsibility (as my current students attribute to Uncle Ben in *Spiderman, au lieu de* Voltaire), not only for how we study, but increasingly for how we must engage with the documentation of world politics through images.

I learned this lesson the hard way, early in my career as a teacher, researcher, and aspiring image-maker of world politics. After desperately trying to avoid an academic life – in the belief that those who can do and those who cannot teach World Politics 101 – and a failed career as a photographer in New York City, I got a real job at the University of Massachusetts (UMASS), Amherst. This, of course, meant teaching World Politics 101. To ease my fear of the eternal recurrence and death of creativity, I decided to add a media component to the course, a weekly public-access television program on current events that I produced with some enthused students. It aspired to *Bill Moyers*, but looked more like *Wayne's World* (there might be a few pirated episodes on YouTube).

Right about that time, UMASS started one of the first BA programs for the criminally incarcerated in the United States – a vast population that has since grown from enormous to obscene. After the first teacher got fired – reportedly, contraband (possibly planted) was found during a body search – the word went out for a volunteer. After everyone else took a step backwards, I found myself a couple of weeks later commuting every week to Gardner State Prison. The class went well: I got to teach some very smart Nation of Islam converts, radical Latino revisionists, and a few self-selected white guys. By the third year, I asked and was granted permission by the warden to combine my UMASS class with my prison course, now called 'World Politics and Media'. This was pre-Skype and, indeed, pre-e-mail, so the mode of collaboration was to be my new 'portable' video system, a battery-operated recording deck on one shoulder, a Panasonic camera on the other, and a bag full of blank VHS videotapes.

Good to go, I thought, except for the guards who worked the trap and resented (understandably) the opportunity I represented of a (free) college education for the 'cons'. Every week the guards came up with a new reason to 'safeguard' (i.e., take) my video equipment – an inspection team had just arrived, there had been a knifing, a lockdown had been declared. Finally, fed up, and on the week the students were to give their final presentations on the Prisoner's Dilemma (PD), I decided not to present the equipment for inspection at the trap. I was glad I had not: the students did a remarkable deconstruction of the International Relations (IR) model of PD, bringing in unsuspecting prisoners from the yard to stage a series of simulations (with Boston cream pies offered as the reward), demonstrating that subjective perceptions of identity – who would snitch, who would not – worked better than supposedly objective predictions of interest.

I was eager to share what I had captured on video with my UMASS class, and on the service road out to the highway, I thought it might be a good idea to get some 'establishment shots'. I decided to get arty (always a mistake), and shot video from the car window with one hand while driving with the other, while the *Violent Femmes* – the best band to come out of Milwaukee, Wisconsin – blasted on the tape player. Halfway past the double fence topped by concertina wire, an unmarked car zoomed by and abruptly braked; another car pulled up from behind, effectively boxing me in. Two guys in civvies got out, ordered me out of my car, hands on the hood; they proceeded to search, top to bottom, my car, the trunk, the ashtrays. They found and took the video equipment, tapes, and me back to the prison, where I was put in a room alone for a couple of hours, giving me plenty of time to think about my situation.

When they finally reappeared, they presented two options: I could leave, but I would be permanently banned from the prison; or I could stay, get written up for an 'incident report', and deal with the consequences, which were left unspecified. No official charges had been made so far, except a verbal statement that I had violated prison policies. My protests about having permission from the warden to videotape the class fell on deaf ears. Not willing to risk the prospect of spending more time behind the walls, I took the option to leave, with tail tucked between my legs.

What followed was a lesson in the power of the media to create realities, to do good as well as bad, with intended as well as unintended consequences. After a series of letters and phone calls, the issue went up the chain of command and through various state bureaucracies, until I was finally informed of my 'crime': I had violated the privacy rights of the convicts. When I pointed out that I had media releases from those on camera, and had blank-screened those whom I did not, I was next informed that I had shot the face of a prisoner through the fenced perimeter who was in a protection program; my videotaping had potentially endangered his life. I thought and said this was a lot of bull, because I had been shooting while moving, and from a long distance through two chain-link fences. I decided that I would set things right. I would fight media with media.

I gave the story to a friend on a Boston news program, who passed it on to the national news program, *60 Minutes*. After several meetings with producers, I found myself back in Gardner State Prison with a full TV crew, sitting across from *60 Minutes*' venerable correspondent, Morley Safer, who grilled me on the costs and benefits of prison education programs. I did my best to highlight the numbers – recidivist rates go down substantially among prisoners in the programs – and downplay the incident. However, the interview went south when Safer probed my decision to join – and then leave – the program. At one point he demanded to know how much of the taxpayer's money was going to my salary. My reply was less than diplomatic: '$1,800 per semester, probably less than you are getting per minute.' My interview got cut from the segment; they decided to go with the kind seventy-year-old nun who was teaching a literacy course.

But it got worse. As it turns out, Jesse Helms, the then arch-conservative Senator from North Carolina, was a fan of *60 Minutes* (I presume it gave him fodder for his weekly tirades against the cultural decline of America). When he learned from the show that Pell Grants were being used to help defray book expenses for the prisoners, he attached a rider to a bill to defund all such programs. I would learn several years later from Senator Pell himself that the funds were shortly reinstated by another bill that he submitted. But I went through life for several years believing that my efforts yielded disastrous results, with prison education programs across America taking a big hit. Chastened and banned from all Massachusetts prisons, my righteous urge to do good through film also took a hit.

It took some time, but I eventually got back up on my high horse and behind the video camera, producing five documentary films over the past decade. But I had learned my lesson. Trafficking in images can be hazardous as well as beneficial to the public good. When entering the fast lane of mass media, good intentions alone do not suffice; indeed, they can be counterproductive. Positive outcomes require technical competence, visual fluency, self-reflexivity, and personal acceptance of responsibility for one's work.

A lasting image

Documenting World Politics is a timely and worthy addition not only to the field of International Relations, but to the extra-discipline of life in a quantum age. The authors raise all the right questions, avoid simple answers, and recognize that no single theory nor single medium can address the most pressing global issues. As images flood the infosphere, the essays collected in this book throw a lifeline out to the viewer seeking a signal of knowledge amidst a sea of informational noise. The authors do not assume documentary film to be a mere record of reality. To do so asserts a sameness of motives and identity in geopolitics, biopolitics, and infopolitics that nullifies difference and curtails the possibilities of change. It would also assume a universal view of a single reality debunked by quantum theory and continental philosophy alike in the interwar. Instead, these essays deepen the depth of field, to investigate how documentary film uses aesthetic, technological, and political reconstructions of space and time to undermine and transfigure the reality principles of world politics. I wish I had been able to read it before picking up my first video camera; I am delighted that others have opportunity to do so now.

Notes

1 Others have prepared the ground and plowed parallel furrows in film and world politics. Michael Shapiro has been a pathbreaker, traversing and undermining the boundaries of fictional and non-fictional formats of representation in geopolitics and biopolitics to forge new imaginaries for peaceful coexistence (a concept overdue for rehabilitation). By opening up the canon to cinema, Cynthia Weber has forged a powerful new critical pedagogy for IR. Lene Hansen is leading yet another Copenhagen interpretation (NB: this is a school-free zone) on visualizations of security (with Megan MacKenzie at the University of Sydney making it a transhemispheric project).
2 For a quick primer on the relevance of quantum theory to world politics, see qsymposium.net. A fuller account can be found in Der Derian (2013) and Der Derian (2011).
3 For a fuller account of the mimetic and creative functions of realism and constructivism, see Der Derian (2000).
4 The official motto of the US Army Simulation, Training and Instrumentation Command (STRICOM), the unique US military command post created to model and represent war through multiple media. See Der Derian (2010) and *Project Z: The Final Global Event* (Bullfrog Films 2014).
5 Sontag (1975). Sontag emphasizes the point in an interview from the new documentary, *Regarding Susan Sontag* (2014): 'I guess I go to war because I think it is my duty to be in contact with as much reality as I can, and war is a tremendous reality in our world.'
6 I attempt an answer to this question with Phillip Gara in our new documentary film, *Project Z: The Final Global Event* (Bullfrog Films 2014).

References

Benjamin, Walter (1991) 'Das Kunstwerk im Zeitalter seiner technischen Reproduzierbarkeit' (Dritte Fassung), in Walter Benjamin, *Gesammelte Schriften* I.2, eds Rolf Tiedemann and Hermann Schweppenhauser. Frankfurt am Main: Suhrkamp, 471–508.

Benjamin, Walter (1999) *The Arcades Project*. Harvard: Harvard University Press.
Benjamin, Walter (2008) *The World of Art in the Age of its Technological Reproducibility and Other Writings on Media*, eds Michael Jennings, Brigid Doherty, and Thomas Y. Levin. Cambridge, MA: Harvard University Press.
Der Derian, James (2000) 'The Art of War and the Construction of Peace: Toward a Virtual Theory of International Relations', in Morten Kelstrup and Michael Williams (eds) *International Relations Theory and the Politics of European Integration*. London Routledge, 72–105.
Der Derian, James (2010) *Virtuous War: Mapping the Military-Industrial-Media-Network*. London and Oxford: Routledge.
Der Derian, James (2011) 'Quantum Diplomacy, German-American Relations, and the Psychogeography of Berlin', *Hague Journal of Diplomacy*, 6, 373–392.
Der Derian, James (2013) 'From War 2.0 to Quantum War: The Superpositionality of Global Violence', *Australian Journal of International Affairs*, 67, 570–585.
Heidegger, Martin (1977 [1938]) 'The Age of the World Picture', reprinted in Martin Heidegger, *The Question Concerning Technology and Other Essays*, ed. W. Lovitt. New York, NY: Harper Torchbooks, 115–154.
Rentschler, Eric (1996) *The Ministry of Illusion: Nazi Cinema and its Afterlife*. Cambridge, MA: Harvard University Press.
Sontag, Susan (1975) 'Fascinating Fascism', *New York Review of Books*, 6 February 1975.
Thomson, David (2010) *The New Biographical Dictionary of Film, Fifth Edition*. New York, NY: Knopf.
Virilio, Paul (1989) *War and Cinema: The Logistics of Perception*. New York, NY: Verso.

List of QR codes included in the volume

When the QR codes are scanned, they will direct readers to excerpts or trailers of films discussed in the chapters.

1	*An Inconvenient Truth*	3
2	*The Fog of War*	23
3	*Inside Job*	43
4	*The Food Speculator*	58
5	*The Forgotten Space*	78
6	*Countdown to Zero*	95
7	*Restrepo*	114
8	*The Invisible War*	133
9	*Burma VJ*	150
10	*The Reckoning*	166
11	*The Ambassador*	183
12	*Act of Killing*	201
13	*Love on Delivery*	213
14	*Human Terrain*	223

Index

Page numbers in *italics* denote tables, those in **bold** denote figures.

Act of Killing, The (film) 16, 37, 201–12, **202**, **207**
actor-network theory 84
Afghanistan 12, 15, 23, 114–28, 147n13, 151, 158–60
Africa, representations of 134, 170–1, 177, 189–91, 213
Ambassador, The (film) *10*, 183, 188–91
ambiguity 8, *10*, 95
anthropology 120, 129n14, 213–15, 218–19, 225
Armadillo (film) *10*, 12, 23–4, 115–16, 118–22, **122**, 125–7, 129n21, n22
Atomic Café (film) *10*, 14, 101–3, **101**
Aitken, Rob 16n3, 44–5, 52, 59, 61
Ashcroft, Ross 48–50, 52–5
assemblage 50, 54, 59–63, 67, 70–4
Atomic Energy Commission (AEC) 95
audience 8–11, 30–7, 117–19, 124–8, 159–61, 168–71, 215–18, 221–2; contract with 9, 61; expectations 4, 16n3; mobilization of 4, 8, 10–11, 13, 46, 97–9, 102, 115, 215; walk-outs 23

Bender, Lawrence 104
Benjamin, Walter 66, 75n1, 95, 225
Black Sea Files (film) 13, 58, 62, 68–72, **69**, **71**, 74
Bourdieu, Pierre 26–7
Brouwer, Kees 65–6
Brügger, Mads 183–91
Burch, Noël 82–7, 91
Burke, John 152, 158–61
Burke + Norfolk (film) 15, 150–2, 158–61
Burma VJ (film) 15, 150–1, 152–8, 160–2, 163n9

Butler, Judith 5, 60, 62, 141, 146n7, 147n14, 183, 186, 191, 196

camera: effect of 141, 144, 155–6, 202–4, 220; frame of 13, 102, 118–19, 125, 142–3, 185; as lens/eye 8, 79, 81–2, 87–8; technology 13, 28, 87, 223–4; video 146n5, 150–8, 228–30; as weapon 153–4, 157
Campbell, David 60, 62, 125, 129n22
Capra, Frank 9, 27, 114–15
capitalism 43–56, 60, 64, 83–6, 92
Capitalism: A Love Story (film) 15, 43, 47–9, 53, 55
'cartoon crisis' 188
Castaing-Taylor, Lucien 24, 87–9
cinema vérité 9, 28, 135, 190, 203, 224–6
civil defense 95, 97, 99
comedy 101, 184, 186
communication 6, 123, 150, 183, 187–96
counterinsurgency (COIN), doctrine of 115–28, 129n14
Countdown to Zero (film) *10*, 104–7, **105**, 110n16
Court, The (film) 166–8, **167**
critique 37, 43–4, 51, 61–4, 73, 101–2, 127, 135
culpability 70, 72
currency 50, 53

Darwin's Nightmare (film) 72–4
democracy 9, 50, 107, 154–5, 175, 183, 186–8, 196
documentary film: and art 7, 13, 26–7, 30, 68, 73, 78, 108, 136, 145, 159–60, 185, 190, 193, 211–12, 217, 224–5; industry 7, 12, 30–6; characteristics and history

Index

documentary film *continued*
   7–14, 27–30, 201–4, 211–12, 224–7;
   and democracy 9; subgenres *10*, 18n18,
   32, 104
Der Derian, James 12, 16n5, 124, 184,
   189, 192, 194
diplomacy 9, 183, 188–9, 191, 194, 198
direct cinema 9, 28, 203
Dr. Strangelove (film) 100

ecology 89, 91
economy, global 54, 55n4, 58, 72, 74–5
education 5, 9, 16n6, 24, 27, 29–30, 43,
   51, 98–100, 168–70, 181n26, 211
embedded liberalism 44–5, 51, 55n4
embedded media *see* media
everyday, the 43–4, 47, 52, 54–5, 59, 74,
   108, 117, 125, 144, 216, 218
evil 61, 74, 171, 184, 204–8
exposure *10*, 13, 65, 115, 153, 189–90

Fahrenheit 9/11 (film) 13, 23
feminism 14, 134–7
Ferencz, Ben 166, 171, 174, 176–7
Ferguson, Charles 43, 46, 49, 51, 54, 56n5,
   58, 63
fiction 7–8, 17n12, 24, 60, 96, 119, 126,
   193, 195, 217–19, 225
finance: embeddedness of 44, 52, 54–5;
   financial crisis 5, 43, 55, 58, 60–5, 74
financial industry 46, 49, 51, 55, 64–5
Fog of War, The (film) 12, 37, 103, 115
Food Speculator, The (film) 65–9, 72, 64
Forgotten Space, The (film) *10*, 82–7, 91–2
Four Horsemen (film) 43, 47–51, 55
framework for analysis 9–11, 18n18

Gibney, Alex 23, 24
gender 55n4, 61, 64, 99, 108n1, 134–6,
   138, 145
globalization 45, 48, 49, 71, 73, 150, 213,
   216, 217–18
Globalization Tapes, The (film) 211
gold standard 50
Gore, Al 3, 18n23, 23
Grierson, John 8–9, 13, 27, 45, 119

hearts and minds 115, 120–4, 170
Heidegger, Martin 223–5
Hetherington, Tim 24, 114–15, 119, 124,
   129n22, 147n13
human rights 134, 137, 166–79, 205, 209
humanity, representations of 89, 107–8,
   166–79, 185, 188, 205

ideology *10*, 11, 53, 86, 99, 114, 142, 175,
   178, 184, 226
Inconvenient Truth, An (film) 3, 12, 17n10,
   18n23, 104
Indonesia 204–5, 207–11
Inside Job (film) *10*, 13, 43, 46–52, 54,
   58–9, 63–5, 72, 74
International Criminal Court (ICC) 15,
   137, 166–79
International Documentary Film Festival
   (IDFA) 25, 30–5, 161
international law 78, 166–79; the
   profession of 172, 174, 176
International Political Economy (IPE)
   43–5, 55, 59, 72
International Relations (IR) 3–7, 13–14,
   15, 24, 70, 78, 114, 136, 162n1, 228
Into Eternity (film) 103, 191–5
injustice 53, 133, 142, 143
Iraq War 23, 115–17, 128n6, n8, 162n1,
   227
irony *10*, 14, 37, 97, 100–3, 184, 186, 188
Invisible War, The (film) 10, 13, 133–4,
   136, 138–42, 145, 146n4

journalism 7, 24, 26–7, 65, 115–18, 124,
   151–62, 211; *see also* media
Junger, Sebastian 23–4, 115, 119, 147n13
justice 15, 70, 133, 137–46, 166–79,
   180n12; *see also* injustice

Kony2012 (film) 3, 8, 166, 168
kino-eye 82; *see also* camera
Kissinger, Henry 104, 106–7, 109–10n14
Kuran, Peter 103

Lagarde, Christine 50
Leviathan (film) *10*, 14, 87–92
Love on Delivery (film) 213, **215**, 216, 220

Masco, Joseph 96, 97, 99, 104, 127
markets 43–5, 48–50, 52, 53, 54, 55, 72,
   74, 90; financial 59, 61, 53, 64, 65–8;
   for documentary film 25, 26, 29–37, 43;
   marketing 11, 12, 24, 43, 45, 91, 124,
   126, 145, 175
media: embedded 115–19, 121, 124,
   128n4, n8 (*see also* journalism); power
   of 154–5, 229
mediation 114, 135, 150–1, 153, 154, 178,
   183, 194, 225; meta-mediation 151–2,
   160–2; remediation 154–6, 162
Metz, Janus 23–4, 115, 118–19, 121,
   125–6, 129n21, 213–22

Index 235

migration 213–14, 217–19
Mitchell, W.J.T. 6, 151–2, 163n17
Moby Dick (novel) 88–90
Moore, Michael 9, 23–4, 47, 49, 52–3, 163n16
Morris, Errol 11, 23–4, 37, 103, 115, 146n7
Mortgage Backed Securities (MBSs) 58, 65
Movies that Matter 166

Nichols, Bill 8, 10, 13–14, 16n6, 18n17, 133, 136–7, 180n16
Nixon, Richard 109–10n14
Norfolk, Simon 151–2, 158–62
norms 5, 15, 33, 92, 147n14, 170, 172, 191, 196
North Korea, representations of 183–8, 197n5
Nuclear Security Project 104, 106
Nuclear Threat Initiative 104
Nuclear Tipping Point (film) 104–7
nuclear waste 103, 192, 195
nuclear weapons 95–108; and nuclear zero 104, 106, 108; and nukespeak 102; and terrorism 105–6; and testing 96, 99–100, 102
Nuclear Weapons Film Declassification Project 99

Ocampo, Luis Moreno 166, 168, 171, 174–7
ocean, the 78–92
Occupy Wall Street 46, 49, 53
oil 68–72, 74
Operation Fine Girl (film) 133–4, 142–6
Oppenheimer, Joshua 16, 37, 201–12
Orientalism 188
Østergaard, Anders 150, 158, 162

Paravel, Verena 24, 87–91
Plambech, Sine 213–22
Plantinga, Carl 10
perceptibility 12, 58, 96, 99, 104, 107
perception 8, 43, 58, 117, 118, 120, 213, 228
popular culture 5–7, 14, 17n8, 110, 114, 128
propaganda 27–9, 53, 116, 118, 138, 207; enemy 117; government 9, 18n17, 24, 38n3, 45, 102, 106, 107, 114–15, 155–6, 175, 181n26, 186, 206

Radio Bikini (film) *10*, 14, 100–3
rape 14, 133–46, 218–19

Reagan, Ronald 47–8, 64, 100, 102, 128n1
reality 4–5, 7–8, 10–14, 16, 17n13, 24–5, 28, 42, 65, 81, 88, 108, 119, 124, 135–6, 155–6, 161–2, 174–5, 185, 201–3, 217, 224–7, 230
Reckoning, The (film) *10*, 11, 137, 166–79
Red Chapel, The (film) 13, 183–8
reenactments 84, 156–62, 163n16, 206–7
reflexivity 12, 14, 36, 43, 45, 50, 54, 134, 136, 138, 145–6, 151–2, 162, 229
Renov, Michael 18n18, 81
research and filmmaking 4, 213–22, 227–9
resistance 52–4, 85, 102, 157–8, 160–2
responsibility 54, 58–75, 219–22, 227, 229
Restrepo (film) *10*, 11, 14, 23–4, 115–16, 118–28, **123**, **125**, 147n13
Riefenshtahl, Leni 8, 27, 114, 226

satire 102, 190–1
sea, the *see* ocean, the
security: discourse 104, 106, 108; global 107; homeland 91, 109n6; Cold War 109–10n14; and the Other 188, 196; and stability 115, 160, 189; politics 3, 107, 150, 191; studies 223, 230n1
Sekula, Allan 82–7
sex industry 221
sexual military assault 133–46
Shapiro, Michael J. 6–7, 58–9, 159, 230n1
shock effects 101–2
soldiers, representations of 114–28, 138, 147n13
space 45, 78–82, 85–7, 91–2, 187
Spurlock, Morgan 9, 23–4
Standard Operating Procedure (film) 23, 129n16, 146n16
subjectivity 135–7
suffering 134, 137–8, 143–6, 205

Taxi to the Dark Side (film) 23, 129n16
teaching IR 4, 6–7, 16–17n7, 227
tears 134, 137–46
territory 78, 80
terrorism 105–6
Thailand 213–22
Thatcher, Margaret 48
Ticket to Paradise (film) 213, 216, 220–2, **221**
time 80–2, 85, 90–1, 183, 186, 190–6
totalitarianism 16, 114, 186, 187, 195
trade 37, 45, 64, 66–8, 78, 83, 84, 190; trader 61, 64, 74; *see also The Food Speculator* (film)
trafficking, human 213, 221, 229

truth 4–5, 7–8, 10–14, 17n6, 25, 81

Uganda 3, 176, 178

Vertov, Dziga 8, 28, 81–2, 84, 88, 92, 224
victimhood 177–8, 213
video recording 15, 68–9, 134, 143, 150–7, 163n15, 228–30
violence 12, 15, 114–28, 133–46, 185, 209, 225–7
vision 6, 74, 87, 152
visual agency 150–1, 158

visual culture 5–6, 152
visualization 14, 58–74, 114, 124, 216, 230n1
viewing, the practice of 61–3, 135–6, 159, 195
voice-over 10, 16n6, 63, 71, 174, 184, 190–1, 211, 215

Wall Street 47, 49, 63–4
war 6, 12, 15, 24, 97–9, 114–28, 133, 138, 151–2, 159, 224–7
Weber, Cynthia 16n5, 17n8, n10, 230n1